Vygotskian Approaches To Second Language Research

Second Language Learning

A Series Dedicated to Studies
in Acquisition
and Principled Language Instruction

Elizabeth B. Bernhardt, Series Editor

Vygotskian Approaches To Second Language Research

Edited by

James P. Lantolf
Cornell University

Gabriela Appel
Cornell University

 Ablex Publishing Corporation
Norwood, New Jersey

Second Printing 1996

Printed in the United States of America

Library of Congress Cataloging-in-Publication Data

Vygotskian approaches to second language research / [edited by] James
  P. Lantolf, Gabriela Appel.
      p.   cm.—(Second language learning)
  Includes bibliographical references and index.
  ISBN 1–56750–024–2 (cl).—ISBN 1–56750–025–0 (ppk.)
  1. Second language acquisition. 2. Vygotskiĭ, L. S. (Lev
Semenovich), 1896–1934. I. Lantolf, James P. II. Appel, Gabriela.
III. Series.
P118.2.V94   1994
418'.007—dc20   93–49680
                                                      CIP

Ablex Publishing Company
355 Chestnut Street
Norwood, New Jersey 07648

We dedicate this volume to the memory of
Robert J. Di Pietro,
a treasured colleague and dear friend

Contents

Part III: Activity Theory

1

Theoretical Framework: An Introduction to Vygotskian Approaches to Second Language Research

James P. Lantolf
Gabriela Appel

*Department of Modern Languages and
    Linguistics
Cornell University
Ithaca, NY*

Lev Semenovitch Vygotsky was born on November 5, 1896, in Orsha, a small rural town near the city of Minsk. He graduated from Moscow University in 1917 with a specialization in literature and returned to what he considered to be his native town of Gomel, where he took up a teaching position at the local teachers college. Although during his stay in Gomel, which ended with his return to Moscow in 1924, Vygotsky worked as a theater critic for the local newspaper, his interest in psychology began to crystallize at this time (Van der Veer & Valsiner, 1991). The link between literary analysis and psychology seemed clear for Vygotsky. Vygotsky asked how it could be that a work such as *Hamlet* could appeal equally to slave-owing, capitalist, and socialist societies, in a direct challenge to the "Marxist theory that social superstructures, mentalities included, change with transformations of the social base" (Joravsky, 1989, p. 257). Furthermore, he asked why the enactment of incongruities between "the expected and the actual pattern of life" in works of fiction intrigues the adult mind (Joravsky, 1989, p. 256). It was questions such as these that stimulated Vygotsky to explore the role of art in the formation of the "new man" in his 1925 dissertation "The Psychology of Art" presented at Moscow University (Van der Veer & Valsiner, 1991, p. 34).

In 1924, Vygotsky presented his first major psychological study at the Second Russian Neuropsychological Congress in Leningrad—a paper that challenged the relevance of reflexology for understanding the nature of human thinking, the theory favored by the leading psychologists and political figures of the day (see Joravsky, 1989, Kozulin, 1990).[1] Although the circumstances of how Vygotsky, supposedly working in virtual seclusion at Gomel, managed to be included in the program of such a prestigious conference remain cloudy, his lecture had a profound and lasting impact on psychology, both inside and outside of the Soviet Union.[2]

Vygotsky's enterprise was to unify semiotics, neurolinguistics, psychology, and psycholinguistics into a stable theoretical framework that had as its goal the scientific exploration and explanation of the development and function of the human mind.[3] Between

---

[1] There is a degree of uncertainty as to the precise paper that Vygotsky delivered at the Leningrad congress. Some biographers have assumed that the title of the paper was "Consciousness As a Problem of The Psychology of Behavior." (See, for example, the translators remarks regarding the English version of this paper published in the journal *Soviet Psychology*, 17(4), 3–35). As Van der Veer and Valsiner (1991, p. 40) point out, however, Vygotsky actually delivered this paper somewhat later in the same year at a conference in Moscow. The tile of the paper presented in Leningrad was "The Methods of Reflexological and Psychological Investigation." To be sure, in both papers Vygotsky broached the problem of higher forms of cognition, but from slightly different perspectives.

[2] Even before his Leningrad speech, Vygotsky had already carried out and published the results from a number of psychological experiments at the laboratory he had set up at Gomel; consequently, he apparently was not unknown in the Moscow psychological community (Van der Veer & Valsiner, 1991, p. 39).

[3] At least one psychologist, Peter Galperin, whose work was heavily influenced by Vygotsky, challenged Vygotsky's contention that real scientific progress could only be achieved through a synthesis of various branches of knowledge instead of through indepth specialization in solely one area (Van der Veer & Valsiner, 1991, p. 185).

1925 and 1934, the year of his untimely death from tuberculosis, Vygotsky and a number of colleagues, including A. R. Luria and A. N. Leont'ev, undertook a vigorous research program to refine Vygotsky's ideas into a sociocultural theory of human mental processing.

Vygotsky argued that because psychology had largely refused to study consciousness, it had deprived itself of access to "some rather important and complex problems of human behavior. [Furthermore, it means that] it [psychology] is forced to restrict itself to explaining no more than the most elementary connections between a living being and the world" (Vygotsky, 1979, p. 5). For Vygotsky, consciousness distinguishes the behavior of humans from that of other living beings (for example, apes), and it links the individual's knowledge to his or her behavior; as such, it constitutes the object of study of psychological research. Vygotsky viewed consciousness as more than awareness of one's cognitive abilities; he conceived of it as comprised of the *self-regulatory* mechanisms that humans deploy in solving problems. This latter understanding is more akin to what in modern jargon is called metacognition, and incorporates such functions as planning, voluntary attention, logical memory, problem solving, and evaluation. What was required, according to Vygotsky, was to discover the appropriate unit of analysis of consciousness, the theoretical principle to explain its formation and operation, as well as a methodological paradigm to carry out the necessary research.

In what follows, we first consider Vygotsky's attempt to develop an explanatory framework. We then address the issue of the unit of analysis, and, finally, we present a summary of the research paradigm that has its origins in Vygotsky's writings. None of these critical issues, however, were fully worked out during Vygotsky's lifetime, and each eventually became the focus of intense debate and controversy in sociocultural psychology.

EXPLANATORY FRAMEWORK

The Roots of Activity Theory

The task Vygotsky set for psychology was to explain consciousness neither by returning to the introspective mentalistic psychology of the Wurzburg School (Luria, 1979, p. 21), nor by accepting the reflexology position of V. Pavlov and other eminent Russian psychologists of the day (Luria, 1979, p. 44). In the former approach,

Vygotsky saw the need for overcoming the cycle of explaining states of consciousness through consciousness itself, and in the latter, he opposed the reduction of psychological phenomena to reflex-like behavior: "a human being is not at all a skin sack filled with reflexes, and the brain is not a hotel for a series of conditioned reflexes accidentally stopping in" (Joravsky, 1989, p. 262). Vygotsky clearly recognized that it was necessary for psychology to establish an explanatory principle "that reflects a reality and on the basis of which the totality of mental processes is explained" (Davydov & Radzikhovskii, 1985, p. 59). Here Vygotsky turned to philosophy, not on some serendipitous fishing expedition, but because he was convinced that philosophical concepts are inherently relevant to psychology. As Vygotsky (1986) remakes, "facts are always examined in light of some theory and therefore cannot be disentangled from philosophy" (p. 11).

It was the writings of Spinoza, along with those of Marx, Engels, and Hegel, that provided Vygotsky with the foundations for an explanatory principle of consciousness. Spinoza rejected "all talk of thought first arising and then, 'being embodied in words,' in 'terms' and 'statements,' and later in actions, in deeds and their results" as senseless (Ilyvenkov, 1977, p. 44). For Spinoza, thinking cannot be explained by describing the structure of the human brain any more than walking can be explained by detailing the structure of the leg. Thinking, like walking, is a proper *function* of its relevant organ: "the fullest description of the *structure of an organ*, i.e., a description of it in an *inactive* state, however, has no right of present itself as a description, however approximate, of the *function* that the organ performs, as a description of the *real thing* that it does" (Ilyvenkov, 1977, p. 45).

Following Spinoza, Vygotsky proposed that since thinking is the function of the cerebral organ, the explanation of the process is not to be found in the internal structure of the organ, but in the interaction between thinking bodies (humans) and between thinking bodies and objects (humans and socioculturally constructed artifacts). Consciousness "arises, functions, and develops in the process of people's interaction with reality, on the basis of their sensuously objective activity, their socio-historical practice" (Spirkin, 1983, p. 153). Vygotsky insisted that socially meaningful activity, as a materialistic unit, has to be considered as the explanatory principle for understanding consciousness, since it was only through activity that consciousness developed in the first place. Thus, at its core, Vygotsky's theory rejected any attempt to decouple consciousness from behavior and searched for the explanation of consciousness in the interaction (that is, concrete and symbolic activity), which links humans to each other and to their artifacts.

Vygotsky was convinced that no theory that aimed at explaining complex psychological functioning by reducing it to a single factor qualified as an adequate scientific account of the mind. Rather than view cognitive development as an evolutionary, quantitative process within a "preformistic model," Vygotsky argued for a "stratificational model" (Vygotsky, 1981b, p. 155), which assumes that in the course of child development, ontogentically prior, and thus *lower order*, biologically specified, mental functions are retained but develop into more complex, or *higher order*, socioculturally determined mental functions. Included among the lower order functions are input systems (that is, vision, hearing, tactile, and olfactory systems) as well as natural memory and involuntary attention.[4] The higher order functions encompass logical memory, voluntary attention, conceptual thought, planning, perception, problem solving, and voluntary inhibitory and disinhibitory faculties. Although biological factors constitute the necessary prerequisite for elementary processes to *emerge*, sociocultural factors, in contrast, constitute the necessary condition for the elementary, natural processes to *develop*. In other words, development does not proceed solely, or even primarily, as the unfolding of inborn faculties, but as the *transformation* of these innately specified processes once they intertwine with socioculturally determined factors.[5]

While most theories of mental development recognize the presence of the social milieu in which cognitive growth occurs,

---

[4] In his own work, Vygotsky failed to fully specify his understanding of what constitutes lower order or natural mental functions, and left much of this aspect of sociocultural theory for others, such as Luria, to work out. As was mentioned, Vygotsky did not focus much of his research on the biological line of development, preferring instead to concentrate on the sociocultural aspect of ontogenesis. Wertsch (1985b) points out, Vygotsky failed "to provide an adequate account of the natural line of development, and failed to specify what it is that is transformed by social forces." (p. 197). Perhaps, however, Wertsch is too harsh in his criticism of Vygotsky on this count. After all, as Wertsch himself notes, little was known about the natural line of development in Vygotsky's time. We still do not know all there is to know about the human brain, some 60 years after Vygotsky's death. Moreover, since Vygotsky was attempting to develop a view of mind as mediated, it seems to us quite natural that he should focus his initial efforts on the socially derived side of the equation.

[5] Luria (1973) discusses, in some detail, how biologically specified neural systems are reorganized into a complex and powerful mental functional system as a result of the appropriation of sociocultural processes.

Vygotsky argued for the uniqueness of the social milieu. He conceived of the sociocultural setting as the primary, and determining, factor in the development of higher forms of human mental activity and called for the redefinition of development from a quantitative to a qualitative problem, thereby renouncing the characterization of the child in terms of the adult. Such "negative characterization" (Vygotsky, 1981c, p. 149) could not reveal any positive features assessing essential differences between children and adults, but only equate differences with deficiencies.

Furthermore, Vygotsky rejected child development as exclusively a slow and gradual accumulation of change—an evolutionary process. He argued, on the contrary, that cognitive change is also brought about through abrupt occurrences—revolutionary processes. Here he drew a critical analogy between cognitive development and cultural–historical development: "Historical development seems to proceed along a straight path. When revolution, the rupture of the historical fabric, occurs, naive observers see nothing but catastrophe, gasps, and precipices. For them, historical progression stops at this point until it alights anew on a straight and smooth path" (Vygotsky, 1981b, p. 150).[6]

Vygotsky saw the transformation of elementary processes into higher order ones as possible through the mediating function of culturally constructed artifacts including tools, symbols, and more elaborate sign systems, such as language. Children learning to master their own psychological behavior proceed from dependency on other people to independence and self-regulation as a consequence of gaining control over culturally fabricated semiotic tools. It was on the nature of the mediating link that Vygotsky and his followers eventually parted company, as we will see.

---

[6] In assuming that radical, as well as gradual, changes are at work in the formation of higher mental functions, Vygotsky undoubtedly relied upon the standard understanding of the development in dialectical-materialist thinking. Development, from this perspective, is conceived of as a dialectical entity consisting of continuous changes of a quantitative nature and discontinuous changes of a qualitative nature. The quantitative changes allow for qualitative changes to arise, or, phrased differently, natural capacities operate as necessary conditions for cognitive development, but they do not constitute sufficient conditions for such growth. Furthermore, dialectical development, according to Kussmann (1976), is teleological, in that it is not a circular movement, or an endless repetition of past forms, but a movement on an *ascending spiral*, encapsulating the assumption that it is directed towards improvement.

Mediation

Tools and Signs. Explicitly acknowledging dialectical materialism as the source of his elaborations, Vygotsky theorized that human consciousness is fundamentally *mediated* mental activity. Beginning with the theorem that humans affect reality and, in transforming reality, establish new conditions for their being and consequently change themselves, Vygotsky repudiated the contemplative conceptions of the individual. If humans were to be regarded as consciously acting beings, whose acting brings about changes in their surrounding world, then humans, in general, and their activities in particular, cannot be adequately understood within a behavioristic framework, since even the most unchallenging activity is not merely a passive reaction by the individual but an action aimed at a specific goal. Therefore, psychological processes have to be explained as part of active participation in the everyday world, and not in the world of the experimental laboratory.

Historically, Vygotsky argued, while humans sought to adapt to their external world through assimilating the laws of nature, they also attempted to control and master nature. The need for control led to the creation and invention of tools, technical as well as mechanical. Tools allowed individuals, in collaboration with other individuals, to shape their world according to their own motives and goals, and thus to alter processes that, without human intrusion, would have taken a different course. Tools used in work—the prototype of human goal-directed activity—function as mediators, as instruments which stand between the subject (the individual) and the object (the goal towards which the individual's action is directed). Vygotsky (1978) explained that "the tool's function is to serve as the conductor of human influence on the object of activity; it is *externally* oriented; it must lead to changes in objects. It is a means by which human external activity is aimed at mastering, and triumphing over, nature" (p. 55).

Tools are created by people under specific cultural and historical conditions. As such, they carry with them the characteristics of the culture in, for example, reflecting the state and level of labor activities. Tools are used to accomplish something, to aid in solving problems that cannot be solved in the same way in their absence. Since they are directed at objects, they influence and thereby change objects. In turn, they also exert an influence on the individual in that they give rise to previously unknown activities and previously unknown ways of conceptualizing phenomena in the world.[7]

Vygotsky extended the notion of instrumental mediation by drawing an analogy between the role of technical and mechanical tools and what he called "psychological tools" (Vygotsky, 1981b, p. 136). Psychological tools are artifacts, including mnemonic techniques, algebraic symbols, diagrams, schemes, and, of course, language, all of which serve as mediators for the individual's mental activity. Vygotsky's principal claim was that just as individuals use technical tools for manipulating their environment, they use psychological tools for directing and controlling their physical and mental behavior. Although Vygotsky established the link between mechanical/concrete tools and psychological tools, or signs, he also observed that "this analogy, like any other, does not imply the identity of these similar concepts," and that one "should not expect to find *many* similarities with tools in those means of adaptation we call signs" (Vygotsky, 1978, pp. 52–53)

For one thing, unlike technical tools, which are externally oriented at the *object* of activity, signs are internally oriented at the *subject* of activity, that is, directed at causing changes in the behavior of other people or oneself (Vygotsky, 1978, p. 55). By virtue of its inclusion in a particular activity, the sign alters the process and the structure of mental functions necessary for carrying out the activity. In natural, or biologically specified memory, two stimuli are connected via a direct link, in an A to B relationship. Thus, to remember someone's phone number we repeat it a sufficient number of times to imprint it directly in our memory. Perhaps, more dramatically, most of us who are old enough can remember what we were wearing, whom we were with, and the time of day when we heard the news of JFK's assassination. The link between A, the Assassination, and B, our attire at that particular time, is direct—that is, nonmediated. In higher order, or symbolically mediated memory, the two stimuli are connected via new

---

[7] Recent developments in computer science are a case in point. When computers were created to aid people in achieving more efficiency and accuracy in carrying out certain tasks, their continual refinement made them such sophisticated machines that they opened a multitude of new avenues for use. The emergence of AI as a scientific discipline is the most recent effect this development has had. The dialectics of this development is reflected in the fact that cognitive processes are now conceptualized on analogy to the processes of a sophisticated electronic machine.

links, A–X and B–X is thus replaced by the new connections. That is, A is linked to B via X. This means that a new path is created so that in the case of retrieving information from voluntary, or mediated, memory, previously unrecoverable segments of information can be retrieved because of the utilization of a mediating device that then basically functions as a heuristic element with respect to the goal to be achieved. This is what happens when we tie a string around our finger in order to remember something, use paper and pencil to write down a phone number we wish to remember, or sketch an outline for a text to assist comprehension. Vygotsky insisted that mental and sociocultural activity in humans are bound together in a dependent, symbolically mediated, relationship that develops during ontogenesis. The mechanism through which external, sociocultural, activity is transformed into internal, mental, functioning is considered in the ensuing section.

Regulation and the Zone of Proximal Development. Higher psychological functions, because they are symbolically mediated, ultimately come under control of the individual (for example, self-initiated and self-inhibited). Gaining and maintaining control over complex mental processes, however, has to be acquired by the individual and begins with the child learning to act willfully. This process is characterized by two important features: (a) it originates outside the individual, and (b) it is directed by language as the most powerful of semiotic systems.

Vygotsky conceived of the child as learning from society those activities (for example work, play, education, literacy, and so on) that society has constructed and placed value on. The sociocultural environment presents the child with a variety of tasks and demands and engages the child primarily—though not exclusively—through the use of language, itself a socially constituted and historically developed artifact. In the early stages of ontogenesis, the child is completely dependent on other people, usually the parents, who initiate the child's acting by instructing the child in what to do, how to do it, and what not to do. Parents, as representatives of the culture, and the conduit through which the culture passes into the child, actualize these instructions primarily by talking to their offspring.

Parents' linguistic activity functions to direct the child's attention to certain objects in his/her environment—those that are the target of the act in which the child is to engage. The child's voluntary act, then, starts out as a motor act beginning with the adult's speech and ending with the child's movement. On a narrow scale, the adult guides the child's motor act; on a broader scale, however, the adult organizes the child's world. The adult aids the child in learning how to differentiate his or her immediate environment by establishing constants in a state of flux and by pointing out, through symbolic means, saliencies and patterns, in the surroundings that would otherwise remain amorphous for the child. These saliencies and patterns are determined by the norms, values, and motives of the respective sociocultural milieu that the adult represents (see Wertsch, Minick, & Arns, 1984).

Critical to Vygotsky's theory is that the process of voluntary acting is distributed between two people, one of whom (the adult or expert) already knows how to perform a particular act and one who (the child or novic) does not. Equally important is the fact that speech serves to direct, or mediate, the interactive process that transpires between the two. This conceptualization of the conditions for the mental growth of the child led Vygotsky to formulate a distinction between the child's *actual* and *potential* levels of development. The former characterizes the child's ability to perform certain tasks independently of another person (that is, without help) and, in essence, reflects those processes or functions that have been established and stabilized in the child. The latter level of development characterizes those functions that the child can carry out *with* the help of another person. These are not sufficiently stabilized to allow the child to perform independently in a given-task. The difference between what the child, or novice, is capable of when acting alone and what he or she is capable of when acting under the guidance of a more experienced other is referred to as the *zone of proximal development*, which is defined as follows: "It is the distance between the actual developmental level as determined by independent problem solving and the level of potential development as determined through problem solving under adult guidance or in collaboration with more capable peers" (Vygotsky, 1978, p. 86). To emphasize again, it is not the carrying out of a specific task that is the important feature of *interpersonal* activity, but the higher cognitive process that emerges as a result of the interaction.

During the first stages of ontogenesis, the volitional act is carried out by another person and the child acting together as a functional system (Luria, 1932), in which the capacity to think strategically is vested exclusively in the adult knower or expert. At the next stage, the activity gradually changes its structure as the child or novice begins to *appropriate* the necessary mental functions from the expert (Leont'ev, 1981b).[8] Vygotsky formulated the transition that occurs during this stage as a *general law of cultural development*:

> Any function in the child's cultural development appears twice, or on two planes, first it appears on the social plane, and then on the psychological plane, first it appears between people as an inter-psychological category, and then within the child as an intrapsychological category. This is equally true with regard to voluntary attention., logical memory, and the formation of concepts, and the development of volition. (Vygotsky, 1981a, p. 163)

The shift from the intermental to the intramental plane marks the beginning of the child's control over his or her own behavior—that is, self-regulation. The role of language in the appropriation process as the primary symbolic cultural artifact is critical. Thus, cognitive development is a question of individual children gaining symbolically mediated control over, or regulation of, strategic mental processes.

Initially, children are incapable of exerting much control over their environment. In fact, the environment, in the early stages of mental growth, exerts its influence on the child and the child is said to be *object-regulated*. While children at an early age are capable of carrying out certain kinds of independent actions that do not require a decontextualized representation, they are not able to pursue independent action whenever a particular goal is not "directly suggested by the environment" (Wertsch, 1979b, p. 89). Children can engage in actions directed toward a decontextualized goal only if their mental processes are mediated by an adult. In the very early stages of mental growth, however, even adult mediation may be ineffective. When, for example, a parent instructs a child to

---

[8] The process by which mental activity passes from the expert to the novice is one of the most controversial points of Vygotsky's theory. It is on this point that the theory has been open to criticism from cognitive scientists espousing a nativist view of cognitive growth. Essentially, their argument is that even though children and adults may interact in a zone of proximal development, it remains to be explained how that joint activity is *internalized* by the child and how a more complex cognitive system can develop from a simpler system over time. However, the very concept of *internationalization* is based on a view of the child as a solipsistic biological organism whose cognitive powers simply unfold or ripen with the passage of time, rather than as someone who experiences "productive participation in joint activity" (Griffin, & Cole, 1989, p. 68). For further discussion of this provocative issue see Wertsch (1985b) and Newman, Griffin, and Cole. (1989).

fetch a toy located at some distance from the child's present position, the child is often easily distracted on the way to complying with the parent's request by other intervening objects. The child may completely forget that he or she was instructed to do something, or may return with the wrong toy. Similarly, Wertsch and Hickmann (1987) found that in a puzzle-copying task, an object-regulated child instructed by his mother to look at a window piece in the puzzle (a decontextualized frame) failed to do so and instead looked at the real window (a contextualized frame) in the room where the task was being carried out.

At the next stage of development, the child is able to carry out certain tasks, but only with appropriate linguistically mediated assistance from a parent, or older and more capable peer. At this stage the metacognition of the child is controlled by a surrogate who has the ability to perform the task. This function is referred to as *other-regulation*. The primary means of carrying out other-regulatory functions is through dialogic speech. Eventually, the child begins to take over a larger portion of the responsibility for strategic functions, until *self-regulation*, or independent strategic functioning, is achieved. The attaining of self-regulation, however, is not an absolute. That is, if a child gains self-regulation in a specific kind of task, he or she does not necessarily have self-regulation in all tasks and for all time; nor is self-regulation achieved at a specific point in ontogenetic growth. It is often the case that a child of four will have gained self-regulation in a given task, while another child, of the same age, will require other-regulated to solve the same task. What is more, an older child may well be other-regulated in the same task (see Wertsch, 1985a; Wertsch & Hickmann, 1987). Self-regulation is a relative phenomenon.

The transition from other-regulation, or intermental activity, to self-regulation, or intramental activity, takes place, as we have said, in the zone of proximal development where child and adult engage in the dialogic process—a process in which the adult undertakes to direct the child through a task, and where the child provides feedback to the adult, who then makes the necessary adjustments in the kind of direction offered to the child. The adult's purpose in directing the child, however, is not simply to have the child complete the task, but to instruct the child in how to solve the task strategically.[9] The adult attempts to guide the child toward a

---

[9] The precise nature of the interaction between the child and the adult is dependent on sociocultural factors. Research by Wertsch and his colleagues, for instance, has disclosed a marked difference in the dialogic mediation provided by

definition of situation that parallels that of the adult. In the early stages of transition, the child's perspective on the purpose of the communicative interaction (definition of situation) does not match that of the adult. Consequently, the child may be able to perform the required task, but without realizing that he or she is involved in a goal-directed (strategic) activity. The point is that the child does not complete the task because of a shared situation definition with the adult; rather, the child comes to understand the adult's perspective on the task "as a result of behaving (under someone else's guidance) *as if* she/he understood it and of trying to create a coherent account of the relationship between speech and action" (Wertsch, 1979a, p. 21).

Empirical support for the above model of dialogic interaction comes from the work of Wertsch and his colleagues, which shows that when attempting to direct children in a puzzle-copying task, middle-class educated adults consistently employ strategic statements, such as "now look at the model to see what comes next," and only if the children are unable to respond to the directive do the adults shift to a more referential mode of speaking, as in "try the red piece here." Interestingly, however, even if the strategic mode fails with a given child, the adults continue to return to this mode of other-regulation. On the other hand, Wertsch et al. (1984) found that rural uneducated Brazilian mothers tended to employ a lower frequency of strategic and a higher frequency of referential speech in order to regulate the behavior of their children in a similar puzzle-solving task.

Eventually, of course, children, under normal circumstances, learn to function independently of adult guidance, and utterances that were once produced by the adults are appropriated by the children, as they take control of their own conscious activity, as in the following excerpt uttered by a single child drawn from one of Wertsch's puzzle-copying studies: "Where's the white? In the middle of the puzzle?" The child's speech in its self-regulatory function has a social cast to it; this is because the origin of the strategic function, which it mirrors, is ultimately social (that is, it originates in the adult–child dialogue of an earlier developmental sage). This leads us to consideration of how Vygotsky conceptualized the development of inner speech and its strategic mediational function.

Inner Speech and Private Speech. The primary, and ontogenetically earlier, function of speech is its communicative or

a rural peasant mother and that provided by an urban teacher and mothers from an educated middle-class background.

interpersonal function. It serves to establish social contact, carry out social interactions, and coordinate behavior in social encounters or joint activities. The secondary, or egocentric, function of speech (secondary only because it is ontogenetically later and derivative from the primary function and not because it is less important) is intrapersonal and cognitive. Egocentric speech is a phenomenon that has been studied by numerous researchers over the years. Its specific function, however, has been a matter of considerable debate. Piaget, for instance, concluded that egocentric speech serves no specific function and merely represents an ontogenetic stage in the transition from individual to social speech and eventually disappears.

For Vygotsky, however, egocentric speech plays a central function in the development and conduct of mental activity; what is more, it does not disappear, but goes *underground* as verbal thought, or inner speech, in elliptical form. As egocentric speech is transformed into inner speech, it loses its structural equivalence to social speech, its progenitor:

> In the beginning, egocentric speech is identical in structure with social speech, but in the process of transformation into inner speech it gradually becomes less complete and coherent as it becomes governed by an almost entirely predicative syntax...the child talks about the things he sees or hears or does at a given moment. As a result, he tends to leave out the subject and all words connected with it, condensing his speech more and more until only predicates are left. (Vygotsky, 1986, p. 145)

In discussing inner speech, Vygotsky makes a critical distinction between word sense, *smysl* in Russian, and word meaning, *znachenis*. Sense is highly individual and variable in semantic content; the sense of a word is contextualized, in that it absorbs, so to speak, an entire situation. Word sense is highly idiosyncratic to the extent that lexical units acquire nuances and merge with others so that new meanings arise within a speaker. The semantic structure of inner speech is thus characterized by a predominance of new information over given, or known information (Wertsch, 1979b). In its most condensed form, inner speech is reduced to a single word packed with meaning—a cognitive "black hole." An individual engaged in a puzzle task, for example, might form an inner-speech utterance such as "Green" rather than a fully syntactic utterance like "Now, I need to put the green piece above the blue piece."[10]

Word meaning, in contrast, is more stable and decontextualized and can be thought of as the conventionalized dictionary definition of a world:

> The interaction between sense and meaning constitutes the inner *dialogue* between two different subjects of one thought. One subject accommodates his or her thought to the pre-existing system of meaning, while the other immediately turns them into idiosyncratic sense, which later will be transformed again into intelligible words. The subject of thoughts is therefore simultaneously engaged in two conversations, one outbound, the other inbound. The outbound thought and speech are oriented toward real or imaginary interlocutors [private speech], while the inbound thought brings the meaning of others back to the subject. The coexistence of these inbound and outbound processes ensures the dialogical nature of human thought. (Kozulin, 1990, p. 268)

Continuous Access.   The emergence of self-regulated activity does not, in Vygotskian theory, signal the end of the developmental process. On the contrary, development is conceived of as dynamic and fluid. Thus, once egocentric speech is transformed into inner speech and goes "underground," it does not remain underground forever, but it can, and does, resurface as *private speech* whenever an individual engages in a task of enhanced difficulty.[11] Private speech has a strategic function, just a social speech has a strategic function in other-regulation. The more difficult the task, the more fully structured (social-like) private speech becomes (Sokolov, 1972). It represents an externalization of the inner order as the individual attempts to regain control of his or her cognitive functioning to carry out the task. From this perspective, an adult is not an autonomous, finalized knower, but an organism that recovers and utilizes earlier knowing strategies in situations that cannot be

---

[10] Actually, Wertsch has shown that private speech, the externalized form of inner speech (see below), is not exclusively marked by new information and often contains utterances with marks of given information, such as definite NPs and pronoun subjects (Wertsch, 1979b).

[11] The term *private speech* was first coined by Flavell (1966). At Wertsch's recommendation, it has become more widely used today in lieu of egocentric speech.

dealt with by self-regulation along. This is in direct contrast to a Piagetian model, which postulates the adult as some sort of cognitive debutant who "comes out" at age seven, reaches the final stage of knowing, and forgets the knowing strategies of the past. According to the Vygotskian view of mental growth, in difficult knowing situations the adult reverts to child-like knowing strategies to control the situation and gain self-regulation. We refer to this dynamic quality of mental activity as the *principle of continuous access* (Frawley & Lantolf, 1985). Research on verbal mediation conducted by Luria, Sokolov, and more recently by Appel (1986), de Guerrero (1990), Frawley and Lantolf (1984), and McCafferty (1992), provides significant empirical support for this principle.

ACTIVITY THEORY

Shortly after Vygotsky's death, a group of his colleagues and students, finding the political climate in Moscow not conducive to the continuation of their research, established a center in the Ukranian city of Kharkov. Included among the Kharkovites, as they were known, were A. N. Leont'ev, Peter Galperin, and Peter Zinchenko. Within a short period of time, perhaps due, in part, to political pressure exerted from Moscow (Joravsky, 1989), but perhaps also due to a legitimate disagreement with their mentor and predecessor, the Kharkovites veered away from Vygotsky's position regarding symbolic mediation of mental life and embraced the notion that mediation arises fundamentally from practical activity with the world of objects (Kozulin, 1990, p. 245). Zinchenko, for example, maintained that Vygotsky had separated himself from a truly Marxist psychology by insisting that culture rather than actual relationships to reality determined the mind. Such a stance, despite their insistence to the contrary, placed the Kharkovites dangerously close to Piaget's conceptualization of cognition as developing from the sensory motor activity of children with objects, rather than on the basis of socioculturally mediated activity as insisted upon by Vygotsky. This, as we will see, would have important consequences for Leont'ev's formulation of Activity Theory.

There is, of course, no reason to insist that mediation has to be exclusively symbolic or exclusively practical. Vygotsky apparently recognized this possibility by allowing for individual activity and interpersonal relationships to play mediational roles, in addition to symbolic systems, the major focus of his own research (Kozulin,

1990, p. 246). We find it is difficult to conceive of any form of human activity, practical or symbolic, as free of sociocultural influence. Indeed, as Schrage (1986) remarks, "human actions tell the story of the social practices of which they are organically a part... human actions are fibers embedded in the texture of social practices and display a contextualized sense" (p. 45). That this is a view of human actions not without some merit is amply attested by Ratner (1991), who shows, among other things, that even phenomena such as human emotions and mental disorders are determined by sociocultural circumstances.

Eventually the Kharkovites, largely in the person of A. N. Leont'ev, proposed a formal theory of activity designed to provide a more "Marxian" explanatory basis of higher mental functioning than Vygotsky seemingly had developed. According to Wertsch (1985b, p. 211), the fundamental question raised by Activity Theory is "What is the individual or group doing in a particular setting?" On the face of it, this seems to be a rather banal question, until we begin to consider what is involved in developing an acceptable answer, because, as Leont'ev showed, the response must be formulated on three distinct levels of analysis. The three levels proposed by Leont'ev as comprising the explanatory framework of Activity Theory are: activity, action, and operation.[12]

The highest level of analysis within the theory, the level of *activity*, is defined as the social institutionally determined setting or context based on a set of assumptions about the appropriate roles, goals, and means to be used by the participants in that setting. Setting, in Leont'ev's framework, does not mean the physical or perceptual context in which humans function; rather, it refers to the sociocultural interpretation or creation that is imposed on the context by the participants (Wertsch, 1985b, pp. 203, 212). Examples of activity settings include play, work, education, worship, and leisure time.

The level of activity is inextricably linked to the concept of *motive*, because without motive there can be no activity (Leont'ev, 1981a, p. 59). Motives specify what is to "maximized" in a setting (Wertsch, 1985b, p. 212) and arise out of the system of relations individuals maintain with other individuals and the world. Thus, the motive of labor is productivity and the motive of formal

---

[12] Leont'ev uses the term *activity* not only to characterize the overall theory (Activity Theory), but also to label the highest of the three strata that constitute the levels of analysis.

schooling is learning for learning's sake (Wertsch, 1985b, p. 212).[13] In labor activity, productivity is maximized and error is minimized, because the latter represents expensive interference with the former (Wertsch, 1985b, p. 212). Moreover, activity settings and their accompanying motives are transparent to the participants and are, thus, not readily accessible to conscious reflection (Wertsch, 1985b, p. 213).

In the puzzle experiment carried out by Wertsch and his colleagues in Brazil discussed earlier, the rural mother interpreted the context in which she and her child were to interact from the perspective of labor activity rather than formal schooling, which is how the teacher in the same experiment (and middle-class parents in Wertsch's other experiments) construed the same context. In rural peasant cultures learning is "inextricably linked to productive or economic activity" (Wertsch, et al., 1984, p. 169). Erroneous performance in such a setting is viewed as potentially costly in economic terms. Learning then is highly contextualized. One way of maximizing production and minimizing costly errors is for the mother to take responsibility for the most difficult parts of the task and guide the child's behavior via directive referential speech, for example, "Pick up the red piece and put it here!" (Wertsch, 1985b, p. 182). There is, of course, a tradeoff here because "independent functioning is not encouraged until it is likely to be error-free" (Wertsch, et al., 1984, p. 155). Hence, the child ought to have less opportunity to learn to think strategically. In the case at hand, the child solved the puzzle, but learned little about solving *puzzles*. In educated middle-class cultures and in formal schooling (at least in Wertsch's interpretation of the school setting) on the other hand, education is usually separated from production activity, and in such circumstances, mistakes are much less likely to be seen as having negative economic consequences. Thus, the child's performance is permitted to diverge from the correct outcome, but the child is, at the same time, afforded the opportunity to function independently of the adult at an earlier stage.

The second level of analysis consists of *actions*. Activities are always directed towards some goal. To say that an individual is

---

[13] While we do not necessarily disagree with Wertsch on the motive of labor, we feel that his conceptualization of the motive of education is too narrow. Although we cannot pursue the issue here, in our view people can have very different motives for education. In a capitalist society, for example, the motive for learning can be the capital into which the learning, or symbolic capital accumulated during educational activity (Bourdieu, 1990), can be converted at the conclusion of the process.

engaged in a particular activity tells us nothing of the means—end relationship involved; it just tells us that the individual is functioning in a socioculturally defined context (Wertsch, 1985b, p. 203). The level of action is the level of an activity at which the process is subordinated to a concrete goal (Leont'ev, 1981). Without an object toward which it is directed, an activity is "devoid of sense" (Leont'ev, 1981a, p. 48). The goal of an activity functions as a kind of regulator of the activity, and itself can be segmented into subgoals. Thus, an individual may have the goal of building a house, but in order to carry this out, he or she must first attain the subgoal of learning how to use the requisite tools. On a more complex scale, an individual may have the goal of becoming a lawyer, but in order to fulfill this goal, he or she must realize the subgoal of passing the bar exam, which, in turn, depends on realizing the subgoal of graduating from law school which, in turn, depends on fulfilling the subgoal of obtaining a bachelor's degree, which, in turn, depends on fulfilling the subgoal of complying with major and general education requirements, which, in turn, may depend on a subgoal of passing a foreign language course, and so on.

In the sense exemplified here, goals are not physical objects but phenomena of "anticipatory reflection" and, as such, permit one to compare and evaluate intended and actual outcomes of activity before the activity is concretely operationalized (Lomov, 1982, p. 72). Vygotsky, attempting to make this point much earlier, borrowed Marx's well-known contrast between human and insect behavior. The human architect or weaver sees his or her intended construction in the mind's eye long before putting hand to paper or physical structure on the ground or the loom. The unerring bee and spider, on the other hand, are much simpler machines, excreting their hives or webs in unchanging stereotypes without intentional preliminaries (Joravsky, 1989, p. 259).

Another important feature of actions is that any given action can be embedded in a different activity. For example, the goal of building a wooden table can be realized in an educational, labor, or play activity setting. Significantly, in each case the building of the table can take on a very different meaning. Another important feature of goals is that, once formed, they are not necessarily stable. Individuals, as agents active in creating their world, can modify, postpone, or even abandon goals altogether.[14]

---

[14] According to Leont'ev (1981a), there remains a great deal of work to be done on how goal formation takes place in the first place.

The final dimension of an activity is its operational level. *Operations* largely determine the means, physical or mental, through which an action is carried out; they are bound to the actual circumstances and conditions under which a goal is realized. The same goal can be achieved through a different set of operations. If one is hungry and has the goal of obtaining food to satisfy the hunger, provided the option is available, one can drive to a supermarket and purchase the necessary food. On the other hand, one may construct a fishing or hunting apparatus of some type in order to satisfy the goal. Here it can be seen that operations under which some goal is realized may themselves at some point be a necessary subgoal. Such was the case in our earlier example of learning how to use tools (a subgoal, later transformed into operations) to build a house.

An essential feature of operations is that they usually become automatized procedures, but once they attain this status, they do not necessarily remain so forever. If a carpenter is building a house with the assistance of a power saw, normally an automatic procedure for such a skilled artisan, and the saw unexpectedly develops a problem, the carpenter then must focus attention on regaining the proper function of the tool. In this case, the proper functioning of the tool becomes a subgoal and what had been an automatized operation loses this quality, at least temporarily. Once the saw's function is recovered, the tool again takes its place as a condition for building the house and its use returns to its automatic status. Similarly, even though native speakers usually exercise automatic control over the formal properties of their language, in the process of achieving some communicative goal they occasionally experience difficulties deploying this linguistic system, such as in the case of lexical access problems. On these occasions, the linguistic system (that is, the tool used to carry out their communicative intent) becomes the focus of their attention and intention, and access to the appropriate lexical item is formed into a temporary subgoal. Once the search is completed, assuming it is successful, use of the formal system again takes on its normal role at the level of operation. It should be clear, at this point, that because operations can be converted into goals or subgoals as actions are carried out, one must look at actions and operations and their interaction simultaneously to fully understand a given activity (Wertsch, 1985b, p. 205).

Leont'ev's decentering of the importance of semiotic mediation in human activity in favor of practical activity meant that there was no way of linking individual actions with sociocultural systems

(Kozulin, 1990, p. 252). On the level of activity, Leont'ev relied heavily on Marxist concepts, including labor, productivity, and appropriation, to stress that human subjects are sociohistorical beings and not abstract, idealized entities (Kozulin, 1990, p. 251). At the same time, however, as we have already pointed out, on the two remaining levels—actions and operations—he employed Piagetian-like argumentation that conceived of development as the internalization of sensorimotor actions as mental schemas (Kozulin, 1990, p. 251). Thus, there was no way of binding the latter two levels to sociocultural categories. In other words, Activity Theory, as originally conceived by Leont'ev, had no mechanism for higher forms of consciousness to arise from sociocultural practices. Vygotsky clearly saw this potential problem and for this reason established symbolic mediation, the link between sociocultural practice and mental functioning, as the centerpiece of his theoretical thinking.[15]

Another problem eventually arose with respect to Activity Theory—a problem that we can only mention here, since a full discussion of it would take us too far afield. The distinction between the theory as an explanatory principle of higher forms of cognition and as itself a legitimate object of psychological research became blurred (Kozulin, 1990, p. 253). Researchers in sociocultural psychology fell victim to the same set of circumstances that Vygotsky had warned about at the outset of his career: Activity cannot be an object of study and simultaneously serve as an explanatory principle of consciousness, unless it has its own unit of analysis as well as its own explanatory principles (Judin, 1984).

To summarize this brief examination of Activity Theory, human sociocultural activity that gives rise to higher forms of cognition, is comprised of contextual, intentional, and circumstantial dimensions. The motive and goal constitute a "kind of vector," determining the direction and amount of effort an individual exerts in carrying out the activity (Lomov, 1982, p. 69). Motives "energize" an activity and goals impart directionality (Leont'ev, 1981a, p. 60). The actual realization of the activity is achieved through specific material circumstances at the operational level. Thus, the level of motive answers why something is done, the level of goal answers what is done, and the level of operations answers how it is done. The link between socioculturally defined motives and concrete

---

[15] Leont'ev (1981a, p. 57) appears to at least acknowledge the role semiotic mediation plays in activity.

actions and operations is provided by semiotic systems, of which language is the most powerful and pervasive.

UNIT OF ANALYSIS

To this point we have avoided mention of a point of confusion and difficulty with Vygotsky's position on what constitutes the proper unit of analysis of higher forms of cognitive functioning. In his writings he proposed that in order to carry out the necessary research on the nature and function of consciousness, a minimal unit of analysis needed to be established, which was itself a microcosm of consciousness. This is a very important point, since for Vygotsky consciousness could not be understood if it were reduced to its component elements. To do so would destroy the very object that psychology was to study. Trying to understand consciousness by reducing it to its elementary components was, for Vygotsky, as useless as trying to answer why water extinguishes fire by reducing water to its component elements of hydrogen and oxygen—hydrogen burns and oxygen nourishes the process (Wertsch, 1985b, p. 193). Vygotsky proposed the linguistic sign, or more appropriately, the inner speech word, as the minimal unit in which the form, function, and genesis of consciousness could be investigated. As Wertsch (1985b) has pointed out, however, this presents real problems, since it is difficult to observe functions such as planning, voluntary attention, and voluntary memory in word meaning, even if we construe meaning to entail idiosyncratic *smysl* sense, as Vygotsky proposed. Furthermore, if the mediating link between sociocultural history and mind is provided by sign systems, then to insist, as Vygotsky does, that the same sign systems can serve as the unit of analysis of consciousness is quite problematic, and in fact violates his own criterion of avoiding circularity in scientific psychological research.

Wertsch (1985b, p. 207) following V. P. Zinchenko, proposed tool-mediated action as the proper unit of analysis for consciousness. This proposal has some merit, because such action can occur on both the intermental (that is, joint action) as well as the intramental plain. Furthermore, one can observe planning, memory, attention, and so on, at work in tool-mediated action, whether it involves physical or symbolic tools, including intrapersonal as well as interpersonal dialogue, more readily than in individual words, as originally proposed by Vygotsky (cf. Wertsch & Hickman, 1987).

METHODOLOGICAL PARADIGM[16]

Vygotsky believed that an understanding of mediated forms of human behavior could not be achieved through exclusive reliance on *phenotypic*, or descriptive, research alone. If it were possible to uncover the essence of objects and processes in their outer manifestation, science would be superfluous and scientific analysis could be replaced by everyday experience (Vygotsky, 1978, p. 63). Furthermore, since Vygotsky's stated aim was to *understand* rather than to *predict* "what is uniquely human in human behavior," he was convinced of the need for a research methodology that transcended models borrowed from the natural sciences (Kozulin, 1990, p. 263). Vygotsky's general approach to psychological research is, we believe, nicely reflected in Israel's (1979) condemnation of experimental laboratory research that transforms humans into inert objects of analysis rather than allowing them to behave as real agents in control of their own mental activity

To contrast his approach to psycholinguistic research with what he perceived as phenotypic approaches used, for example, by introspectionists, Vygotsky coined the term *genetic method*, which was a way of understanding, rather than predicting, mental functioning (Vygotsky, 1981a). Although he saw descriptive research as necessary, he considered *genotype* analysis to be indispensable. For Vygotsky, genotypic research was a means of understanding mental processes through disclosure of their emergence and subsequent growth. An analysis that was not genetic in nature could not take account of the "inner workings and causal dynamics" of the phenomenon under study (Wertsch, 1985b, p. 18).[17] The only

---

[16] There exists a potential point of confusion in the Vygotskian literature having to do with the term "methodology." Russian psychologists, such as Davydov and Radzikhovskii (1985), when writing about Vygotsky often distinguish Vygotsky the psychologist from Vygotsky the methodologist. Their understanding of "methodologist," however, is quite different from the way western scholars use the term. It is much closer to our understanding of "theoretician" (cf. Wertsch, 1985b). In the following discussion, we intend methodology to have its usual meaning of a way of doing research.

[17] Recently, Gould (1983) has advocated an approach to scientific research quite similar to Vygotsky's. Like Vygotsky, he states that a developmental perspective permits researchers to differentiate between "superficial appearance and knowledge of underlying causes" (Gould, 1983, p. 317). He illustrates his point with a discussion of whether zebras are black with white stripes or white with black stripes. Gould argues that one cannot determine this by studying normal adult zebras (aberrant patternings in adults might also shed some light on the problem, a viewpoint which Vygotsky would surely embrace) but by following the development of stripes from the embryo.

complete analysis of mental functioning, according to Vygotsky, has to incorporate evidence from the four genetic domains in which semiotic mediation plays a central role: phylogenesis, sociocultural history, ontogenesis, and microgenesis.

Our earlier discussion of mediation and tool use provides a glimpse of what Vygotsky understood as the phylogenetic domain. He assumed, on the basis of the evidence available during his day, drawn largely from the primate research of Köhler and Yerkes, that only humans are capable of using cultural artifacts (tools and symbols) to mediate their behavior and thinking. By studying the ways in which apes use or fail to use tools, Vygotsky reasoned that we could learn more about how humans ultimately developed this unique capacity. As for the sociocultural domain, with the notable and controversial exception of Luria's (1976) study of the impact of schooled literacy on cognitive functioning among the Uzbek people of Soviet Central Asia, Vygotsky and his colleagues carried out little research in this area, relying instead on the earlier writings of others, including Durkheim, Levy-Bruhl, and Weber (Wertsch, 1985, p. 30).[18]

It is in the final two domains that the most interesting differences between Vygotsky's approach to experimentation and more traditional approaches surface. Vygotsky reasoned that if psychology is to explain (that is, to understand) higher forms of socioculturally derived consciousness, it could not study mind in its fully formed and smoothly functioning adult state. Vygotsky (1978, p. 63) referred to this as the "problem of fossilized behavior" and believed that it was fruitless for psychology to attempt to study automated cognitive processes. Therefore, he rejected introspective methods claiming that, at best, they provide confirmation of the existence of natural, biologically specified forms of mental behavior and, at worst, they often confuse the subject's feelings with true description. In any event, introspection offers psychology nothing in the way of explanation (understanding) of higher mental functions (Vygotsky, 1978, pp. 60, 67). Vygotsky also expressed a lack of confidence in the reaction time paradigm of experimental psychol-

---

[18] Between 1931 and 1932 Luria set out to test Vygotsky's theoretical claim that a change in sociocultural circumstances would have profound consequences for the functioning of higher mental processes. Luria's was a study of the decontextualization of mediational means as a result of schooled literacy among the Uzbeks of Soviet Central Asia (Luria, 1976). Scribner and Cole (1981) report on an attempt to replicate Luria's findings on the impact of schooled literacy on higher mental processes.

ogy. He argued that reaction time measures could only provide evidence of quantitative variations in psychological processes, the source of which must still be the object of speculation. More importantly, however, he seriously questioned the truth of the assumption that "a complex reaction consists of a chain of separate processes which may be arbitrarily added and subtracted" and argued that reaction time research converts experimental procedures into "surrogates for psychological processes" (Vygotsky, 1978, pp. 66–77).

As an alternative research paradigm, Vygotsky advocated a "developmental approach...to experimental psychology" (Vygotsky, 1978, p. 61)., Here he not only included the study of ontogenetic processes in children, the major component of his own research program, he also construed development to comprise the changes that occur in mental functioning over the span of a few weeks, a few days or even a few seconds (Vygotsky, 1978, p. 61). Wertsch (1985b) refers to this latter domain of experimentation as the study of "microgenesis." In the ontogenetic domain, the task of psychology was to tract the ontogenesis of mind from the point at which natural processes begin to merge with sociocultural processes during childhood. Vygotsky was, therefore, concerned with designing experiments to trace the process through which children incorporate semiotic systems into their cognitive activity in order to mediate that activity in tasks that are beyond their capabilities at any given moment (Vygotsky, 1978, p. 74). His experiments revealing how children of different ages utilize or fail to utilize colored pieces of paper (symbolic mediators) to help them remember forbidden colors in a memory game are typical of this line of research (cf. Vygotsky, 1978, Chapter 4). It seems clear that Vygotsky was not really a developmental psychologist, in the strict sense of the term, as much as he was a cognitive psychologist who used evidence from child development to explain (understand) how the adult mind functions.

With regard to the microgenetic domain, Vygotsky pointed out that when they set up an experiment, researchers often discard the most revealing evidence generated by their subjects—that which emerges as the experimenter trains the subject to criterion prior to actually beginning the experiment. It is here that the researcher has the opportunity to "grasp the process in flight" and study its content while it is being learned (Vygotsky, 1978, p. 68). Vygotsky suggested that researchers abandon pretraining periods, and provide subjects with minimal instructions accompanied by some auxiliary means (that is, mediation) to help them carry out a task.

By observing precisely how subjects integrate the auxiliary means into the task, including linguistic signs, the process under investigation is brought to the surface and made observable. As a variation of this approach to the study of microgenesis, Vygotsky reasoned that it should also be possible to gain access to psychological functions by introducing a complication, or disruption, into what otherwise would be an automatized, smoothly operating process. If, for example, subjects are asked to respond to a red light by pressing a button with the left hand and to a green light by pressing with the right, they will usually have little difficulty in achieving a consistent response. If, however, the response is then made more complicated by asking subjects to respond at times by pressing a button and at times by raising a finger, depending on the sequence in which the lights appear, they frequently externalize, through speaking, their inner order in such a way as to reveal the mental processes used to carry out the task.[19]

Vygotsky's criticism of experimental research notwithstanding, several of his colleagues, especially Luria in his early work, and his more recent followers, including Ushakova (the present volume), have made productive use of reaction time experimentation. Moreover, two of the papers in the present collection (de Guerrero & Gillette) also rely on introspective/retrospective techniques to yield significant information on mental functioning and language learning processes. The point we would like to underscore, however, is Vygotsky's contention that because of its capability to expose mental processes that might otherwise remain opaque, the genetic research paradigm represents a vital complement to orthodox research methods.

To conclude our overview of Vygotskian theory and research methodology, we take the liberty of borrowing from Vocate's (1987) cogent commentary on one of Vygotsky's leading followers, A. R. Luria. For Luria, as for Vygotsky, "'mind' is impossible without its synergetic relationship with spoken language, and that both arise from the physical reality of the human brain and human society" (Vocate, 1987, p. 129). For both scholars, linguistic activity is not simply the means through which mental activity is reflected, but it is the means through which higher mental functions derive their

---

[19] Some have already fruitfully extended this methodology to second language text processing and discourse production research (see, Ahmed, this volume; Appel & Lantolf, 1992; Frawley & Lantolf, 1985; and McCafferty, 1992, and this volume).

sociocultural origins and through which a specifically human mind is organized and functions.[20]

THE PRESENT VOLUME

Although second language research within Vygotskian theory has been carried out for decades in the former Soviet Union (see the paper by Ushakova in the present volume), we believe there are two principal reasons why such research has had only minimal influence on L2 research in the west. First, only recently have scholars working outside of the former Eastern bloc begun to have fuller access to the writings of Vygotsky and his followers. In this regard, we owe a great deal to the efforts of James Wertsch, Michael Cole, Vera John-Steiner, Alex Kozulin, René van der Veer, and Jan Valsiner. Of more immediate relevance, however, is the fact that second language acquisition research has squarely situated itself within the natural science research tradition—a tradition that values predictive explanation and controlled, heavily quantitative experimentation. It is not our intent to criticize the field for embracing this paradigm. On the contrary, we believe that significant progress has been made in understanding the process of second language acquisition as a result of the work carried out within the current paradigm. Our hope, which is shared by the contributors to the present volume, is that second language researchers will begin to explore the potential that sociocultural theory and Vygotskian research methodology have for developing an even fuller understanding of second language phenomena. With this in mind, the research contained in the following pages is presented.

The first set of studies addresses issues relating to mediation in the *zone of proximal development*. Donato, in his paper "Collective Scaffolding," explores the process through which adult foreign language learners mediate each other through collaborative interaction in a classroom learning environment. He distinguishes between "loosely knit groups" and "collective groups" and shows how the latter are able to construct jointly the scaffold necessary to complete a learning task. Schinke-Llano ("Linguistic Accommoda-

---

[20] For an enlightening and stimulating discussion of the need to introduce humanism and humanistic research principles into the social sciences, see Polkinghorne (1988).

tion") analyzes the quantitative and qualitative differences in the linguistic mediation provided by adults interacting with monolingual English-speaking children, LEP children, and learning-disabled children in problem-solving tasks. She reports that adults produce less abbreviated forms of speech when interacting with children in the latter two groups than with those in the former and suggests that use of non-abbreviated speech may impede progress of LEP and LD children. Washburn, in her study "Working in the ZPD," brings to light important differences in the linguistic behavior of fossilized and nonfossilized learners of a second language. She shows that the difference between these two learner types is quantitative rather than qualitative. Fossilized speakers appear to have no ZPD and thus are not able to operate on the input clues provided by a caregiver.

The next series of studies focuses on the function of inner and private speech in second language learning and performance. De Guerrero, in her paper, "Form and Function of Inner Speech," presents the results of a large-scale survey of ESL learners designed to elicit information on their use of inner speech in the second language acquisition process. She supplements her quantitative findings with evidence drawn from a series of interviews of selected subjects. Her data provide important information on the formal and functional properties of inner speech in a second language. She concludes that analysis of inner speech may give us new insights into the nature of the second language learning process. McCafferty, in his study "The Use of Private Speech by Adult ESL Learners," analyzes samples of private speech produced by ESL learners at different proficiency levels. The goal of his research is to replicate the original study of private speech in second language learners carried out by Frawley and Lantolf (1985). He presents evidence to support Frawley and Lantolf's claim that as learners' proficiency increases their use of private speech decreases. He also presents evidence that partially corroborates and partially contradicts the finding reported by Frawley and Lantolf with regard to tense and aspect features of private speech. Furthermore, he suggests that the cultural background of L2 speakers may override proficiency level with respect to the frequency of private speech production. Ushakova, in her study, "Inner Speech and Second Language Acquisition," first presents a brief survey of the research that has been conducted in the former Soviet Union on inner speech in general and then focuses on the work she and her colleagues have been doing specifically in second language learning. She reports on the findings of an experimental study of lexical acquisition in a second language, from which she concludes that the inner speech patterns laid down during first language acquisition serve as hosts onto which second languages are mapped.

The final set of papers are framed within Activity Theory and begin with Ahmed's study "Speaking as Cognitive Regulation," in which he analyzes and compares how L2 and L1 speakers employ language in problem-solving activity. Like McCafferty, he uses Frawley and Lantolf's (1985) research as the starting point for his analysis. Unlike McCafferty, however, he focuses on bringing to light how apparently aberrant linguistic patterns play an important role in a speaker's (L1 or L2) attempt to mediate mental activity in order to complete a difficult puzzle task. Coughlan and Duff, in "Same Task, Different Activities," show that tasks cannot be designed to elicit specific samples of interlanguage data independently of the speaker who engages in communicative linguistic activity. Their L2 protocols support Vygotsky's argument that speakers are agents active in controlling their environment; consequently, *tasks* cannot be predetermined, but *emerge* from the interaction of speakers, settings, motives, and histories. Finally, Gillette, in her study, "The Role of Learner Goals in L2 Success," focuses on individual differences in second language learning from the perspective of Activity Theory. Using personal interviews, class notes, and diaries, she reports findings from a three-month case study of six intermediate university learners of French as a foreign language. Gillette shows how learners' goals and histories play a key role in the type of strategies they deploy to acquire the second language.

REFERENCES

Appel, G., & Lantolf, J.P. (1992). *Comprehension through speaking: A study of L1 and L2 text recall tasks*. Paper presented at the AAAL Conference, Seattle, WA.

Appel, G. (1986). *L1 and L2 narrative and expository discourse production: A Vygotskian analysis*. Unpublished doctoral dissertation, University of Delaware, Newark.

Bourdieu, P. (1990). *Language and symbolic power*. Cambridge, MA: Harvard University Press.

Davydov, D.D., & Radzikhovskii, L.A. (1985). Vygotsky's theory and the activity-oriented approach in psychology. In J. V. Wertsch (Ed.), *Culture, communication, and cognition: Vygotskian perspectives* (pp. 35–65). Cambridge: Cambridge University Press.

Flavell, J.H. (1966). La langue prive. *Bulletin de Psychologie, 19*, 698–701.

Frawley, W., & Lantolf, J.P. (1984). Speaking and self-order: A critique of orthodox L2 research. *Studies in Second Language Acquisition, 6*, 143–159.

Frawley, W., & Lantolf, J.P. (1985). Second language discourse: A Vygotskian perspective. *Applied Linguistics, 6*, 19–44.

de Guerrero, M.C.M. (1990). *Nature of inner speech in mental rehearsal of the second language.* Unpublished doctoral dissertation, Inter American University of Puerto Rico, San German.

Gould, S.J. (1983). *Hens' teeth and horse's toes: Further reflections in natural history.* New York: Norton.

Ilyvenkov, E.V. (1977). *Dialectical logic: Essays on its history and theory.* Moscow: Progress.

Israel, J. (1979). *The language of dialectics and the dialectics of language.* Copenhagen: Humanities Press

Joravsky, D. (1989). *Russian psychology: A critical history.* Oxford: Blackwell.

Judin, E.G. (1984). Das Problem der Taetigkeit in Philosophie und Wissenschaft. The problem of activity in philosophy and science. In *Grundfragen einer Theorie der Sprachlichen Taetigkeit* (pp. 216–270). Stuttgart: Kohlhammer.

Kozulin, A. (1990). *Vygotsky's psychology. A biography of ideas.* Cambridge, MA: Harvard University Press.

Kussmann, T. (1976). The Soviet concept of development and the problem of activity. In K.F. Riegel & J.A. Meacham (Eds.), *The developing individual in a changing world* (pp. 122–130). The Hague: Mouton.

Leont'ev, A.N. (1981a). The problem of activity in psychology. In J.V. Wertsch (Ed.), *The concept of activity in Soviet psychology* (pp. 37–71). Armonk, NY: M.E. Sharpe.

Leont'ev, A.N. (1981b). *Problems of the development of mind.* Moscow: Progress.

Lomov, B.F. (1982). The problem of activity in psychology. *Soviet Psychology, 21*, 55–91

Luria, A.R. (1932). *The nature of human conflicts: On emotion, conflict, and will.* New York: Liveright.

Luria, A.R. (1973). *The working brain: An introduction to neuropsychology.* New York: Basic Books.

Luria, A.R. (1976). *Cognitive development. Its cultural and social foundations.* Cambridge, MA: Harvard University Press.

Luria, A.R. (1979). *The making of mind: A personal account of Soviet psychology.* Cambridge, MA: Harvard University Press.

McCafferty, S. (1992).The use of private speech by adult second language learners: A cross-cultural study. *Modern Language Journal, 76*, 177–189.

Newman, D., Griffin, P., & Cole, M. (1989). *The construction zone: Working for cognitive change in school.* Cambridge, UK: Cambridge University Press.

Polkinghorne, D.E. (1988). *Narrative knowing and the human sciences.* Albany, NY: State University of New York Press.

Ratner, C. (1991). *Vygotsky's sociohistorical psychology and its contemporary applications.* New York: Plenum

Schrage, C.O. (1986). *Communicative praxis and the space of subjectivity.* Bloomington, IN: Indiana University Press.

Scribner, S., & Cole, M. (1981). *The psychological consequences of literacy.* Cambridge, MA: Harvard University Press.

Sokolov, A.N. (1972). *Inner speech and thought.* New York: Plenum.

Spirkin, A. (1983). *Dialectical materialism.* Moscow: Progress.

Van der Veer, R., & Valsiner, J. (1991). *Understanding Vygotsky: A quest for synthesis.* London: Blackwell.

Vocate, D. (1987). *The theory of A.R. Luria: Functions of spoken language in the development of higher mental processes.* Hillsdale, NJ: Erlbaum.

Vygotsky, L.S. (1978). *Mind in Society: The development of higher psychological processes.* Cambridge, MA: Harvard University Press.

Vygotsky, L.S. (1979). Consciousness as a problem in the psychology of behavior. *Soviet Psychology, 17,* 3–35.

Vygotsky, L.S. (1981a). The development of higher forms of attention in childhood. In J.V. Wertsch (Ed.), *The concept of activity in Soviet psychology* (pp. 189–239). Armonk, NY: M.E. Sharp.

Vygotsky, L.S. (1981b). The genesis of higher mental functions. In J. V. Wertsch (Ed.), *The concept of activity in Soviet psychology* (pp. 144–188). Armonk, NY: M.E. Sharpe.

Vygotsky, L.S. (1981c). The instrumental method in psychology. In J. V. Wertsch (Ed.), *The concept of activity in Soviet psychology* (pp. 184–143). Armonk, NY: M.E. Sharpe.

Vygotsky, L.S. (1986) *Thought and language.* Cambridge, MA: MIT Press.

Wertsch, J.V. (1979a). From social interaction to higher psychological processes: A clarification and application of Vygotsky's theory. *Human Development, 22,* 1–22.

Wertsch, J.V. (1979b). The regulation of human action and the given-new organization of private speech. In G. Zivin (Ed.), *The development of self-regulation through private speech* (pp. 79–98). New York: Wiley & Sons

Wertsch, J.V. (1985a). Adult-child interaction as a source of self-regulation in children. In S.R. Yessen (Ed.), *The growth of reflection in children* (pp. 69–97). Orlando, FL: Academic Press.

Wertsch, J.V. (1985b). *Vygotsky and the social formation of mind.* Cambridge, MA: Harvard University Press.

Wertsch, J.V., & Hickmann, M. (1987). Problem solving in social interaction: A microgenetic analysis. In M. Hickmann (Ed.), *Social and functional approaches to thought* (pp. 251–266). Orlando, FL: Academic Press.

Wertsch, J.V., Minick, N., & Arns, F.J. (1984). The creation of context in joint problem-solving. In B. Rogoff & J. Lave (Eds.), *Everyday cognition: Its development in social context* (pp. 151–171). Cambridge, MA: Harvard University Press.

2

Collective Scaffolding in Second Language Learning

Richard Donato

Department of Instruction and Learning
University of Pittsburgh
Pittsburgh, PA

INTRODUCTION*

For almost a decade, the study of non native speaker (NNS) interactions in the second language (L2) classroom has brought attention to the importance of the negotiation of meaning and modification of interaction to L2 development (Long, 1985; Long & Porter, 1985; Porter, 1986; Pica, Holliday, Lewis, & Morgenthaler, 1989). These

* An earlier version of this paper was presented at the International Conference on Pragmatics and Language Learning, University of Illinois, Urbana-Champaign, April 5–7, 1990. My gratitude goes to James P. Lantolf, Department of Modern Languages and Linguistics, Cornell University, and Ellice Forman, Department of Psychology in Education, University of Pittsburgh, for their comments on this paper. My thanks also goes to Isabel L. Beck, Learning Research and Development Center, University of Pittsburgh, who suggested to me the need for this investigation.

studies have maintained that modifying interaction through the negotiation of meaning is a means of providing comprehensible input (Krashen, 1985) to the learner's subconscious language processing mechanisms. Thus, it is argued that the development of the learner's interlanguage system is stimulated by two processes engendered in interaction—first, the need for comprehensible input to the learner; and second, the challenge for the learners to grammatically structure their output (Swain, 1985). The psycholinguistic rationale (Long & Porter, 1985) for classroom group work is derived, therefore, from the theory that negotiating meanings provides the necessary and sufficient conditions for acquisition and mastery of a second language.

It has been asserted that we need to continue to identify ways in which learners produce comprehensible input and comprehensible output and that negotiated interaction is a most vital source of data (Pica, et al., 1989, p. 84). In the context of research, the identification of these discourse processes is generally understood as the description and categorization of repair strategies, or negotiation moves (Pica, et al., 1989) observed in learners during message clarification and comprehension. Although empirical studies of second language interaction have uncovered a profusion of statistical results documenting the relationship between communicative task, negotiation strategies, and grammaticality, they have yet to show the effect that negotiation arising from interaction has on eventual L2 acquisition (Chaudron, 1988, p. 109).

Underlying the construct of L2 input and output in modified interaction is the message model of communication. In this model, the goal of conversational partners during a communicative event is the successful sending and receiving of linguistic tokens. Studies of L2 interaction reflect this theoretical orientation by defining the negotiation process from the perspective of the conduit metaphor of communication; that is, message transmission and reception (Pica, 1987; Porter, 1986; Doughty & Pica, 1986; Ehrlich, Avery, & Yorio, 1989; Pica, et al., 1989). This paper argues that framing the study of L2 interaction in the message model of communication masks fundamentally important mechanisms of L2 development and reduces the social setting to an opportunity for "input crunching" (Donato, 1988). In the end, the social context is impoverished and undervalued as an arena for truly collaborative L2 acquisition. As Savignon (1991) points out, where meaning appears fixed, immutable, to be sent and received, what is lost is the collaborative nature of meaning making.

The message model, predicated upon the conduit metaphor of

communication, is limited in its ability to explain linguistic inter-actions. The problem with this theoretical orientation is that it only *superficially* recognizes the influence of the social context on individual linguistic development. More specifically, it claims that although individuals are socially situated, the process of L2 ac-quisition remains the solipsistic struggle to receive, analyze, and incorporate input into developing linguistic systems. The develop-ment of interlanguage grammar remains an abstract, solitary process hidden in the heads of individuals rather than concretely available in the social relationships among learners (Newman, Griffin, & Cole, 1984; Forman & Kraker, 1985). As Vygotsky claimed, however, all cognitive development is first and foremost interpsychological; that is, it arises as a result of the interaction that occurs between individuals engaged in concrete social interac-tion (Wertsch, 1985).

Politzer's (1974) arguments against abstracting human psycho-logical activity in favor of concrete psychology are relevant to this issue. Politzer states that the problem with abstract approaches to the psychology of human conduct is that they *disregard the individual* in their effort to amplify and categorize processes. As a result, experimental methods are, at the same time, driven too far and not far enough. Too far, because researchers never seem content with the rigor of their method, with the observational details, and accordingly overspecialize their object of study. Not far enough, because one has to drive the experiment to its end, to the very moment in which the drama is encountered. At this point, the researcher is still required to analyze this factual case as found in the particular form in which it unfolds. Politzer goes on to argue that there is a need for an approach that investigates the drama in its concrete actuality and particularity. Van Lier (1988) echoes in part this concern when he states that present research on the discourse of NNSs refers only generally to features of interaction, in this case repair strategies, without offering an explanation of the purposes of these collaborative utterances.

The development of L2 skills in the social context is far more complex than the present approach to the topic acknowledges. Morrison and Low (1983, p. 232) contend that to understand L2 production, we must observe the utterance-building process as it unfolds in real time. Trusting "hard" data from interaction studies, as Forman and Kraker (1985, p. 27) insist, obscures the cognitive processes that are enacted on the social plane during an experi-mental treatment.

In peer problem solving, for example, it is often the case that actions are goal-directed and oriented toward co-constructing an implicit understanding of the task and a set of procedures for solving it (Forman & Kraker, 1985, p. 26). However, in the case of L2 interaction studies, these cooperative actions are not reported since referential communicative tasks yield few, if any, opportunities to collaborate. By externally defining the goals of the experimental task to the sharing of pictorial or verbal information, individuals are coerced into engaging in communicative conduits without the rich network of social support typical of real world learning interactions (Rogoff, 1990). As Bronfenbrenner (1977, p. 513) states, the results of experiments such as these are by-products of short-lived and unfamiliar experiments requiring strange people to do strange things to strangers for the briefest possible period of time.

ACTIVITY THEORY AND THE SOCIAL CONTEXT[1]

Activity Theory (Wertsch, 1979b) directly addresses the issue of individual development, activity, and the social context. In its attempt to grasp the nature of activity, a basic principle of Activity Theory is the claim that human purposeful activity is based on motives; that is, socially and institutionally defined beliefs about a particular activity setting. The theory specifies that to explain the activity of individuals requires uncovering the motive and the interrelationship of this motive with the selection of goal-directed actions and their operational composition. The individual's motive determines which actions will be maximized and selected and how they will be operationalized in a particular setting.[2] Further, the operational composition of a motivated action is believed to be adaptive to physical conditions and material circumstances.

This principle of the theory may elucidate several conclusions inferred from L2 interaction studies and complicate others. According to Activity Theory, variance in motive during communicative activity implies variability in the operational composition of the

---

[1] The purpose of this section is to briefly highlight the major tenets of Activity Theory. It is not intended to introduce or debate the various interpretations the theory is currently receiving.

[2] See Wertsch, Minich, and Arns (1984) for an example of how Brazilian mothers vary in operationalizing the task of model building with children. They argue that the motive for activity, in this case the belief that the model building session is either a labor activity or school activity, has a significant impact on the way these adults approach problem solving with their children.

activity. The motive shapes the communicative event by maximizing one set of linguistic actions over another. For example, the motive could determine cultural or gender specific interaction patterns (Gass & Varonis, 1985), focus on specific levels of language to negotiate, for example, phonological, semantic, or morphosyntactic features (Swain, 1985; Pica & Doughty, 1985; Wesche & Ready, 1985), or ways of dealing with the imposition of the task demands quickly or effortlessly (Ehrlich, Avery, & Yorio, 1989). The point is that the participants' motives shape and guide the particular activity, be it in the laboratory, the classroom, or the street. The motive of the individual, rather than that of the researcher, determines how actions will be constructed, as well as their functional significance. Thus, the variability of activity (that is, the interrelationship of motives, goals, and operations) needs to be taken into consideration when investigating L2 interaction.[3] This theoretical perspective differs significantly from studies that focus solely on the operational composition of speaker output.

Another important concept in Activity Theory that is relevant to learning in the social context is *internalization*. For Vygotsky (1978), social interaction is a mechanism for individual development, since, in the presence of a more capable participant, the novice is drawn into, and operates within, the space of the expert's strategic processes for problem solving. More specifically, the dialogically constituted interpsychological event between individuals of unequal abilities is a way for the novice to extend current competence. During problem solving, the experienced individual is often observed to guide, support, and shape actions of the novice who, in turn, internalizes the expert's strategic processes. The notion of internalization finds support in the work of Palincsar and Brown (1984) on the training of reading strategies through guided participation in hypothesis generation, evaluation, and revision, and the work of Tomasello and Herron (1989) on expert feedback during learner hypothesis testing in second language grammar lessons.

The concepts of motive and internalization emphasize the importance of attributing a more dynamic role to the social context than

---

[3] Although not invoking Activity Theory as an explanatory framework for her findings, Kinginger (1990) reports on the repair sequences in learner-learner conversations in an intermediate French language class. In her study, she found that if learners assumed that conversational tasks were form-oriented, their repair sequences were other-directed and mimicked that of their teachers. On the other hand, if tasks were believed to be open-ended and did not explicitly focus on form, a greater amount of self-monitoring and self-repair was reported to occur.

has yet been achieved in the literature on interaction and L2 acquisition. Although it is a truism to claim that knowledge is constructed actively by the learner, this process often takes place in a variety of ways and with the help of another. According to Activity Theory, the individual's creative construction process of knowledge acquisition suggests, as well, socially mediated activity. As Ellis (1985) has rightly pointed out, simply counting conversational adjustments in search of understanding the process of input may be inaccurate. To this it could be added that to provide a complete picture of the effects of social interaction on individual L2 development requires abandoning the barren notion that the function of L2 interaction is to give the learner access to the hidden black box.

CONSCIOUSNESS AND L2 DEVELOPMENT

Recently some second language researchers have begun to recognize the dimension of consciousness and cognition in the language learning process. This shift in focus from subconscious to conscious cognitive processes is revealed in the studies of learner strategies (Oxford, 1990), research on conscious planning and interlanguage variation (Crookes, 1989), and consciousness raising through systematic attention to the formal regularities of second language structure (Rutherford & Sharwood-Smith, 1988).

This recent interest in consciousness also brings with it the need to reassess assumptions and beliefs concerning the role of social interaction in L2 development. If consciousness is to become the object of study in investigations of L2 acquisition, then the social context exerts and even greater influence than previously believed. For Vygotsky (1986), consciousness is *co-knowledge*; the individual dimension of consciousness is derivatory and secondary. To account for this phenomenon requires studies that capture the evolving and dynamic features of interaction that allow individuals to change and be changed by the concrete particulars of their social context (Rommetveit, 1985). This perspective differs fundamentally from the current view that maintains that social interaction provides opportunities to supply linguistic input to learners who develop solely on the basis of their internal language processing mechanisms. In contrast, the Vygotskian position assigns to social interaction a developmental status; that is, development is situated activity.

In this vein, Lave (1988), following Vygotsky and his colleagues, points out that what we call learning and cognition is a complex social phenomenon. If this is so, studies of verbal interactions in which participants are observed in the process of structuring communicative events jointly, and according to their own self-constructed goals, will provide important insights into the development of linguistic competence.The focus should be, therefore, on observing the construction of co-knowledge and how this co-construction process results in linguistic *change* among and within individuals during joint activity. In this way we can begin to answer the question of how negotiation arising from interaction impacts on L2 development.

PURPOSE OF STUDY

The purpose of this study is twofold. First, the study is an attempt to illustrate how students co-construct language learning experiences in the classroom setting. To this end, students were observed working on an open-ended classroom task that was familiar to them. No attempt was made to coerce the use of L2, to influence the process of task completion, or to structure the interaction in terms of requisite steps or focus of attention (that is, the focus on form or meaning). The decision for planning and structuring the activity was surrendered to the students.

Second, this study attempts to uncover how L2 development is brought about on the social plane. Following Vygotsky's developmental theory, it is hypothesized that learners can, in certain circumstances, provide the same kind of support and guidance for each other that adults provide children (Forman & Kraker, 1985). Specifically, the study seeks to answer the question of whether learners can exert a developmental influence on each other's interlanguage system in observable ways. That is, rather than to theorize that interaction has the potential to result in L2 development, this study attempts to examine how social interactions in the classroom result in the appropriation of linguistic knowledge by the individual.

METHOD

The protocols in this study are taken from a larger study on collaborative planning (Donato, 1988) among third semester students of French at an American university. The three students in the group under study had worked together in class for a period of ten weeks on a variety of small group projects before the data were collected. They knew each other well, enjoyed working on projects together, and seemed to assume a collective orientation to problem solving. Moreover, their discourse often reflected that of a single speaker, further supporting their highly collective orientation to their work. This type of discourse is generally characterized by the lack of overt turn-taking discourse markers, the discursive pre-dominance of comment overt topic, significantly more occurrences of "we" over "I" and "you" when addressing each other, and a flexibility in interchanging discourse roles (Donato, 1988). For this reason, the term *collective* is used to distinguish these students from loosely-knit *groups* in the same class (Petrovsky, 1985).

Their interactions, which were audiotaped and later transcribed for analysis, represent a one-hour planning session for an oral activity.[4] In the protocols to follow, the students helped each other plan what they anticipated they would need in order to participate in the oral activity that would take place during the next class.

THE METAPHOR OF SCAFFOLDING

Before beginning the analysis of the protocols, it is necessary to discuss the discursive mechanism of scaffolding. This concept, which derives from cognitive psychology and L1 research, states that in social interaction a knowledgeable participant can create, by means of speech, supportive conditions in which the novice can participate in, and extend, current skills and knowledge to higher levels of competence (Greenfield, 1984; Wood, Bruner, & Ross, 1976). According to Wood, Bruner, and Ross, scaffolded help is characterized by six features:

---

[4] The oral activity is based on a scenario by Di Pietro (1987). Students were asked to stage to the class the conclusion of a scenario in which a husband purchases a fur coat for another woman. The follow-up interaction reported in this study is the encounter between the husband and the wife after the wife discovers his actions. The one-hour planning session was intended to allow the students to decide on the scenario conclusion. The students were also instructed that their presentation was not to be memorized. As in Crookes' (1989) experiment on interlanguage variation, the students were told to discuss or make notes in French, but were specifically instructed not to attempt to write out everything they would say. They were also told that their presentation would be made without the aid of their notes. In contrast to Crookes' experiment, the planning represents a collective effort rather than individual work.

1. *recruiting* interest in the task,
2. *simplifying* the task,
3. *maintaining* pursuit of the goal,
4. *marking* critical features and discrepancies between what has been produced and the ideal solution,
5. *controlling* frustration during problem solving, and
6. *demonstrating* an idealized version of the act to be performed

Additionally, the metaphor implies the expert's active stance toward continual revisions of the scaffold in response to the emerging capabilities of the novice (Rogoff, 1990). For example, a child's error or limited capabilities can be a signal for the adult to upgrade the scaffolding. Conversely, as the child begins to take on more responsibility for the task, the adult dismantles the scaffold, indicating that the child has benefited from the assisted performance and internalized the problem-solving processes provided by the previous scaffolded episode. According to Wertsch (1979a), scaffolded performance is a dialogically constituted interpsychological mechanism that promotes the novice's internalization of knowledge co-constructed in shared activity.

This concept is relevant to this study, since it will be shown that collaborative work among language learners provides the same opportunity for scaffolded help as in expert–novice relationships in the everyday setting. This finding differs from the majority of research on scaffolding, since it is assumed that scaffolding occurs in the presence of an identifiable and stable expert participant and that this help is unidirectional, that is from knower to non-knower.[5]

Regarding L2 acquisition, the concept of scaffolding has only been reported, to my knowledge, in Hatch's (1978) early research on L2 interaction and, more recently, in Van Lier (1988). Van Lier states that language teaching methodology can benefit from a study of L1 scaffolding to understand how classroom activities already

---

[5] Ochs (1990) has argued that the problem with former accounts of the acquisition of knowledge has been that the novice has little impact on the developed systems of competent speakers/members of a society. She claims that both expert members and novices use language in ways to create contexts of shared understanding. Ochs states that *both* novices and more competent speakers transfer their structures of knowledge and understanding vis-à-vis discourse and culture.

tacitly employ such tactics. No attempt has been made, however, to look qualitatively at this discursive phenomenon in present studies of learning interaction, input, and L2 acquisition. The study of scaffolding in L2 research has focused exclusively on how language teachers provide guided assistance to learners (Ulichny, 1990; Wong-Fillmore, 1985; Ellis, 1985), or how NSs dispense linguistic structures in vertical discourse to the NNS (Hatch, 1978). This study is an attempt to discover if, during open-ended collaborative tasks, second language learners *mutually construct* a scaffold out of the discursive process of negotiating contexts of shared understanding, or what Rommetveit (1985) calls *intersubjectivity.*

ANALYSIS OF PROTOCOLS

This study of learner interaction is developmental to the extent that it seeks to uncover the mutual effects of learners on each other's interlanguage system. For this reason, a microgenetic analysis is used. As defined by Wertsch and Stone (1978), microgenesis refers to the gradual course of skill acquisition during a training session, experiment, or interaction. The need for microgenetic analysis in the study of human development was most forcefully and eloquently stated by Vygotsky (1978) in his argument against restricting ourselves to studying human development, including linguistic development, *postmortem,* or what he referred to as the study of "fossilized behavior." A microgenetic analysis allows us to observe directly how students help each other during the overt planning of L2 utterances and the outcome of these multiple forces of help as they come into contact, and interact, with each other. The power of this collaborative experience has support in the developmental theory of Vygotsky (1978), which maintains that when learners are actively assisted in dialogic events on topics of mutual interest and value, individual and conceptual development occurs.

In this study, scaffolding is operationalized according to the definitions of Wood, Bruner, and Ross (1976). In order to visualize the scaffolded help and to trace its influence on the collective, the help sequences are diagrammed on two axes. The horizontal axis represents interactional time, or the actual time it took the group participants to solve their problem and arrive at a consensus. The vertical axis is an ordinal scale illustrating the constituent parts of the interaction in question from its inception to its resolution. The order of linguistic elements on the vertical axis matches that observed in the group members and reflects the structure of the interaction as it occurred in real time.

The numbers 1, 2, and 3 refer to the three participants themselves. Next to each number is a positive or negative sign. The positive sign represents correct, but not necessarily complete, knowledge; the negative sign reflects incomplete or incorrect knowledge. The sequence of numbers is faithful to the other in which utterances appeared in the conversation. Matching the position of the speaker with the vertical and horizontal axis reveals the contents of the utterance, its correctness or incorrectness, and its sequential relationship to other utterances in the interaction. In addition, the influence of one student on another can be visualized by following the course of negatively and positively marked utterances.

Before turning to the protocols, one caveat is in order. As will be shown, the students negotiate quite spontaneously, among other things, the form of utterances. The selection of these protocols for analysis is not intended, however, to imply that, when left to their own devices, linguistically homogeneous students define their interactions *only* on the basis of the formal properties of the language. These interactions are in fact only another type of negotiation—the negotiation of form rather than meaning (Long, 1991). The critical point is that when students have the opportunity to help each other during nonstructured tasks and on the basis of internal goals for activity, they are observed to create a context of shared understanding in which the negotiation of language form and meaning co-occur. In other words, focusing on form was not a requirement of the task but rather how the students operationalized their motive for activity at the particular point in the interaction. The three protocols for microanalysis represent, therefore, the internally generated and naturally occurring subgoal of the total task.[6]

---

[6] This is a critical point, since the majority of research on L2 interaction overlooks the transforming potential of human activity (Asmolov, 1986). During experimental tasks, subjects are manipulated by the experimental condition itself. This study attempted to avoid such manipulation to gain insight into the internal mental activity of L2 learners. As Newman, Griffin, and Cole (1984) point out, the "laboratory" simply cannot capture the wide variety of content, different degrees of familiarity, various ways of dividing up and carrying out labor, and reliance on conversation as a medium of expression during conversation.

Protocol

A1   Speaker 1   ...and then I'll say... *tu as souvenu notre anniver-saire de marriage*...or should I say *mon anniversaire?*

A2   Speaker 2   *Tu as...*

A3   Speaker 3   *Tu as...*

A4   Speaker 1   *Tu as souvenu*... "you remembered?"

A5   Speaker 3   Yea, but isn't that reflexive? *Tu t'as...*

A6   Speaker 1   Ah, *tu t'as souvenu.*

A7   Speaker 2   Oh, it's *tu es*

A7   Speaker 1   *Tu es*

A9   Speaker 3   *tu es, tu es, tu...*

A10   Speaker 1   *T'es, tu t'es*

A11   Speaker 3   *tu t'es*

A12   Speaker 1   *Tu t'es souvenu.*

Protocol A is an attempt to render "you remembered" into French. The compound past tense formation of reflective verbs in French presents complex linguistic processing, since students are required to choose the auxiliary *être*) instead of *avoir*, select the correct reflexive pronoun to agree with the subject, form the past participle, which in this case is an unpredictable form, and decide if, and how, the past participle will be marked for agreement with the subject. More importantly, the complexity of the verb formation in question can be defined internally on the basis of the extent of processing required of the students to reach an appropriate French utterance. Additionally, this protocol represents the internally generated goals and subgoals of the learners themselves and not the requirement of the task for formal accuracy. That is, the students could have stopped their search for expressing "you remembered" on line A4. However, Speaker 3 sets the goal, or more specifically one of several subgoals of the total task, by questioning the accuracy of the utterance. The need to verify the accuracy of the utterance appears quite spontaneously and is attended to jointly by the other two students. This joint work is illustrated in Figure 2.1.

That the students collaboratively attend to Speaker 1's initial phrase, and Speaker 3's questioning of its legitimacy, is clearly shown here. Remarkably, however, no student alone possesses the

FIGURE 2.1   Scaffolded Help for "You Remembered"

subj-pro-aux-pp			1 −		1 +
subj-aux-pp	1 −				
subj-pro-aux			3 −		1 + 3 +
subj-aux		2 − 3 −		1 + 2 + 3 +	
			interactional time		

ability to construct the French past compound tense of the reflexive verb "to remember." Each student appears to control only a specific aspect of the desired construction. Speaker 1, for example, produces the correct past participle (A1) but the incorrect auxiliary verb. Speaker 2 recognizes the verb as reflexive (A5) but fails to select the appropriate auxiliary *être*. Speaker 3, on the other hand, understands the choice of the auxiliary for reflexive compound past tense forms but does not include the correct reflexive pronoun into his version of the utterance (A7). At this point in the interaction Speakers 1 and 2 synthesize the prior knowledge that has been externalized during the interaction and simultaneously arrive at the correct construction (A9–12).

The interesting point here is that these three learners are able to construct collectively a scaffold for each other's performance. Following the definition of Wood, Bruner, and Ross (1976), they jointly manage components of the problem, mark critical features of discrepancies between what has been produced and the perceived ideal solution (A5, A7, A10), and minimize frustration and risk by relying on the collective resources of the group.

It also appears that the collective scaffold is built on negative evidence. That is, correct knowledge is subsequently secured from incomplete and incorrect knowledge. The interaction shows quite dramatically the dialectical process of collective argumentation (Miller, 1987), which surfaces in the social context. In this regard, if language learning and language processing are thought to be achieved through the competition and resolution of the morphosyntactic and lexical features of the target language (Gass, 1987; MacWhinney, 1987), a fruitful line of investigation is to observe these competitive, dialectical processes as they unfold and are externalized in collective activity.[7] As Vygotskian theory maintains,

---

[7] For a discussion of the problems of observing mental processes, see Donato and Lantolf (1990), Lantolf (1990), Lyons (1987).

the origin of the individual's higher mental functions is situated in the dialectical processes embedded in the social context (Vygotsky, 1978).

The affective markers in this interaction, "Oh," "Ah," and "Yea," reveal, as Schiffrin (1987) points out, task and information management. They are also indicators of orientation to the task (Donato & Lantolf, 1990), thus signifying the point at which joint focus of the attention has been achieved. Each of the participants in this interaction uses one of these affective markers (Speaker 3 in A5, Speaker 1 in A6, and Speaker 2 in A7) indicating the presence of distributed help and mutual orientation to the task. This is not surprising, since, as previously mentioned, these students operationalize their activity collectively as revealed in the high degree of topic continuity and a discourse structure reminiscent of that of a single speaker. Their collectivity is also exhibited by their ability to establish intersubjectivity (Rommetveit, 1985). The convergence of affective markers appears at the critical point in the interaction, when negative evidence is transformed into positive knowledge (A5, A6, A7), indicating a point of development for the participants.

These students have constructed for each other a *collective scaffold*. During this interaction, the speakers are at the same time individually novices and collectively experts, sources of new orientations for each other, and guides through this complex linguistic problem solving. What is most striking is that although marked individual linguistic differences exist at the onset of the interaction, the co-construction of the collective scaffold progressively reduces the distance between the task and individual abilities.

Protocol B provides further evidence of the construction of the collective scaffold among learners.

Protocol B

B1   Speaker 1   *Dé...décou...* How do you say "discovered?"

B2   Speaker 2   *découvert.*

B3   Speaker 1   *J'ai découvert*

B4   Speaker 2   He [referring to the teacher] just told me

B5   that today

B6   Speaker 1   *J'ai...* I have discovered... *J'ai découvert.*

B7   Speaker 2   *J'ai découvert...* I have discovered

B8   Speaker 3   (whispering) *J'ai découvert... vert*

B9   Speaker 1   OK... *J'ai découvert, uhm, votre surprise.*

In Protocol B the same students as in Protocol A are attempting to express "I discovered" in French. Although the answer is supplied relatively early in the interaction (B1-B3) by the direct reply of Speaker 2 (B2) to Speaker 1's request for assistance (B1), the resulting utterances indicate that Speaker 2's utterance functions to demonstrate the idealized version of the act to be performed. On the structural level, it could be argued that Protocol B is a paradigm case of vertical structure, or the novice's incorporation of chunks of speech from the preceding discourse (Ellis, 1984, 1985; Wagner-Gough, 1975). However, on the developmental level, Speaker 2's model of the utterance initiates language play utterances or, more precisely, cognitive dialogue (Lantolf, 1990) in which the past participle is repeated (B3-8), separated into syllables (B7), and subvocalized (B8) by the collective. The psycholinguistic function of Speaker 2's contribution is barely captured if the interpretation focuses solely on how the communicative channel is kept open by means of imitation within the vertical structure of discourse. Ellis's (1986, p. 156) warning that output should never be considered in isolation, but always in context, is clearly illustrated in this protocol. Figure 2.2 represents the developmental influence of Speaker 2's help on the collective.

The discourse in Protocol B reflects Wood, Bruner, and Ross' (1976) definition of the functions of the tutor in scaffolding a child's performance. The diagram reveals the rapid diffusion of Speaker 2's idealized version of the task to be performed throughout the collective. The diagram also represents the development of Speaker 1 from the beginning to the end of the joint activity (B1, 3, 6, 9). The actions of Speaker 1 and 2 are clearly beyond mimicking the repair trajectories typical of teacher-led classroom discourse but are indications of self-initiated attempts to control and internalize the needed knowledge.

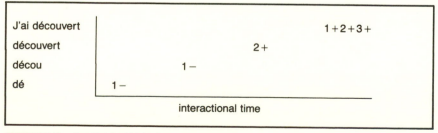

FIGURE 2.2   Scaffolded Help for "I discovered"

The subvocalized utterance (B8) and intersentential translation (B6) are directed to no one other than the speakers themselves and represent private speech. The occurrence of private speech, as documented by Vygotsky (1986), Zivin (1979), and Kohlberg, Yaeger, and Hjertholm (1968), is stimulated and developed by a child's early social experiences, contrary to intuitive notions that private speech is performed in isolation. Within the Vygotskian paradigm, private speech is a discursive developmental mechanism enabling children to push the limits of their current mental ability. In other words, speech to oneself, which overtly expresses the requisite actions to successfully complete the task (in this case the need to produce in French the meaning of "discovered"), is a means of self-guidance in carrying out an activity beyond one's current competence.

In terms of the linguistic development made by Speaker 1 and 3, it appears that the scaffolded help provided by Speaker 2—that is, the model of the ideal answer for the collective—initiated private talk functioning to organize, rehearse, and gain control over their verbal behavior. What is interesting, however, is that unlike children, who frequently display private speech during language learning and problem-solving activities, it has at least been assumed that adults rarely exhibit this behavior in the presence of others.[8] If Speaker 1 and 3 are engaging in private speech, which appears undoubtedly to be the case, it has been stimulated by Speaker 2. Thus, the social context foments the private speech of Speakers 1 and 3, and accordingly provokes their linguistic development and the internalization of collective knowledge.

The preclosing use of "OK" offers the chance to reinstate the earlier topic (Speaker 1 in B8) prior to conversational closure (Schegloff & Sacks, 1973). That the students have attained a collective orientation to the task is indicated in the clustering of utterances containing the correct past participle in B6-8 (see Protocol B). The overall operational composition of the activity also exhibits the motive, or assumption, that for these students, the social setting is indeed the legitimate domain for individual progress in language learning.

---

[8] See Lantolf (1990) for a discussion of private speech and the problem of observing this phenomenon when studying the L2 acquisition process in adults. Based on this study, it appears that L2 collective activity provides the opportunity to observe adult private speech that otherwise remains hidden from the probing eye of the researcher.

Although, at first glance, this protocol appears to be an English translation into French followed by borrowing in vertical discourse, its analysis reveals a complex fabric of interindividual help and the activation of developmental speech not captured within the message model framework. If the negotiation of meaning is defined as mutual efforts at comprehending and clarifying utterances, then Protocol C explains the psycholinguistic influence of these discourse modifications on the linguistic development of conversational participants.

Further support for linguistic development through scaffolded help among this collective is visible in Protocol C, in which Speaker 2 attempts to express the idea that "if he tells her the truth, she (his wife) will divorce him."

Protocol C

C1   Speaker 2   OK, help me say this...and I can say...

C2   Speaker 1   *Rien*

C3   Speaker 2   *rien, rien,* that's right, *rien parce que...*

C4   Speaker 3   *parce que...*

C5   Speaker 2   *si je...lui dis...dire...?*

C6   Speaker 1   *dis, si je lui dis la vérité,* the truth...

C7   Speaker 2   *si je lui dis...*

C8   Speaker 3   *si je lui dis...*what was that? *La* what?

C9   Speaker 2   *la vérité*

C10 Speaker 1   *la vérité.*

C11 Speaker 3   *la vérité* [whispering to himself], *la vérité.* [second repetition almost inaudible]

C12 Speaker 1   *v-e-r-i-t-e, accent aigu...*

C13 Speaker 3   *si je lui dis la vérité...*

C14 Speaker 2   *elle me dit...* [The co-construction continues in French until Speaker 2 states the following]

C15   *elle va, elle va me divorcer.*

Speaker 2's explicit request for assistance (C1) recruits the interest of the others in the task and begins the scaffolded interaction. The request for assistance is not expressed as an interrogative but is embedded in an imperative, indicating that Speaker 2 realizes that help is, indeed, available. This is a dialogic indication that Speaker 2 defines the task on the basis of this motive. In C2–C7 Speaker 2 is supported and guided during his on-line planning through the efforts of Speaker 1 and 3. Speaker 1's use of "rien" (C2) and Speaker 3's use of "parce que" (C4) appears to disinhibit Speaker 2 and initiate his linguistic processing (C5). Disinhibition is clearly in line with the function of scaffolding, since it is one way of allowing a novice to begin or maintain pursuit of the task goal and control frustration during problem solving. Without the disinhibition offered by Speaker 1, Speaker 2 may have abandoned the task entirely.

What is also interesting is the dual scaffolding occurring in this interaction. At the onset of the interaction, Speaker 1 and Speaker 3 scaffold the performance of Speaker 2 by disinhibiting his linguistic processing. Later, Speaker 1 resolves the conflict between two competing verb forms, "dis" and "dire," in the production of Speaker 2. In the middle of the interaction, Speaker 1 and Speaker 2 scaffold the performance of Speaker 3 by providing three models of the lexical item "vérité:, which include its spelling (C8-C12). Private speech by Speaker 3 is also observed in C11 (see Protocol C). At the end of the interaction (C13), Speaker 3 is observed to synthesize the prior help he received (C9–10) and supplied (C4) in the fully expanded utterance. This utterance is completed by Speaker 2 and the utterance expansion of "if I told her the truth, she is going to divorce me" is unchallenged, thus representing a collective consensus. Figure 2.3 depicts the process of development during this peer-scaffolding episode.

As in Protocol A, the dialectical process of development is revealed. A thesis and subsequent antithesis occur in Speaker 2 when he questions the competing forms of the verb ("dis...dire"). The

si je lui dis la vérité				3+
la vérité				2+1+3+
la			3–	
si je lui dis		1+2+3+		
dis	1+			
dis/dire	2–			
	interactional time			

FIGURE 2.3   Scaffolded Help for "If you told him the truth"

competition is resolved and a synthesis is provided by Speaker 1. Through his repetition (C8), Speaker 3 adopts the synthesis embodied in the utterance "si je lui dis" but introduces a new antithesis by questioning the word "vérité" (C8). Both Speakers 1 and 2 provide Speaker 3 with the necessary word (C9–10) resulting in a new synthesis for Speaker 3 embodied in the expanded utterance (C13). Speaker 3's synthesis is accepted as thesis by Speaker 2, who expands and completes the utterance (C14–15). The two shifts from negative evidence to positive evidence are indicative of the process of competition during linguistic development. The scaffolding engendered by the social context is, therefore, one way that this linguistic competition is resolved.

DISCUSSION AND CONCLUSION

It has been shown that learners are capable of providing guided support to their peers during collaborative L2 interactions in ways analogous to expert scaffolding documented in the developmental psychological literature. It has also been posited that collective scaffolding may result in linguistic development in the individual learner. This fact, however, requires independent validation. To discover if the collective scaffolding exhibited in these protocols brings about independent L2 performance at a later time when support is no longer available, the oral activity was recorded and transcribed for analysis. It is assumed that if the same students who had previously engaged in collaborative planning reveal the appropriate use of these collective utterances during the oral activity, evidence for individual linguistic development deriving from social interaction is supported.

In all, 32 cases of scaffolded help were documented in the hour planning session. Of these 32 cases, all but eight of the scaffolded utterances were used during the performance portion of the activity. This means that the contents of the 24 scaffolded help sequences were observed at a later time in the independent performance of the students when help was no longer available. This is not surprising in light of Vygotskian theory, which argues that individual knowledge is socially and dialogically derived, the genesis of which can be observed directly in the interactions among speakers during problem-solving tasks.

Additionally, the independent use of collaboratively constructed utterances is not limited solely to the individual who initially requested the help during the planning session. For example, the word "découvert" (see Protocol B) is used in the speech of Speaker 1 who requested the help. However, as a peripheral participant, Speaker 3 also appears to have benefited from the scaffolded help as demonstrated by his use of "découvert" during the oral activity.

> Speaker 1: J'ai *découvert* ton secret mon amour.
>
> (later in the interaction)
>
> Speaker 3: Comment est-ce que tu l'as *découvert*?

Recall that it was Speaker 2 who modeled the idealized solution to the problem (B2). Clearly, Speakers 1 and 3 benefited from, and internalized, the help supplied by Speaker 2 during the planning session. In this way, independent evidence is given that peer scaffolding results in linguistic development within the individual. Space does not permit a detailed analysis of all the scaffolded episodes and subsequent occurrences of this knowledge in the individual during independent linguistic performance. However, the results of this study indicate that scaffolding occurs routinely as students work together on language learning tasks. The effects of this help are substantial enough to redefine and further cultivate the role played by the social context in L2 development.

This study has underscored the need to account for, and explain, the rich fabric of interindividual help that arises in social interactions. Second language learners appear quite capable and skillful at providing the type of scaffolded help that is associated in the developmental literature with only the most noticeable forms of expert–novice interaction, such as parent and child (Wertsch, 1979a), teacher and student (Wong-Fillmore, 1985), NS and NNS (Hatch, 1978), or master and apprentice (Greenfield, 1984; Goody, 1989; Singelton, 1989). Discussions of the potential benefit of guided participation (Rogoff, 1990) and learning apprenticeships (Brown, Collins, & Duguid, 1989) in the classroom have recently become fashionable. It appears useful, therefore, to consider the learners themselves as a source of knowledge in a social context.

The findings of this study also suggest that changes in linguistic systems are brought about in ways that go beyond mere input crunching by the individual learner. Focusing the investigation on the conversational adjustments of language learners will inevitably obscure the functional significance of collaborative dialogic events. The microgenetic analysis of collective activity has revealed that in the process of peer scaffolding, learners can expand their own L2 knowledge and extend the linguistic development of their peers.

The implication for this finding is that the obdurate nature of some language tasks inhibit learners from engaging in dialogically constituted guided support, or collective scaffolding. By recasting the role of learners during social interaction, the current theoretical position supporting group work in second language classrooms will be expanded beyond simple opportunities to exchange linguistic artifact to that of the collective acquisition of the second language.

REFERENCES

Asmolov, A.G. (1986). Basic principles of a psychological analysis in the theory of activity. *Soviet Psychology, 25*(2), 78–102.

Bronfenbrenner, U. (1977). Toward an experimental ecology of human development. *American Psychologist, 32*, 513–530.

Brown, J.S., Collins, A., & Duguid, D. (1989). Situated cognition and the culture of learning. *Educational Researcher, 18*, 32–42.

Chaudron, C. (1988). *Second language classrooms: Research on teaching and learning.* Cambridge: Cambridge University Press.

Crookes, G. (1989). Planning and interlanguage variation. *Studies in Second Language Acquisition, 11*, 367–383.

Di Pietro, R.J. (1987). *Strategic interaction: Learning languages through scenarios.* Cambridge: Cambridge University Press.

Donato, R. (1988). *A psycholinguistic rationale for collective activity in second language learning.* Unpublished doctoral dissertation, University of Delaware, Newark.

Donato, R., & Lantolf, J. (1990). Dialogic origins of L2 monitoring. In L.F. Bouton & Y. Kachru (Eds.), *Pragmatics and language learning, Vol. 1* (pp. 83–97). Urbana-Champaign, IL: Division of English as an International Language.

Doughty, C., & Pica, T. (1986). Information gap tasks: Do they facilitate second language acquisition? *TESOL Quarterly, 20*, 305–325.

Ehrlich, S., Avery, P., & Yorio, C. (1989). Discourse structure and the negotiation of comprehensible input. *Studies in Second Language Acquisition, 11*, 397–414.

Ellis, R. (1984). *Classroom second language development.* Oxford: Pergamon.

Ellis, R. (1985). Teacher-pupil interaction in second language development. In S. Gass & C.G. Madden (Eds.), *Input in second language acquisition* (pp. 69–85). Cambridge, MA: Newbury House.

Ellis, R. (1986). *Understanding second language acquisition.* Oxford: Oxford University Press.

Forman, E.A., & Kraker, M.J. (1985). The social origins of logic: The contributions of Piaget and Vygotsky. In M.W. Berkowitz (Ed.), *Peer conflict and psychological growth* (pp. 23–39). San Francisco, CA: Jossey-Bass.

Gass, S.M. (1987). The resolution of conflicts among competing systems: A bidirectional perspective. *Applied Linguistics, 8,* 329–350.

Gass, S.M., & Varonis, E.M. (1985). Task variation and nonnative/nonnative negotiation of meaning. In S.M. Gass & C.G. Madden (Eds.), *Input in second language acquisition* (pp. 149–161). Cambridge, MA: Newbury House.

Goody, E.N. (1989). Learning, apprenticeship and the division of labor. In M.W. Coy (Ed.), *Apprenticeship: From theory to method and back again* (pp. 233–256). Albany, NY: State University of New York Press.

Greenfield, P.M. (1984). A theory of the teacher in the learning activities of everyday life. In B. Rogoff & J. Lave (Eds.), *Everyday cognition* (pp. 117–138). Cambridge, MA: Harvard University Press.

Hatch, E. (1978). Discourse analysis and second language acquisition. In E. Hatch (Ed.), *Second language acquisition* (pp. 401–435). Rowley, MA: Newbury House.

Kinginger, C. (1990). *Task variation and the structure of repair sequences in learner/learner conversations.* Paper persented at the Conference on Second Language Acquisition and Foreign Language Learning, University of Illinois, Urbana-Champaign.

Kohlberg, L., Yaeger, J., & Hjertholm, E. (1968). Private speech: four studies and a review of theories. *Child Development, 39,* 691–735.

Krashen, S. (1985). *The input hypothesis: Issues and implications.* New York: Longman:

Lantolf, J.P. (1990). *Language play: A form of cognitive diagolue.* Paper presented at the International Conference on Pragmatics and Language Learning, University of Illinois, Urbana-Champaign.

Lave, J. (1988). *Cognition in practice: Mind, mathematics, and culture in everyday life.* Cambridge: Cambridge University Press.

Long, M. (1985). Input and second language acquisition theory. In S.M. Gass & C.G. Madden (Eds.), *Input in second language acquisition* (pp. 377–393). Cambridge MA: Newbury House.

Long, M. (1991). Focus on form: A design feature in language teaching methodology. In K. de Bot, D. Coste, R. Ginsberg, & C. Kramsch (Eds.), *Foreign language research in cross-cultural perspective* (pp. 39–52). Amsterdam: John Benjamins.

Long, M., & Porter, P. (1985). Group work, interlanguage talk, and second language acquisition. *TESOL Quarterly, 19,* 305–325.

Lyons, W. (1987). *The disappearance of introspection.* Cambridge, MA: MIT Press.

MacWhinney, B. (1987). Applying the competition model to bilingualism. *Applied Linguistics, 8,* 315–327.

Miller, M. (1987). Argumentation and cognition. In M. Hickmann (Ed.), *Social and functional approaches to language and thought* (pp. 225–249). Orlando, FL: Academic Press.

Morrison, D., & Low, G. (1983). Monitoring and the second language learner. In J.C. Richards & R.W. Schmidt (Eds.), *Language and communication* (pp. 228–250). London: Longman.

Newman, D., Griffin, P., & Cole, M. (1984). Social constraints in laboratory and classroom tasks. In B. Rogoff & J. Lave (Eds.), *Everyday cognition* (pp. 172–193). Cambridge, MA: Harvard University Press.

Ochs, E. (1990). Indexicality and socialization. In J.W. Stigler, R. Shweder, & G. Herdt (Eds.), *Cultural psychology* (pp. 287–308). New York: Cambridge University Press.

Oxford, R.L. (1990). *Language learning strategies: What every teacher should know.* New York: Newbury House.

Palincsar, A.S., & Brown, A.L. (1984). Reciprocal teaching of comprehension-fostering and monitoring activities. *Cognition and Instruction, 1*, 117–175.

Petrovsky, A.V. (1985). *The collective and the individual.* Moscow: Progress.

Pica, T. (1987). Second language acquisition, social interaction, and the classroom. *Applied Linguistics, 8*, 1–21.

Pica, T., & Doughty, C. (1985). Input and interaction in the communicative language classroom: A comparision of teacher-fronted and group activities. In S.M. Gass & C.G. Madden (Eds.), *Input in second language acquisition* (pp. 115–132). Cambridge, MA: Newbury House.

Pica, T., Holliday, L., Lewis, N., & Morgenthaler, L. (1989). Comprehensible output as an outcome of linguistic demands on the learner. *Studies in Second Language Acquisition, 11*, 63–90.

Politzer, G. (1974). *Kritik der klassischen Psychologie [Critique of classical psychology].* Cologne: Europaeische Verlagsanstalt.

Porter, P. (1986). How learners talk to each other: Input and interaction in task-centered discussions. In R.R. Day (Ed.), *Talking to learn* (pp. 200–221). Rowley, MA: Newbury House.

Rogoff, B. (1990). *Apprenticeship in thinking.* New York: Cambridge University Press.

Rommetveit, R. (1985). Language acquisition as increasing linguistic structuring of experience and symbolic behavior control. In J.V. Wertsch (Ed.), *Culture, communication, and cognition* (pp. 183–204). Cambridge: Cambridge University Press.

Rutherford, W., & Sharwood-Smith, M. (Eds.). (1988). *Grammar and second language teaching: A book of readings.* New York: Newbury House.

Savignon, S.J. (1991). Research on the role of communication in classroom-based foreign language instruction: On the interpretation, expression, and negotiation of meaning. In B. Freed (Ed.), *Foreign language acquisition research and the classroom* (pp. 31–45). Lexington, MA: D.C. Heath.

Schegloff, E.A., & Sacks, H. (1973). Opening up closings. *Semiotica, 8*, 289–327.

Schriffin, D. (1987). *Discourse markers.* Cambridge: Cambridge University Press.

Singleton, J. (1989). Japanese folkcraft pottery apprenticeship: Cultural patterns of an educational institution. In M.W. Coy (Ed.), *Apprenticeship: From theory to method and back again* (pp. 13–30). Albany, NY: State University of New York Press.

Swain, M. (1985). Communicative competence: Some roles of comprehensible input and comprehensible output in its development. In S.M. Gass & C.G. Madden (Eds.), *Input in second language aquisition* (pp. 235–253). Cambridge, MA: Newbury House.

Tomasello, M., & Herron, C. (1989). Feedback for language transfer errors: The garden path technique. *Studies in Second Language Acquisition, 11*, 385–395.

Ulichny, P. (1990). *Talking literate: Teaching reading to ESL college students.* Unpublished paper, Harvard Graduate School of Education, Cambridge, MA.

Van Lier, L. (1988). *The classroom and the language learner.* New York: Longman.

Vygotsky, L.S. (1986). *Thought and language.* Cambridge, MA: MIT Press.

Vygotsky, L.S. (1978). *Mind in society: The development of higher psychological processes.* Cambridge, MA: Harvard University Press.

Wagner-Gough, J. (1975). Comparative studies in second language learning. In E. Hatch (Ed.), *Second language acquisition* (pp. 155–171). Rowley, MA: Newbury House.

Wertsch, J.V. (1979a). From social interaction to higher psychological processes: A clarification and application of Vygotsky's theory. *Human Development, 22*, 1–22.

Wertsch, J.V. (Ed.) (1979b). *The concept of activity in Soviet psychology.* Armonk, NY: M.E. Sharpe.

Wertsch, J.V. (1985). *Vygotsky and the social formationof mind.* Cambridge, MA: Harvard University Press.

Wertsch, J.V., & Stone, C.A. (1978). Microgenesis as a tool for developmental analysis. *Quarterly Newsletter for the Laboratory of Comparative Human Cognition, 1*, 8–10.

Wertsch, J.V., Minich, N., & Arns, F.J. (1984). The creation of context in joint problem-solving. In B. Rogof & J. Lave (Eds.), *Everyday cognition* (pp. 151–171). Cambridge, MA: Harvard University Press.

Wesche, M.B., & Ready, D. (1985). Foreigner talk in the university classroom. In S.M. Gass & C.G. Madden (Eds.), *Input in second language acquisition* (pp. 89–114). Cambridge, MA: Newbury House.

Wong-Fillmore, L. (1985). When does teacher talk work as input? In S.M. Gass & C.G. Madden (Eds.), *Input in second language acquisition* (pp. 17–50). Cambridge, MA: Newbury House.

Wood, D., Bruner, J.S., & Ross, G. (1976). The role of tutoring in problem solving. *Journal of Child Psychology and Psychiatry, 17*, 89–100.

Zivin, G. (1979). Removing common confusions about egocentric speech, private speech, and self-regulation. In G. Zivin (Ed.), *The development of self regulation through private speech* (pp. 13–49). New York. Wiley & Sons.

3

Linguistic Accommodation With LEP and LD Children*

Linda Schinke-Llano

Department of English
Millikin University
Decatur, IL

INTRODUCTION

It has long been noted (Ferguson, 1971) that adjustments in speech occur with particular groups of interlocutors: children, the elderly, the hearing impaired, and foreigners, for example. A considerable body of literature, in fact, has developed with respect to two of those categories, namely children and foreigners.[1] Subsumed under the classifications of baby talk (BT) and foreigner talk (FT), numerous studies have attempted to identify the characteristics of these simplified registers. Early studies in both areas tended to focus on

* The author would like to thank James V. Wertsch of Clark University for his assistance in the experimental designs of both studies reported here.

[1] Researchers have also begun to focus on speech to the elderly, as is evident in the studies by Coupland, Coupland, and Giles (1991); Coupland, Coupland, Giles, and Henwood (1986); and Hamilton (1986).

phonological, syntactic, and lexical adjustments. More recent studies have investigated variation in discourse strategies. Generally speaking, however, relatively few of the studies investigating linguistic accommodation have been experimental in design, rather than observational. Of those that are experimental, few have utilized similar data-gathering procedures, and even fewer have employed an interactional framework to analyze the data.

It is the purpose of this chapter to review two experimental studies, both of which involve joint problem-solving activities analyzed from a Vygotskian perspective. That is, both utilize the premise forwarded by Vygotsky (1962, 1978, 1981a, 1981b) that higher mental (or sign-mediated) functions develop as a result of the progression from interpsychological (assisted) functioning to intrapsychological (independent) functioning. The role of speech in this progression is, of course, critical. In the first study (Schinke, 1981; Schinke-Llano, 1986), fifth and sixth-grade teachers were observed in dyadic interaction with native English-speaking (NS) and limited English-proficient (LEP) children. In the second (Sammarco, 1984), mothers were observed in problem-solving tasks with preschool normally achieving (NA) and learning disabled (LD) children. In both studies, the major focus was on how the adults utilize language to structure the problem-solving task for the children.

Despite the different ages and characteristics of the children, the results of the studies are strikingly similar. Given the similarities of these studies in both design and outcome, this chapter will forward a description of linguistic accommodation from an interactional perspective, as well as propose an explanation for that accommodation. Further, speculation will be made as to the effect of the interaction patterns observed on the LEP and LD populations represented.

LEP STUDY

Subjects

In the study conducted by Schinke-Llano, subjects were 12 monolingual English-speaking classroom teachers located at four schools. Four were fifth-grade teachers; four were sixth-grade teachers; and four taught fifth and sixth-grade combination classes. All classroom populations consisted of native speakers of English, nonnative speakers fluent in English, and LEP students.

Twenty-four students participated in the experimental study, two from each teacher's class. Twelve students were native speakers of English; 12 were LEP students. All LEP students observed were Spanish-speaking participants in the school district's bilingual education program.

Data Collection

The task selected for the study was one that placed identical demands upon the teacher to communicate with an LEP student and with a student who is a native speaker of English. The task was academic in nature, yet not associated with a specific content area: the filling out of a catalogue order blank. The teachers were informed that observations would be made of them as they explained a task to each of two students. At the beginning of the task, each teacher was given a catalogue page, an order blank, and the following typed instructions:

> Using the accompanying pages, explain to the student how to fill out an order blank. Then, with your assistance if necessary, have the student fill out an order blank by ordering the two items circled. This is *not* a test; completion of the task is not essential.

Each student involved (one LEP and one NS student per teacher) was asked in his or her native language by the researcher to assist in an activity with the teacher. Each was informed that the activity was not a test and would not be graded, and that completion or accuracy was not important.

Teacher–student dyads were audiotaped for approximately 10 to 15 minutes each in private rooms near, or adjacent to, the participating classrooms. Field notes were kept on any pertinent comments the teachers made outside of the taping sessions. The tapes were transcribed for analysis.

Coding and Analysis

Analysis focuses on the organization of the instructional interaction to ascertain if there is any variation in the way teachers utilize language to structure the task for the two groups of students. Both quantitative and qualitative features are considered. First, in order to ascertain any differences in total amount of language used with the two groups, lines of teacher-talk in the transcripts were counted, and tapes timed. Chi-square analysis was used to determine whether the differences were significant.

Next, in order to characterize the nature of the instructional interactions, the concept of abbreviation—that is, the degree to which subdirectives of a task are explicitly mentioned—was utilized. In order to do this, the task at hand, the filling out of a catalogue order blank, was conceived of as a single task having many substeps, or as a directive having many subdirectives. Two sections, both involving filling in the catalogue number, were chosen for more detailed analysis for several reasons. Most importantly, they are relatively difficult sections, since they are the only ones involving both the order form and the picture of the item and its written description on the catalogue page, as well. Further, these sections involve observable behaviors that can be measured objectively. Finally, since each student had to order two items, there were four occurrences of the step for each teacher. Thus, more detailed comparisons both within and across teachers could be done.

In coding and analyzing these data related to the completion of catalogue numbers, each substep explicitly mentioned by the teacher was identified. Explicit mention includes utilization of:

1. nonverbal directives (e.g., pointing);
2. direct directives (e.g., "The number goes in this blank."); or
3. indirect directives (e.g., "Where does that number go?").

Related to the question of abbreviation is that of regulation. The same sections of transcript were coded to determine whether the steps delineated were teacher-regulated or student-regulated. In short, which person—the teacher or the student—is responsible for the proceedings of the task? In this case, for example, does the teacher or the student locate the catalogue number? If it is the student, does he or she accomplish it through mediation (assistance) by the teacher?

Relating the coding of regulatory behavior to that of abbreviation, both nonverbal and direct directives are categorized as teacher-regulated behavior. Statements such as "This catalog number will be down below: 7-10-G-M-B" are labeled as teacher-regulated substeps. Indirect directives, on the other hand, fall into the category of student-regulated behavior that is mediated. Examples of mediated student-regulated behavior are "Can you find the letter?" and "Where's the description?" Finally, pure student-regulated behavior occurs only if the substep is not mentioned (either explicitly or implicitly) by the teacher. It is important to note that abbreviation and regulation are inversely related. That is, the more abbreviated the language used to direct the task, the more student-regulated the task is. The less abbreviated the instructions, the more teacher-regulated the task.

Results of the abbreviation and regulation coding were reported in grid form, weighted, and tabulated in order to ascertain any differences in treatment of the two groups of students. A Mann-Whitney U Test was utilized to determine the significance of differences obtained.

Results

With respect to the quantity of speech used (as indicated by the number of lines per transcript), chi-square calculations reveal that the amount of language utilized with LEP students as a group is significantly greater than the amount used with non-LEP students as a group ($p<.001$). Results are not significant, however, with respect to the amount of time used in each dyad.

In addition to talking more to LEP students, the teachers organized the task quite differently for them with respect to abbreviation. Despite individual variation in teachers' instructional strategies, certain patterns are evident. One such pattern is the change in degree of abbreviation from the first items ordered to the second. In the NS dyads, 11 of the 12 teachers were more abbreviated in their instructions when ordering the second items than when ordering the first item. In the LEP dyads, nine teachers showed increased abbreviation of the instructional task when progressing from the first to the second item ordered. Thus, with both types of student, there is a consistent pattern of increased abbreviation as the task situation progresses. That is, fewer task steps were specified, and less teacher-regulation was utilized for both NS and LEP students when the second item was ordered.

Despite this common pattern, important differences emerge when one compares speech to the two groups for each item ordered. With respect to the first item, ten of the 12 teachers were more abbreviated in their speech to native speakers, with two evidencing no difference in their speech to the two types of students. Regarding the second item, nine NS interactions were more abbreviated than the corresponding LEP interactions; two showed no difference. (One teacher was not included because the LEP student was not requested to order a second item.)

When the Mann-Whitney U test is used to analyze the ranked data, the differences are found to be significant (p = .0028). Therefore, as a group, teachers structure the instructional task situation in a significantly more abbreviated manner for NS students than for LEP students. In other words, the interactions with LEP students are more teacher-regulated, and the steps of the task are made more explicit, than they are for the native speakers.

LD STUDY

Subjects

In the Sammarco study, subjects were 12 mother–child dyads, all from Anglo-American homes where English is the primary language. All the mothers had at least a high school education. The children were all males, ages 3–7 to 3–11, matched for nonverbal intelligence, social-emotional status, and sensory acuity. Six of the children were categorized as normally achieving (NA) and six as significantly below average (LD) as determined by the Peabody Picture Vocabulary Test—Revised. Thus, two groups of six dyads each were utilized for the experiment.

Data Collection

Each dyad was presented with the identical problem-solving task, one chosen to be appropriate for both the age and interest level of the children. Dyads were seated side-by-side at a table in an empty classroom. On the table were two three-dimensional airport scenes, one a model and the other a copy, each having 12 vehicles (four sets of three each of helicopters, airplanes, baggage cars, and cars).

Mothers were read the following instructions by the researcher:

> Here we have two toy airports [point to the model and then point to the copy]. As you can see, the two toy airports are exactly alike. All of the pieces are the same. They are also in exactly the same places [point to the cars in the model and then in the copy]. We know this piece goes here [pick up a baggage car from the copy], because there is a dot here [point to the dot]. These toys [point to the model] don't come out because they're glued. In a minute, I will take this airport [point to the copy] apart. I want [child's name] to make this airport [point to the

copy] look exactly like this airport [point to the model] with all the pieces in the same places. In the end, both of them should look just like they do now. I will put some extra pieces here also [present board with extra pieces]. They do not fit into the airport. So, in the end, they will be left out. If ____ doesn't know how to put the airport together, I would like you to help him. Provide any assistance that you think is necessary for ____ to complete the airport. There is no hurry. Take as long as you need. Do you have any questions? [Dismantle the copy and randomly place the pieces on the board with the extra pieces.] You may begin. (Sammarco, 1984, p. 89)

Dyads were then videotaped for approximately 20 minutes each. Tapes were transcribed in preparation for analysis; nonverbal elements such as gazes, pointing, handling of pieces, and general gestures were all noted. In addition to the formal task, mothers of LD children were asked to complete a questionnaire regarding the nature and severity of the child's problem, as well as the age at which it was diagnosed and the length of time spent in special programs.

Coding and Analysis

Similar to the first study reported, the data were analyzed to determine whether mothers utilize language to structure the problem-solving situation any differently for the two groups of children.[2] Both quantitative and qualitative aspects of the interactions were considered. As a quantitative feature, total time spent per task was calculated. A Mann-Whitney U test was utilized to determine if differences between the two groups were significant.

In characterizing the nature of the interactions, the concepts of regulation and abbreviation were used as in the first study. The total task of completing the airport copy was viewed as consisting of 12 episodes (for the 12 vehicles), each of which comprised three substeps—consult the model, select the piece, and insert the piece. In a four-level analysis, data were coded to determine:

1. who is physically responsible (mother or child) for each substep of each episode;
2. if the child is responsible, whether the behavior is self-regulated or other-regulated;

---

[2] A number of research questions were posed. Only those directly relating to language usage are reported here.

3. if the behavior is other-regulated, whether the regulation is direct ("Look over there.") or indirect ("Find the next piece.");
4. again if the behavior is other-regulated, whether the regulation consists of direct versus indirect pointing or direct versus indirect speech. (Recall that indirect speech equates with abbreviated directives.)

Unless otherwise noted, a Mann-Whitney U test was used in each instance to determine if differences were significant in the way in which the two groups divided up responsibility for the task.

A related analysis determined the level of direct responsibility for each dyad. The mother was viewed as responsible if she physically performed a step or provided direct other-regulation. The child was responsible if either self-regulation or indirect other-regulation occurred. A Mann Whitney U Test was again used to determine if differences were significant.

Results

In the analysis of time needed to complete the task, there were no significant differences between the two groups. With respect to regulation of the problem-solving task, however, strong differences between the NA and LD dyads were shown. Regarding level one (physical responsibility for the task), NA children were physically responsible for consulting the model, selecting the piece, and inserting the piece nearly 100 percent of the time. LD children, on the other hand, were responsible 68, 91, and 79 percent of the time for each respective step. Differences were significant ($p<.008$, $p<.032$, and $p<.008$, respectively). In short, mothers in LD dyads were physically responsible for task steps significantly more often than were mothers in NA dyads.

Results for level two (self- versus other-regulation) are similar. While 87 percent of the LD children's looks to the model were other-regulated, only 37 percent of the NA children's looks were. Ninety-one percent of the LD children's and 63 percent of the NA children's selection of pieces were other-regulated. Ninety-seven percent of the placement of pieces by LD children were other-regulated, while only 49 percent of the NA placements were. Differences for each substep were significant ($p<.047$, $p<.047$, and $p<.008$, respectively). Thus, other-regulation (that is, regulation by the mothers) occurred significantly more often in the LD dyads than in the NA dyads.

The pattern of differences continues in the level three analysis (direct versus indirect other-regulation). While differences were not significant for the substep of consulting the model, they were for the other two substeps. Sixty-five percent of the LD children experienced direct other-regulation in picking up the pieces; 0 percent of the NA children did (p<.001). Sixty-nine percent of the LD children as opposed to 30 percent of the NA children received direct other-regulation in placing the pieces (p<.009). Thus, mothers in the LD dyads utilize direct other-regulation significantly more often than do their counterparts in NA dyads.[3]

Further differences were revealed in the level four analysis (direct versus indirect pointing and speech). With respect to direct pointing versus direct speech, differences were significant (p<.012) for the substep of placing the piece. That is, while 50 percent of the NA dyads involved direct speech for this substep, only 10 percent of the LD dyads did. With respect to indirect pointing versus indirect speech, differences were significant (p=.008, chi square) for the substep of selecting the piece. While 33 percent of the NA dyads utilized indirect speech for this substep, 0 percent of the LD dyads did. Thus, in substeps where differences were significant, mothers in LD dyads relied almost exclusively on pointing (whether direct or indirect) rather than on language for other-direction. Mothers in NA dyads, while also utilizing pointing behaviors, incorporated both indirect and direct speech into their regulatory behavior.

Finally, with respect to the level of direct responsibility manifested in the tasks, it was found that mothers in the LD dyads assumed a greater part of the strategic responsibility (physical responsibility or direct other-regulation) than did their counterparts in the NA dyads. Differences were significant for each substep (p<.001, p<.001, and p<.004, respectively).

DISCUSSION AND CONCLUSIONS

The differences between the two studies cited are obvious: the age of the children (3 years versus 10 and 11 years); the gender mix (all male versus male and female); the distinguishing characteristic of the children (LD versus LEP); the characteristics of the adults (mother versus teacher, all female versus male and female); and the task (completing a model versus filling out a form).

---

[3] In a post hoc analysis, it was found that 25 percent of the mothers in the LD group manifested ineffective other-regulation; only 2 percent of the mothers in the NA group did (p<.047).

Despite these differences, the overriding similarities between the studies justify attempting to interpret the results under the single broad category of linguistic accommodation. One such similarity is that of design. Both are experimental studies involving a joint problem-solving task divided into substeps (a directive with subdirectives). Further, both employ a Vygotskian framework for analysis. Who regulates the substeps, the child or the adult? How is language used to mediate the task? Is the language direct or indirect (nonabbreviated or abbreviated)? Finally, the results are strikingly similar. As groups, adults in both LEP and LD dyads structure the task situation in a significantly different way than they do in NS and NA dyads. Interactions with both LEP and LD children are more other-regulated, and the steps of the task are made more explicit than for the NS and NA children.

Thus, as a result of the evidence presented, the following description of linguistic accommodation is offered from an interactional perspective:

> With particular groups of interlocutors, adult native speakers will modify their interaction patterns so that they take responsibility for joint problem-solving tasks. Further, their speech will be less abbreviated; that is, more substeps of the task will be specified.

At the outset of this chapter it was stated that an explanation for this interactional pattern would be forwarded in addition to a description of the pattern. Key to this explanation is the issue of perception. In the studies both LEP and LD children were perceived by their adult interlocutors to be in need of assistance in the task situation, and the linguistic accommodation as described above ensued. Thus, the description just given could be revised as follows:

> With particular groups of interlocutors perceived to be less than fully capable of participating in verbal interactions, adult native speakers will modify their interaction patterns so that they take more responsibility for joint problem-solving tasks. Further, their speech will be less abbreviated; that is, more substeps of the task will be specified.[4]

---

[4] To a degree these statements illustrate the model presented by Coupland et al. (1986). Utilizing their terms, the adult interlocutor whose sociopsychological orientation is convergent and whose interactional goal is to promote communication efficiency will be accommodative (perhaps over-accommodative) when the evaluation of the child interlocutor's performance is negative.

A critical issue raised by these studies is whether perceptions of a need for assistance (as opposed to perceptions of differences) are accurate. Certainly one cannot refute that normally achieving and learning disabled children differ in a particular way. Similarly, native English-speaking and limited English-proficient children differ in an obvious characteristic. While perceptions of these differences among children may be accurate, are the perceptions of need for assistance accurate as well? Both researchers question whether the linguistic accommodation evidenced is necessary. Schinke-Llano, for example, cites the fact that all LEP children completed the tasks regardless of the degree of other-regulation and abbreviation. Sammarco cites instances when mothers in LD dyads continued to assume responsibility when it was evident from earlier episodes that such other-regulation was not necessary. Thus, while it can be argued that linguistic accommodation occurs because of perceived inabilities on the part of the interlocutor to participate in the interaction, the question remains as to the necessity of the degree of accommodation.

Related to the question just posed is that of the potential consequences of such interaction patterns, if indeed they are unwarranted.[5] In the case of LEP children, for example, Schinke-Llano speculates that overly modified input may impede the second language acquisition process. In the case of LD children, Sammarco questions whether reliance on nonverbal strategies and ineffective other-regulation may exacerbate the children's underlying language deficiencies. Finally, in the case of both populations studied, excessive over-regulation and nonabbreviated language may impede the children's progress from interpsychological to intrapsychological functioning. While these final questions raised are by no means answered by the studies reported, they are sufficiently serious to merit further attention from researchers.

REFERENCES

Coupland, N., Coupland, J., & Giles, H. (1991). *Language, society, and the elderly: Discourse, identity, and aging.* Oxford: Basil Blackwell.
Coupland, N., Coupland, J., Giles, H., & Henwood, K. (1986). *Accommodating the elderly: Aspects of intergenerational miscommunication.* Paper presented at the Minnesota Linguistics Conference, MN.

---

[5] Hamilton (1986) expresses similar concerns regarding the effects of particular kinds of linguistic accommodation in speech to Alzheimer's patients.

Ferguson, C. (1971). Absence of copula and the notion of simplicity: A study of normal speech, baby talk, foreigner talk, and pidgins. In D. Hymes (Ed.), *Pidginization and creolization of languages* (pp. 141–150). Cambridge: Cambridge University Press.

Hamilton, H. (1986). *Problems in accommodating the other: Content convergence and Alzheimer's Disease.* Paper presented at the Minnesota Linguistics Conference, MN.

Sammarco, J. (1984). *Joint problem-solving activity in mother-child dyads: A comparative study of normally achieving and language disordered preschoolers.* Unpublished doctoral dissertation: Northwestern University, Evanston, IL.

Schinke, L. (1981). *English foreigner talk in content classrooms.* Unpublished doctoral dissertation, Northwestern University, Evanston, IL.

Schinke-Llano, L. (1986). Foreigner talk in joint cognitive activities. In R. Day (Ed.), *Talking to learn: Conversation in second language acquisition* (pp. 99–117). Rowley, MA: Newbury House.

Vygotsky, L.S. (1962). *Thought and language.* Cambridge, MA: Harvard University Press.

Vygotsky, L.S. (1978). *Mind in society: The development of higher psychological processes.* Cambridge, MA: Harvard University Press.

Vygotsky, L.S. (1981a). The development of higher forms of attention. In J. Wertsch (Ed.), *The concept of activity in Soviet psychology* (pp. 189–239). Armonk, NY: M.E. Sharpe.

Vygotsky, L.S. (1981b). The genesis of higher mental functions. In J. Wertsch (Ed.), *The concept of activity in Soviet psychology* (pp. 144–188). Armonk, NY: M.E. Sharpe.

4

Working in the ZPD: Fossilized and Nonfossilized Nonnative Speakers

Gay N. Washburn

English Language Programs
University of Pennsylvania
Philadelphia, PA

INTRODUCTION

Although fossilization is generally accepted as both a theoretical concept and a factual occurrence in second language acquisition, we still seem far from understanding it on either the practical or the theoretical level. As a concept, fossilization is, as Hyltenstam said, "scientifically undeveloped" (1988, p. 68). Even the definitions differ, ranging from Celce-Murcia's description of fossilization as second language acquisition that has "prematurely plateaued" (1991, p. 462) to Selinker's definition of fossilization as "...a mechanism which is assumed also to exist in the latent psychological structure" (1972, p. 215) to Johnston's definition of fossilization as "a consistently nonstandard pattern of speech of the kind that teachers frequently call *fractured...*" (emphasis in original, 1987, p. 29). All the definitions do agree that when fossilization occurs, the second language acquisition process, or some aspect of this process, has ceased at least temporarily.

Empirical research on fossilization, for the most part, has focused on case studies, which have told us a great deal about these particular second language speakers and their learning environments (e.g., Agnello, 1977; Bean, 1990; Bruzzese, 1977; Lennon, 1991; Sotillo, 1987). In general, these studies have described the percentage of targetlike usage for selected structures on one or more tasks for their subjects, and/or have described subjects' past and present learning environments. For example, Lennon tracks the use of five structures over a period of months and reports that his subject, an advanced learner of English, develops more targetlike use in all but one of the structures. For the fifth structure, future time forms, the subject shows no change and Lennon concludes that she seems to have fossilized in that structure. However, none of these studies has described the linguistic behavior or (non)learning behavior of second language learners whose second language acquisition process has fossilized (hereafter referred to as fossilized speakers), which distinguishes them from those who are still in the process of learning (nonfossilized speakers). Thus, fossilized speakers must still be identified, as they were for this study, by nonlinguistic criteria, such as length of residence and learning history.

Similarly, pedagogical discussions of fossilization encounter problems because they have no strong empirical research on which to base their advice for instructing the fossilized speaker or avoiding the onset of fossilization. For example, a recent article, "Proficiency and the Prevention of Fossilization—An Editorial" by Valette (1991), considers the problem of the poor proficiency of foreign language undergraduate majors in the United States. She suggests that oral proficiency interviews be analyzed "to determine whether the speech shows signs of fossilization or whether the mistakes are more random and simply indicative of material not yet mastered" (p. 327). This is an interesting suggestion but it rests on the assumption, not yet verified by research, that the pattern of errors of fossilized speakers is somehow noticeably different, in particular, as Valette suggests, that it is less random. It remains an empirical question whether the performance of fossilized speakers on an oral proficiency interview task is even (or easily) distinguishable from that of nonfossilized speakers. Valette concludes by calling for a focus on "minimizing all possibility of fossilization" (1991, p. 328), certainly a laudable goal, but not necessarily a practical one given our current state of knowledge.

The articles by Valette (1991) and Lennon (1991) illustrate some of the difficulties SLA researchers and teachers face when trying to study or remedy fossilization. In addition, Valette's article highlights the need in SLA research to be able to identify the fossilized speaker, in part to arrive at a definition of fossilization that can be applied in research, but also to better understand and assist learning, or acquisition.

However, fossilization is not a term unique to SLA. Vygotsky defined fossilization in the 1930s when discussing the "problems of method" (1978, p. 63). He states that when some mental processes undergo prolonged development, they then become fossilized. Furthermore, he claims that processes that have fossilized are difficult to study because "they have lost their original appearance, and their outer appearance tells us nothing about their internal nature" (1978, p. 64). He offers us the example of voluntary and involuntary attention; well-established voluntary attention appears the same as involuntary attention. So too was second language acquisition viewed for many years as " . . . simply a mechanical process of habit-formation . . . " (Allen & Widdowson, 1975, p. 46). Vygotsky adds that if we want to study a fossilized behavior it is not sufficient merely to examine that behavior as it is, but we must "alter the automatic, mechanized fossilized character of the higher form of behavior and to turn it back to its source through experiment" (1978, p. 64).

Vygotskian theory also suggests an approach to the problem of fossilization through its emphasis on the basic social nature of language learning. For Vygotsky, language is learned first through social speech and then is internalized. Although SLA theories also acknowledge that the negotiation that occurs in the course of interaction is probably a necessary condition for SLA (Hatch, 1983; Krashen, 1982; Long, 1981), to date studies on negotiation (e.g., Gass & Varonis 1985, 1989; Pica 1987, 1991; Pica, Holliday, Lewis, & Morgenthaler, 1989; Pica, Holliday, Lewis, Berducci, & Newman, 1991) assume their subjects are all still in the process of learning the target language. In addition, the tasks they employ emphasize communication and thus do not encourage any attention to, or focus on, form.[1]

Furthermore, Vygotsky's insistence that we must consider the

---

[1] However, see Pica (1991) for a call for more variation in task type and consideration of subject's current level of development.

zone of proximal development, as well as the actual level of development, in order to understand what a person is ready to learn suggests that differences between fossilized speakers (or non-learners) and nonfossilized speakers (or learners) may well be found in tasks done in the ZPD, rather than at the actual level of development. Considering fossilization then from a Vygotskian perspective suggests that examination of the zone of proximal development of both fossilized and nonfossilized speakers should reveal differences between the two groups since the fossilized speaker is presumably not acquiring or learning—not using the available input (as Lennon, 1991, suggested) or not exploiting opportunities for comprehensible output (Swain 1985). In addition, examination of the ZPD entails comparison of fossilized and non-fossilized speakers' performance on the interpsychological and intrapsychological levels; that is, what the speaker can do with and without help. Thus, we need to examine the productions of speakers while they are trying to learn, while they are being given help, and while their linguistic skills are being challenged, as well as while they are doing tasks independently, in order to understand fossilization at all.

To illustrate the usefulness of Vygotskian theory to the study of fossilization in SLA, I would like to report on findings from a study that was based in Vygotskian theory and attempted to find differences in performance between fossilized and nonfossilized speakers on several tasks.

THE STUDY

The subjects (n = 18) were all matriculated undergraduates at a large urban public university. At the time of the study all were enrolled in the highest-level English as a Second Language (ESL) writing class. Since there is no operationalized definition of fossilized speakers based on linguistic behavior, a working definition was employed. Fossilized speakers (n = 9) were identified from among the volunteers by their length of residence in the United States (five years or more) and a history of failure in ESL at their school (they had failed at least one ESL course previously). Non-fossilized speakers (n = 9) had lived in the United States for a shorter time, 6 months to $4\frac{1}{2}$ years, and had no history of failure. Half were male and half female. Their native languages were Spanish (n = 7), Cantonese (n = 8), and Mandarin Chinese (n = 3). Although all had been placed by a writing exam (scored globally) in the same level for their ESL writing, the fossilized subjects scored significantly lower on a cloze test given by the researcher to determine global proficiency (p = .0007, df = 15, Two sample T test). The cloze test was given near the end of the semester, so the difference in scores between the two groups could have been due to differential progress over the semester, or it may have been due to a difference between their global language skills and their writing skills. It is also possible that the difference may reflect a real difference in proficiency between the two groups, which the class placement failed to capture.

The data reported here were gathered over the course of three meetings. Each lasted about 45 minutes. In the first meeting, subjects were led through a structured interview designed to elicit certain grammatical structures, which a pilot study had suggested were problematic for these students. The structures chosen for the tasks were: negation (in all tenses and aspects and with nouns), present perfect and present perfect continuous, if- clauses (both real and unreal conditionals), embedded wh- questions (such as "I don't know where he went."). Sentence negation was chosen because SLA research has identified clear developmental stages in its acquisition (Cancino, Rosansky, & Schumann, 1978; Schumann, 1978). Present perfect tense and if- clauses were used because the initial interviews indicated that many subjects had failed to use these structures in targetlike fashion, in terms of both the form and their use in the obligatory contexts. Embedded wh- questions were chosen because the pilot study suggested that placement of the auxiliary verb in this structure is often problematic for advanced learners.

In the subsequent meetings, the subjects were given the cloze test, a combined grammaticality judgment and imitation task (hereafter abbreviated GJI Task), and a short-term learning task. The results reported here consider subjects' performance in the structured interview, the GJI Task, and the short-term learning task.

The GJI Task asked the subjects to listen to a model utterance, decide if it was grammatical or not, and then to repeat it if it was grammatical; if it was not grammatical, they were to change it to a grammatical form, keeping to the meaning that they understood. The model sentences were mostly taken from utterances subjects had produced in their initial meeting with the researcher. Some were generated by the researcher in order to fill out the various paradigms.

In the short-term learning task, utterances that the subjects produced in the GJI Task but that were not targetlike were used as the interviewer/investigator attempted to teach the targetlike form by the following means, used successively as needed: (a) provision of the correct model, (b) repetition of the correct model with emphasis, (c) breaking the utterances into smaller chunks, (d) backwards build-up, and (e) overt correction. This attempt to teach was considered working in the subject's ZPD, since the subject had demonstrated that he/she could not produce the sentence after being supplied with just one model, and since the help given was varied until the subject could produce the target utterance.

RESULTS

Comparison of the performance of the fossilized and nonfossilized subjects on work in the ZPD revealed some similarities and differences.

Performance on the short-term learning task for the two groups was superficially similar, as can be seen through a quick reading of Examples 1 and 2. All subjects repeated some previously non-targetlike utterances perfectly; other utterances required a series of turns for the subject to produce a targetlike imitation. The number of turns it took each subject to produce the model utterance in targetlike fashion was counted and changes within each turn and between turns were examined as well.

Example 1. S10, nonfossilized speaker

I   (Interviewer): If her parents hadn't decided that, she wouldn't be here in the United States.

S10:   If—if her parents [pause] ha... haven't, that's what you say? haven't decided that, she wouldn't be in United States.

I: Uh, okay. If her parents hadn't decided that, she wouldn't be here in the United States.

S10:   Oh, okay. If here parents hadn't decided that, she wouldn't be-be in the United States.

Example 2. S3, fossilized speaker

I: The Mainlanders thought if they didn't do it, there would be a rebellion.

S3:   [pause] The Mainlander thought if they... Should I change it?

I: No, I have it corrected. So repeat it exactly as I said it.

S3: The Mainlanders think- thought if they don't if they didn't do it, there will be a rebellion.

I: The Mainlanders thought if they didn't do it, there would be a rebellion.

S3: The Mainlander thought if they... if they didn't do it, there would be a rebellion.

I: Okay, one more time.

S3: The Mainlander thought if they... if they didn't do it, there would be a rebellion.

Both groups had high turn takers and low turn takers—those who needed many turns (more than 15) to imitate the model sentence and those who needed few turns (less than 13) on the average. The fossilized group had one high turn taker and the nonfossilized group had two high turn takers. They averaged 24.9 turns and 23.5 turns, respectively. This difference is not significant. It could be supposed that these subjects were working outside their ZPD, and thus had equal difficulty in learning.

However, closer analysis revealed some differences between fossilized and nonfossilized speakers. Among the low turn takers, the fossilized speakers needed significantly more turns than the nonfossilized to produce the model utterance in targetlike fashion. As can be seen in Table 4.1, the low turn nonfossilized subjects averaged 5.7 turns while the low turn fossilized subjects averaged 8.4 turns. This difference is statistically significant.

One reason that the fossilized speakers needed more turns appears to be that their production of structures seemed to be less stable. In other words, they would produce a form, for example, irregular past tense, in one turn, and then one or two turns later, they would not produce it when required. This giving up of previously targetlike forms or alternation of targetlike with non-targetlike forms has been labeled *regression* in this study. Only loss of targetlike forms from required contexts was counted as regression. A count of the number of regressions used by all subjects (see Column 4 of Table 4.1) showed a significant difference between the nonfossilized and fossilized groups: 2.66 mean versus 8.66 mean, respectively. This pattern held for both high and low turn takers and the difference was statistically significant.

Finally, the performance of the fossilized and nonfossilized subjects in the first interview and the GJI Task was compared for

TABLE 4.1
Cloze Scores, Average Number of Turns, Number of Regressions.

	Cloze Score	Average Number of Turns	Number of Regressions
Nonfossilized subjects			
S10	68%	3.33	1
S9	90%	4.15	2
S1	76.5%	4.76	1
S12	67%	4.86	1
S8	79.5%	5.86	2
S7	46%	8.0	0
S4	65%	9.27	2
SUBGROUP MEAN		***5.74**	**1.28**
S.D.		2.15	0.76
S13	68%	21	8
S16	50%	26	7
SUBGROUP MEAN		**23.5**	**7.5**
S.D.		12.7	3.5
NONFOSSILIZED GROUP MEAN		**9.69**	****2.66**
S.D.		10.9	2.8
Fossilized subjects			
S2	44%	6	6
S3	68%	6	4
S18	34%	6.2	5
S6	46%	7.27	6
S11	47%	8.12	5
S17	41%	9.57	12
S14	27%	11.5	13
S15	38%	12.58	11
SUBGROUP MEAN		***8.40**	**7.76**
S.D.		2.57	3.62
S19	37%	24.9	16
FOSSILIZED GROUP MEAN		**10.24**	****8.66**
S.D.		6.0	4.36

*Difference between these two means is statistically significant ($p = .05, t = -2.18$, df = 12, Twosample T, Minitab, 1988).
**Difference between these two means is statistically significant ($p = .0042, t = 3.46$, df = 13, Twosample T, Minitab, 1988).

the following structures: copula, past and present; affirmative and negative simple present; affirmative and negative present continuous; affirmative regular past; irregular past; past with negative; negative or affirmative past continuous; and present perfect, both affirmative or negative. Analysis showed that all subjects tended to produce targetlike forms more consistently in the GJI Task than in the structured interview. This has been found in other studies in SLA (e.g., Ellis, 1985; Tarone, 1983), which report that use of targetlike forms varies across task.

However, as in the production of regressions in the short-term learning task, the fossilized subjects tended to produce non-targetlike forms to a greater extent in the first interview even though they could imitate them in targetlike form when they were given a model. The fossilized subjects were consistent in their targetlike use across tasks for only 36.5 percent of the structures. In contrast, for those structures that were produced targetlike when a model was given (the GJI task), the nonfossilized subjects, as a group, had 52 percent of these structures also targetlike in the interview. This difference was not statistically significant (see Table 4.2). Nonetheless, it follows the pattern set in the short-term

TABLE 4.2

Count of C, Z, O, and—in Interview 1 and GJI Task for Nonfossilized and Fossilized Subjects.

NONFOSSILIZED: INT. 1	C	Z	O	—	GJI Task	C	Z	O	—
S1	2	5	1	2	6	3	0	1	
S4	3	6	0	1	7	3	0	0	
S7	6	3	0	1	8	1	0	1	
S8	7	3	0	0	9	0	0	1	
S9	3	4	2	1	8	1	0	1	
S10	3	7	0	0	8	2	0	0	
S12	2	6	1	1	7	3	0	0	
S13	5	4	0	1	6	3	0	1	
S16	2	4	1	3	4	3	—	3	
Mean	*3.7	4.7	0.6	1.1	7.0	2.1	0	0.9	
S.D.	1.9	1.4	0.7	0.9	1.5	1.2	0	0.9	

FOSSILIZED: INT. 1	C	Z	O	—	GJI Task	C	Z	O	—
S2	3	7	0	0	4	5	1	0	
S3	0	6	3	1	7	2	0	1	
S6	4	6	0	0	9	1	0	0	
S11	3	6	0	1	4	4	1	1	
S14	2	6	1	1	4	4	0	2	
S15	1	8	1	0	4	5	1	0	
S17	0	6	3	1	3	3	2	2	
S18	3	6	0	1	7	2	0	1	
S19	1	7	2	0	6	2	0	2	
Mean	*1.9	6.4	1.1	0.5	5.3	3.1	0.5	1.0	
S.D.	1.4	0.7	1.3	0.5	2.0	1.4	0.7	0.9	

*These differences are NOT significant ($p = 0.22$, $t = -1.29$, df = 14, Twosample T, Minitab, 1988).

learning task by the fossilized subjects for production of more regressions.

Table 4.2 shows comparisons for individual subjects in production of targetlike forms across the two tasks. *C* indicates production was always targetlike, *Z* indicates it was sometimes targetlike, *O* that it was never targetlike, and those structures that were avoided are marked −.

An example of this pattern can be seen by comparing subjects from the two groups across the tasks. For example, both S6 (fossilized) and S8 (nonfossilized) produced nine (out of ten) structures consistently targetlike on the GJI Task. But in Interview 1, only four of them were targetlike for S6 (fossilized) while S8 (nonfossilized) produced seven of those structures targetlike. Similarly, S19 and S13 both produced six (out of ten) structures targetlike on the GJI Task, but in the first interview only one of them was targetlike for S19 (fossilized) compared to five for S13 (nonfossilized).

DISCUSSION

The results of this study indicate that fossilization can be approached and differences in behavior found through observation of performance across tasks and across groups (fossilized and nonfossilized). Furthermore, the tasks must vary in the degree to which subjects work on the interpsychological and intrapsychological planes in order to give us insight into the ZPD. This should not be surprising considering that most definitions of fossilization focus on its relation to the learning process. In other words, until we can describe the linguistic behavior or characteristics of fossilized speakers, we can only observe fossilization in contrast to its opposite—learning.

Second, the results of this study suggest that the "errors" produced by the fossilized speakers are not in themselves distinct, as Valette's editorial (1991) seems to suggest. All differences found between the fossilized and nonfossilized speakers were quantitative rather than qualitative. In other words, fossilized and nonfossilized speakers may produce exactly the same nontargetlike utterance (for example, "I living here four years"). The difference cannot be seen in the one error but in the pattern of errors across tasks. The fossilized speakers will produce targetlike structures less consistently in less structured situations even though on an imitation task, they have shown they can produce the structure accurately.

Finally, in a learning task the fossilized speakers generally need more turns to learn to produce an utterance because of this difficulty in maintaining the targetlike form across turns.

Few researchers have attempted to describe the distinctive behavior of fossilized speakers. Selinker's *backsliding* (1972), however, does seem to be very similar to the phenomenon labeled regression in this study. Selinker stated that the fossilized speakers produced nontargetlike forms on occasion although at other times they were able to produce targetlike forms for that very structure. On the other hand, Valette (1991) characterized the mistakes of learners as more random than those of fossilized speakers, but if Valette meant random to mean occurring unexpectedly or occasionally, then it seems that it is the errors of the fossilized speakers that are more random.

Finally, Lennon's observation that his fossilized subject seemed insensitive to the input available is confirmed by the behavior of the fossilized subjects studied here, who seemed not to perceive some forms until their presence was emphasized or pointed out in some way. For example, in the interview they did not pick up cues in the linguistic input that might have guided their choice of tense and aspect ("How long have you lived here?" "I live here five years."), but when they were given an explicit model and/or emphasis on their differences from the model (as in the short-term learning task and/or in the GJI Task), they were able to produce the required forms. Perhaps the forms are in their interlanguage competence, but they have different rules governing the necessary contexts for use.

In conclusion, although fossilization has long been recognized as an important phenomenon in SLA, few studies to date have been able to shed much light on it. That this study was able to find some differences between fossilized and nonfossilized speakers owes much to the use of Vygotskian theory, which emphasizes the importance of method and the need for researchers to look at the development of processes by working in the ZPD.

REFERENCES

Agnello, F. (1977). Exploring the pidginization hypothesis: A study of three fossilized negation systems. In C. Henning (Ed.), *Proceedings of the Los Angeles Second Language Research Forum 1977* (pp. 246–261). Los Angeles, CA: Dept. of English, UCLA.

Allen, J., & Widdowson, H. (1975). Grammar and language teaching. In J. Allen & S.P. Corder (Eds.), *The Edinburgh course in applied linguis-*

tics: Vol. 2. Papers in applied linguistics (pp. 45–97). London: Oxford University Press.

Bean, M. (1990). *Personal identity and the pragmatic personality: Case study of a fossilized adult.* Unpublished manuscript. University of Southern California, Department of Linguistics, Los Angeles, CA.

Bruzzese, G. (1977). English/Italian secondary hybridization: A case study of the pidginization of a second language learner's speech. In C. Henning (Ed.), *Proceedings of the Los Angeles Second Language Research Forum 1977* (pp. 235–245). Los Angeles, CA: Dept. of English, UCLA.

Cancino, H., Rosansky, E.J., & Schumann, J.H. (1978). The acquisition of English negatives and interrogatives by native Spanish speakers. In E. Hatch (Ed.), *Second language acquisition: A book of readings* (pp. 207–230). Rowley, MA: Newbury House.

Celce-Murcia, M. (1991). Grammar pedagogy in second and foreign language teaching. *TESOL Quarterly, 25,* 459–480.

Ellis, R. (1985). A variable competence model of second language acquisition. *International Review of Applied Linguistics, 23,* 47–65.

Gass, S., & Varonis, E. (1985). Task variation and NNS/NNS negotiation of meaning. In S. Gass & C. Madden (Eds.), *Input in second language acquisition* (pp. 149–161). Rowley, MA: Newbury House.

Gass, S., & Varonis, E. (1989). Incorporated repairs in nonnative discourse. In M. Eisenstein (Ed.), *The dynamic interlanguage: Empirical studies in second language variation* (pp. 71–86). New York: Plenum.

Hatch, E. (1983). Simplified input and second language acquisition. In R. Andersen (Ed.), *Pidginization and creolization as language acquisition* (pp. 64–86). Rowley, MA: Newbury House.

Hyltenstam, K. (1988). Lexical characteristics of near-native second language learners of Swedish. *Journal of Multilingual and Multicultural Development, 9*(1 & 2), 7–84.

Johnston, M. (1987). Understanding learner language. In D. Nunan (Ed.), *Applying second language acquisition research* (pp. 5–41). Adelaide: National Curriculum Resource Centre.

Krashen, S. (1982). *Principles and practice in second language acquisition. Oxford: Pergamon.*

Lennon, P. (1991). Error elimination and error fossilization: A study of an advanced learner in the L2 community. *ITL Review of Applied Linguistics, 93-94,* 129–151.

Long, M. (1981). Input, interaction, and second language acquisition. In H. Winitz (Ed.), *Annals of the New York Academy of Science: Native language and foreign language acquisition* (pp. 259–278). New York: New York Academy of Sciences.

Pica, T. (1987). Interlanguage adjustments as an outcome of NS-NNS negotiated interaction. *Language Learning, 38,* 45–73.

Pica, T. (1991). *Do second language learners need negotiation?* Paper presented at the Second Language Research Forum, Los Angeles, CA.

Pica, T., Holliday, L., Lewis, N., Berducci, D, & Newman, J. (1991). Language learning through interaction: What role does gender play? *Studies in Second Language Acquisition, 13,* 343–376.

Pica, T., Holliday, L., Lewis, N., & Morgenthaler, L. (1989). Comprehensible output as an outcome of linguistic demands on the learner. *Studies in Second Language Acquisition, 11,* 63–90.

Schumann, J. (1978). The acquistion of English negation by speakers of Spanish: A review of the literature. In R. Anderson (Ed.), *The acquisition and use of Spanish and English as first and second languages* (pp. 3–33).

Selinker, L. (1972). Interlangauge. *International Review of Applied Linguistics, 10,* 209–231.

Sotillo, S. (1987). *The impact of job-related instruction on language use: The case of a long-term resident second language learner.* Paper presented at LSA/AAAL Annual Meeting, San Francisco, CA.

Swain, M. (1985). Communicative competence: Some roles of comprehensible input and comprehensible output in its development. In S. Gass & C. Madden (Eds.), *Input in second language acquisition* (pp. 235–253). Rowley, MA: Newbury House.

Tarone, E. (1983). On the variability of interlanguage systems. *Applied Linguistics, 4,* 143–163.

Valette, R. (1991). Proficiency and the prevention of fossilization—An editorial. *Modern Language Journal, 74,* 325–328.

Vygotsky, L. (1978). *Mind in society: The development of higher psychological processes.* Cambridge, MA: Harvard University Press.

5

Form and Functions of Inner Speech in Adult Second Language Learning

María C. M. de Guerrero

English Department
Inter American University of Puerto Rico
San Juan, PR

BACKGROUND FOR THE STUDY OF INNER SPEECH IN THE SECOND LANGUAGE

Despite its recognized status as an important object of research from a first language (L1) perspective, inner speech has been conspicuously absent from the scope of second language (L2) research. Only a few scholarly works, nonempirical in nature, have established a direct link between inner speech and second (or foreign) language acquisition (Hellmich & Esser, 1975; Murphy, 1989; Rohrer, 1987). Why L2 acquisition researchers have not taken notice of inner speech is somewhat of a puzzle in the face of indisputable L1 evidence of its crucial role in language comprehension, production, and development. It may have been the researchers' behavioristically skewed interest with regard to the learner's observable language production that diverted them for years from the mental, covert processes of learning a language that accounted for their neglect of L2 inner speech. It may have simply been their lack of familiarity with the major and voluminous work of Soviet psychology on inner speech (Luria, 1982; Sokolov, 1972; Vygotsky, 1962, 1979). At any rate, the revitalized interest in introspective methods that has resulted from the cognitive revolution in language acquisition research has also made an impact on the study of the mental processes involved in L2 acquisition (Cohen, 1991; Cohen & Hosenfeld, 1981; Faerch & Kasper, 1987; Grotjahn, 1987, 1991). Obviously, inner speech, as a mind –language mechanism, must be present in many covert L2 processes. One such process is mental rehearsal, a language learning strategy that involves the covert practice of the second language (Chamot, 1987; de Guerrero, 1987; Murphy, 1991, O'Malley, Chamot, Stewner-Manzanares, Russo, & Küpper, 1985; Rubin, 1987).

As an internal language activity, mental rehearsal falls naturally within the realm of inner speech. Given the widespread use of mental rehearsal among L2 and FL learners (Bedford, 1985; Chapman & Krashen, 1986; de Guerrero, 1987) and its obvious connection to inner speech, mental rehearsal appears as fertile ground to explore and observe L2 inner speech. Of particular interest to L2 research would be those characteristics of form and function in the nature of L2 inner speech that might reveal something about how a second language is comprehended and produced, and how it develops towards a target language norm. This article reports the results of a study on the characteristics and functions of inner speech during mental rehearsal of the L2 among adult L2 learners.

The study of form and function in L2 inner speech finds a sound theoretical framework in Vygotsky (1962, 1979), among the earliest to delve experimentally into these aspects in L1 inner speech. Other propositions, coming from followers of Vygotsky as well as from scholars in other fields,[1] contribute to build a composite picture of inner speech that might serve as the basis for its exploration as an

---

[1] Although it is difficult to draw boundaries among fields of research, the following classification of references on L1 inner speech according to research areas has been attempted: psychology (Luria, 1982; McGuigan, 1970, 1978; Rosenblatt & Meyer, 1986; Sokolov, 1972; Vygotsky, 1962; 1979; Wertsch, 1977, 1980), psycholinguistics (Beggs & Howarth, 1985; Hardyck & Petrinovich, 1970; McNeill, 1987; Yaden, 1984), communication theory (Honeycutt, Zagacki, & Edwards, 1989; Johnson, 1984; Korba, 1987, 1989), and language education (Moffet, 1982, 1985; Smith, 1983; Streff, 1984; Trimbur, 1987).

L2 phenomenon. Occurring at an exceedingly fast pace, inner speech is remarkably different from external speech. Briefly, research has led to the discovery of the following formal characteristics of L1 inner speech: (a) typical abbreviated syntactic forms, (b) occasional expanded syntactic structures, (c) inner dialogue or conversation as a possible discourse pattern, (d) the usual absence of phonologically overt sounds, (e) concomitant auditory speech images and covert speech movements, and (f) the organization of highly condensed semantic complexes.

Functionally, inner speech appears to be, first and foremost, the medium for the formation, expression, and development of verbal thought. Hence its major role as an ideational tool. Inner speech, however, also performs a distinct threefold communicative function: as the means of turning inwards the social manifestations of language, as the vehicle for self-communication, and as antecedent for communication with others. Furthermore, inner speech is a major cognitive instrument for the planning, guiding, and evaluation of action. Because of its intrinsic relation to verbal thought and communication, inner speech is thus inextricably involved in the four modes of language perception and production: listening, speaking, reading, and writing.

AN EMPIRICAL STUDY OF L2 INNER SPEECH

A two-phased study of the inner speech of adult English as a second language (ESL) students was conducted (for further details, see de Guerrero, 1991/1990). The purpose of the study was to explore the nature of the inner speech that Puerto Rican ESL college students on three levels of proficiency (low, intermediate, and high) experienced while mentally rehearsing in the second language. "Nature of inner speech" was operationally defined as the linguistic characteristics of inner speech related to sound, structure, meaning, and vocabulary, as well as the functional role, or roles, of inner speech in learning the L2.

Method

The Research Design.   The study was carried out in two phases: Phase I, in which mainly a quantitative approach[2] was employed to

---

[2] In addition to the quantitative analysis of the 35 items of the questionnaire, a qualitative study was done on the comments section of the questionnaire.

analyze the responses to a questionnaire obtained from a large sample of the population (n = 426); and Phase II, in which a qualitative analysis was performed on interview protocols generated by nine "rehearsers" (participants who showed a tendency to rehearse mentally in English) who had participated in two classroom communicative activities.

Instruments and Activities.   A 35-item questionnaire and an interview form were constructed to tap those aspects of form and function included in the operational definition of "nature of inner speech." To ensure full understanding by all the participants, the instruments used—the questionnaire and the interview form— were in Spanish, the participants' native language (see Appendices A and B for an English version of these instruments). Two communicative activities (based on Littlewood, 1981) were designed to carry out Phase II of the study. In Communicative Activity 1, pairs of students, adopting the roles of interviewer and applicant, simulated a job interview based on a newspaper ad. In Communicative Activity 2, the students, also in pairs, had to discover the differences between two versions of the same picture.

Sampling and Data Collection Procedures.   From a target population of 2,108 Inter American University of Puerto Rico students enrolled in ESL courses representative of three levels of proficiency, a sample of 426 was obtained by means of the proportional stratified sampling technique, with a resulting distribution of 161 in the low proficiency group, 192 in the intermediate proficiency group, and 73 in the high proficiency group.[3] In Phase I of the study, the questionnaire was administered to the 426 sample population. In Phase II, all "high rehearsers" (students with an average of 4–5 points in their responses to Items 1, 19, 21, 25, and 34 of the questionnaire) were identified. Of these, 18 were randomly selected, and nine remained after the second interview. A week before each of the two communicative activities, the selected participants received all the necessary guidelines for the activities together with preliminary instructions for the interview that would be conducted the day following each activity. A random ordering of the activities was used. The day after the activities took place, the students were

---

[3] The students' ESL proficiency had been determined (prior to their placement in different ESL courses) by their scores on the College Board's English as a Second Language Test (ESLAT), as follows: low proficiency, <400; intermediate proficiency, 400–499; high proficiency, 500–599.

interviewed by the researcher. During these interviews the participants were questioned about the inner speech they had experienced
while mentally rehearsing for the activities. The interviews were
scheduled a day after the activities so as to facilitate the observation
of any after-the-task inner speech.

Data Analysis:

Phase I.   Responses to the questionnaire were distributed along a
five-category rating scale ranging from *never* to *always*. To analyze
the questionnaire responses, descriptive and inferential statistics
were used. The descriptive statistics consisted of frequencies,
percentages, and the median for each item on the questionnaire.
The inferential statistics included the one-sample chi-square test to
observe whether significant differences existed in the way the total
sample (n = 426) distributed along the five-category rating scale,
and the following tests to observe differences among the three
proficiency samples: chi-square (multiple sample), K-sample median, Cramer's V, and Kendall's tau c.

The multiple-sample chi-square test indicated whether the variable "proficiency level" and the variables contained in each item of
the questionnaire were significantly related. Chi-square tests were
run using the five-category distribution and two additional two-
category distributions: (a) the No/Yes distribution, where No included all the *never* and *almost never* responses and Yes all the
sometimes, often, and *always* responses, and (b) the Low/High
distribution, where the all the *never, almost never,* and *sometimes*
responses were collapsed as Low and all the *often* and *always*
responses were collapsed as High. The K-sample median test, which
is computed as a chi-square statistic, tested whether the three level
samples came from populations having different medians. When
statistical differences among the samples were found, two measures of association—Cramer's V and Kendall's tau c—were applied. While Cramer's V indicated the strength of the relationship
between the variables, Kendall's tau c indicated the direction,
positive or negative, of the association (or correlation) between the
variables. Significance levels were set at $p<.05$. In addition, 130
comments to the questionnaire were received and qualitatively
analyzed.

Phase II.   In depth "content" analysis (Kerlinger, 1973; Wenden,
1987) was used to examine the 18 retrospective verbal reports
produced by the nine rehearsers during the interviews. A classification scheme for coding the protocols was developed. Two major

classifications were linguistic characteristic (LC) and functional role (FR). To label the roles, the literature provided many of the terms used, for example, Halliday's (1973) "ideational," "interpersonal," and "textual" (macro)functions of language; Sokolov's (1972) "mnemonic" function of inner speech; and Smith's (1983) "affective" reason for talking to oneself.

Analysis of the Data

Phase I. The analysis of the data began with examination of the nature of inner speech as perceived globally by the 426 participants. Both the linguistic characteristics (sound, structure, vocabulary, and meaning) as well as the functional roles of inner speech were examined. The reader is referred to Table 5.1 for information on specific figures.

Table 5.1 offers a listing of the focus or purpose of each item, the chi-square one-sample test values for the five-category scale distribution, percentages of Yes and No responses, the chi-square values for the No/Yes distribution, and the medians. Following is a summary of the results.

First, it was found that a significant majority (84%) of the participants admitted to having experienced inner speech in the L2 (Item 1). In relation to sound, the significant presence of the following features was ascertained: the sounds of English could be heard in the mind (Item 7), voices of other people in English could also be heard (Item 14), and inner speech could be audibly vocalized when the person was alone (Item 15).

In terms of structure, significantly more affirmative than negative answers were given for the use of words (Item 3), phrases (Item 4), and sentences (Item 5) in the participants' L2 inner speech. Although a 53.10 percent of affirmative answers was found for the conversation/dialogue structure type (Item 6), the difference between Yes and No answers was nonsignificant. Moreover, the data showed that as the complexity of inner speech structures increased so did the number of No responses (see Table 5.2). This finding was confirmed by the fact that there were significantly more Yes than No responses to short thoughts (Item 17) and significantly more No than Yes responses to long thoughts (Item 18; see Table 5.1).

In relation to vocabulary, the data yielded significant values for the presence of the following types of words in the students' inner speech (see values in Table 5.1): words they repeated in order to learn (Item 8), words whose pronunciation they tried to imitate (Item 9), words they tried to recall (Item 11), and words with an

TABLE 5.1
Inner Speech (IS) Linguistic Characteristics and Functional Roles.
Questionnaire Figures for Total Sample[a]

Item	Focus or Purpose	χ^2 one-sample[b]	No %	Yes %	χ^2 No/Yes[c]	Mdn
1	frequency of IS	321.371*	16.00	84.00	197.418*	3
2	use of L1	84.657*	31.45	68.55	58.601*	3
3	structure	175.737*	14.10	85.90	219.803*	3
4	structure	209.939*	20.90	79.10	144.376*	3
5	structure	147.145*	30.30	69.70	66.254*	3
6	structure	99.634*	46.90	53.10	1.587	2
7	sound	159.352*	13.85	86.15	222.685*	4
8	vocab., mnemonic r.	257.920*	4.22	95.78	357.042*	4
9	vocab., instructional r.	288.624*	3.52	96.48	368.113*	4
10	vocab., instructional r.	157.897*	18.54	81.46	168.601*	3
11	vocab., mnemonic r.	143.258*	2.35	97.65	386.939*	4
12	vocab.	256.770*	14.55	85.45	214.094*	3
13	meaning	285.408*	4.70	95.30	349.756*	4
14	sound	92.474*	41.55	58.45	12.169*	3
15	sound	121.418*	27.23	72.77	88.347*	3
16	vocab.	58.577*	37.60	62.40	26.376*	3
17	structure	270.526*	15.26	84.74	205.671*	3
18	structure	249.235*	65.26	34.74	39.671*	2
19	textural r.	335.220*	7.75	92.25	304.225*	5
20	textural r.	312.145*	6.57	93.43	321.361*	4
21	textural r.	326.991*	6.57	93.43	321.361*	4
22	textural r.	212.756*	7.75	92.25	304.225*	4
23	textural r.	186.559*	10.56	89.44	265.014*	4
24	textural r.	188.390*	8.45	91.45	294.169*	4
25	evaluative r.	202.920*	16.90	83.10	186.676*	3
26	evaluative r.	227.638*	5.63	94.37	335.408*	4
27	evaluative r.	154.466*	18.31	81.69	171.127*	3
28	instructional r.	133.437*	24.41	75.59	111.559*	3
29	evaluative r.	171.019*	10.09	89.91	271.361*	4
30	ideational r.	267.192*	2.82	97.18	379.352*	4
31	class-unrelated IS	129.892*	37.09	62.91	28.404*	3
32	class-related IS	98.859*	23.47	76.53	119.897*	3
33	evaluative r.	252.521*	4.00	96.90	360.713*	4
34	interpersonal r.	116.840*	30.52	69.48	64.685*	3
35	intrapersonal r.	97.357*	38.03	61.97	24.423*	3

Note. Mdn = Median. vocab = vocabulary. r. = role.
[a]n = 426. [b]Based on the five-category scale distribution, df = 4. [c]Based on the No/Yes distribution, df = 1.
*$p < .001$.

TABLE 5.2
Extent to Which Inner Speech Adopted Various Structures.

Frequency category	Words	Phrases	Sentences	Convs./Dialogues
Never	16 (3.76)	27 (6.34)	34 (7.98)	75 (17.61)
Almost never	44 (10.33)	62 (14.55)	95 (22.30)	151 (35.45)
Sometimes	154 (36.15)	186 (43.66)	167 (39.20)	102 (23.94)
Often	144 (33.80)	118 (27.70)	99 (23.24)	73 (17.14)
Always	68 (15.96)	33 (7.75)	31 (7.28)	25 (5.86)

Note. All figures are for observed responses. The figure for expected responses in the chi-square one-sample test was 85.20 for each category. Figures in parentheses are percentages. Convs. = conversations.

unfamiliar meaning (Item 12). Furthermore, there was a significantly higher percentage of affirmative answers to the following vocabulary related strategies: mentally constructing sentences with certain words (Item 10), and looking up in a book or dictionary the meaning of unfamiliar words that came to mind (Item 16).

As regards meaning, the data revealed a significantly greater percentage of affirmative responses for the existence of words with an unfamiliar meaning in the participants' inner speech (Item 12), although there was an even greater percentage and higher median for thoughts making sense in English (Item 13; see Table 5.1).

The extent of L1 use within inner speech in the L2, a formal characteristic which would entail some kind of semantic, syntactic, and/or lexical breakdown in the learner's L2 inner speech, was measured by Item 2. Significantly more affirmative than negative responses and a median of three (*sometimes*) were produced for this item, but when responses were distributed as Low/High, there was a significantly greater percentage of Low responses (66.20%) than High responses (33.80%).

In addition, a significantly higher number of affirmative responses was given to the following functional roles in the participants' inner speech: the use of inner speech as an aid to memory (*mnemonic* role) both to store and retrieve verbal data (Items 8 and 11); the use of inner speech as a tool for self-teaching (*instructional* role, Items 9, 10, 28); the use of inner speech to self- or other-evaluate language, correct errors and find out how well or how much of the second language was known (*evaluative* role, Items 25, 26, 27, 29, and 33); the use of inner speech to clarify thought (*ideational* role, Item 30); the use of inner speech to create, organize, and experiment with the form of oral and written texts (*textual* role, Items 19-24); the use of inner speech to imagine conversations with others (*interpersonal* role, Item 34); and the use of inner speech to talk to oneself (*intrapersonal* role, Item 35). Another finding was the existence of both class-related (Item 32) and class-unrelated (Item 31) inner speech among the participants.

Second, differences among the three proficiency samples (low proficiency, $n = 161$; intermediate proficiency, $n = 192$; high proficiency $n = 73$) were observed with attention to the linguistic characteristics of inner speech and to its functional roles. Table 5.3 presents the statistical values obtained for those questionnaire items where significant differences among the samples were observed. These values are for the chi-square test based on the five-category distribution, Cramer's V test, Kendall's tau c test, the chi-square test based on the No/Yes distribution, and the K-sample median test. Below is a summary of the results.

The multiple-sample chi-square tests showed a significant difference in the frequency with which the different samples experienced L2 inner speech. Cramer's V and Kendall's tau c tests further revealed a significant positive association between the variables

TABLE 5.3
Statistical Values for Questionnaire Items Showing Significant Differences in the Nature of Inner Speech Among Three Proficiency Samples[a]

Item	χ^2 (df = 8)[b]	V[c]	Tau c	χ^2 (df = 2)[d]	K-sample median
1	29.482*	.186*	.210	15.293*	18.694*
2	16.224***	.138***	−.047	.574	3.735
4	15.285****	.134	.136	11.545**	5.357
5	25.317*	.172*	.192	16.595*	15.776*
6	41.182*	.220*	.197	14.837*	14.837*
7	20.991**	.157**	.176	7.907***	6.534***
13	48.444*e	.238*	.271	10.413**	10.650**
18	21.250**	.158**	.170	11.312**	11.312**
27	15.991***	.137**	.054	7.891***	3.311
30	15.365****e	.134	.010	10.534**	4.077
31	31.051*	.191*	.183	7.046***	24.056*
34	12.888	.123	.097	6.633***	3.892
35	11.687	.117	.138	9.477**	1.832

[a]low $n = 161$, intermediate $n = 192$, high $n = 73$.
[b]Chi-square based on the five-category scale distribution.
[c]In Cramer's V, probability levels were approximate.
[d]Chi-square based on the No/Yes distribution.
[e]More than 20% of the cells had an expected frequency lower than five.
*$p < .001$. **$p < .01$. ***$p < .05$. ****$p < .10$.

"proficiency level" and "frequency of inner speech." In other words, as the proficiency level increased, so did the frequency of inner speech. These results are clearly seen in Table 5.4.

In terms of sound, there was a significant difference in the extent to which the different samples could hear the sounds of English in their minds (Items 7, see Table 5.1). In this item, a significant positive association between the variables "proficiency level" and "hearing the sounds of English in the mind" was found. In terms of structure, there were significant differences in the frequency of phrases (Item 4), sentences (Item 5), and conversation/dialogues (Item 6) as well as in the frequency of long, elaborate thoughts (Item 18). In all these cases there was a positive association with proficiency level. In other words, as the proficiency of the participants' increased, so did the frequency of such variables. Table 5.5 shows this tendency. No statistically significant differences in terms of vocabulary were observed. As regards meaning, a significant difference was found in the extent to which the participants' thoughts in English made sense (Item 13, see Table 5.1), a significant positive association existing between this variable and proficiency level. When the extent of use of the native language within L2 inner speech (Item 2) was observed in the five-category distribution, a significant difference and a negative association were found among the samples. However, when responses were distributed as No/Yes and Low/High, no significant differences were found for Item 2.

The following functions of inner speech revealed significant differences among the three proficiency samples (see Table 5.3 for statistical values); correction of grammar errors (an *evaluative* role, Item 27), using inner speech to clarify thought (an *ideational* role, Item 30), imagining conversations with others (*interpersonal* role, Item 34), and talking to oneself (*intrapersonal* role, Item 35). A positive correlation (nonsignificant in some cases) was found between all these roles and proficiency.

TABLE 5.4
Frequency of Inner Speech by Levels with a No/Yes Distribution.

| Frequency category | Levels | | |
	Low	Intermediate	High
No	40 (24.8)	21 (10.9)	7 (9.6)
Yes	121 (75.2)	171 (89.1)	66 (90.4)

Note. Figures in parentheses are percentages.

TABLE 5.5
Percentages of Responses Distributed as No/Yes by Levels for Four Types of Structures.

Type of structure	Frequency category	Low	Levels Intermediate	High
Words (Item 3)				
	No	16.1	12.0	15.1
	Yes	83.9	88.0	84.9
Phrases (Item 4)				
	No	29.2	17.2	12.3
	Yes	70.8	82.8	87.7
Sentences (Item 5)				
	No	41.6	25.0	19.2
	Yes	58.4	75.0	80.8
Convs./dialogues (Item 6)				
	No	64.6	47.9	41.1
	Yes	35.4	52.1	58.9

Phase II. This section presents a brief analysis of the data gathered during interviews with nine rehearsers after two communicative activities. As in Phase I, the nature of the inner speech generated by the communicative activities will be examined, first, in terms of its linguistic characteristics and, second, in terms of its functional roles. A sample of an interview protocol analysis is provided in Appendix C.

As regards sound, most students reported they could hear the sound of speech in their minds, either in their own voices or in the voice of their professor or interlocutor. Some students also reported hearing in their minds a better, more native-like, pronunciation than their own and being able to detect incorrect pronunciations in their minds.

As far as structure, it was found that inner speech could adopt the form of words, phrases, sentences, dialogues, or conversations, although lengthy constructions (sentences and dialogues/conversations) tended to be reported more often in relation to the inner speech associated with Communicative Activity 1, which involved a simulated job interview. The students also reported using the following types of sentences in their inner speech: statements, questions, commands, and some incomplete constructions.

In terms of vocabulary, it was found that the students' inner speech lexicon was highly related to the thematic content of the communicative activities, that it was retrieved from the students' memories or some outside source (dictionaries, book, other people), that it was sometimes mixed with Spanish, and that it could contain words coined by the students. In the case of Communicative Activity 2, which involved the use of pictures, all students reported observing the image and trying to translate the visual stimuli into words. Some students also reported substituting words with graphic images.

As for meaning, the students' inner speech was found to be usually meaningful although they sometimes reportedly had to process difficult words or resort to the native language to make sense.

As far as the functional roles of the inner speech related to the communicative activities, six major categories emerged: the ideational, the textual, the evaluative, the mnemonic, the affective, and the interpersonal. The affective role, which had not been tested through the questionnaire, appeared in five specific functions: to derive self-satisfaction, to acquire self-confidence, to reduce nervousness, to obtain self-diversion, and to improve the self-image. Some differences were observed in the inner speech roles associated with the activities; for example, while in Activity 1 inner speech adopted a dialogic pattern, with a typical threefold structure (opening greeting, body, and farewell), in Activity 2 inner speech followed a descriptive pattern based on spatial order. Moreover, while in most cases in Activity 1 the students were highly aware of the interlocutor's role and even imagined their possible text, in Activity 2 only one student reported thinking of what the interlocutor might say. In addition, while the mnemonic role was basically the same for both activities, in Activity 2 language recall was aided by recall of the visual image.

No obvious differences in the nature of the rehearsers' inner speech were found among the three proficiency groups, except for the fact that lengthy constructions, such as dialogues or conversations, were more frequently reported among the intermediate and high proficiency students than among the low ones.

Figures 5.1, 5.2, and 5.3 below summarize the results of both phases of the study. An interpretation of the most salient results is provided in the next section.

Interpretation of the Results

The fact that 84 percent of the participants admitted to having experienced inner speech in their L2 was a crucial finding, establishing sound empirical evidence of the existence of L2 inner speech among adult ESL learners. The discovery of a rising trend in

FIGURE 5.1 Linguistic characteristics of inner speech in mental rehearsal of the second language.

A. CHARACTERISTICS RELATED TO SOUND

   1. inner speech is usually sonorous in the mind

   2. inner speech may be polyphonic

   3. inner speech may be overtly vocalized

   4. inner speech may appear to sound more native-like than the learner's overt production

B. CHARACTERISTICS RELATED TO STRUCTURE

   1. inner speech may adopt the following structures:

      a. words

      b. phrases

      c. sentences

      d. dialogues/conversations

   2. inner speech sentences may be:

      a. statements

      b. commands

      c. questions

      d. predicated (incomplete)

   3. inner speech is usually abbreviated

   4. inner speech may be unabbreviated during dialogues or when processing difficult text

   5. inner speech may have a mixed verbal-pictorial structure

C. CHARACTERISTICS RELATED TO VOCABULARY

   1. inner speech may contain the following types of words:

      a. words the learner repeats in order to learn

      b. words whose pronunciation the learner imitates

      c. words the learner tries to recall

      d. words with an unfamiliar meaning

      e. words in the native language

      f. words coined by the learner

   2. the learner may try out new words constructing sentences with them

   3. the learner may consult a dictionary/person to resolve a lexical gap in inner speech

4. inner speech vocabulary is highly contextualized when task-related

5. some words may be substituted by graphic symbols in inner speech

D. CHARACTERISTICS RELATED TO MEANING

1. inner speech is usually meaningful

2. inner speech sometimes has to process difficult words

3. inner speech sometimes switches to the native language to make meaning

FIGURE 5.1 (Continued)

FIGURE 5.2 Functional roles of inner speech in mental rehearsal of the second language.

ROLES	SPECIFIC FUNCTIONS
1. Ideational	to create ideas
	to analyze ideas
	to clarify thoughts
2. Mnemonic	to store language in memory
	to retrieve language from memory
3. Textual	to create/give structure to oral or written texts
	to organize verbal data in sequence
	to experiment with language
4. Instructional	to imitate pronounciation
	to apply grammar rules
	to make sentences with words
5. Evaluative	to assess extent and quality of language knowledge
	to self-evaluate and self-correct language
	to other-evaluate and other-correct language
6. Affective	to obtain self-satisfaction
	to reduce nervousness
	to acquire self-confidence
	to obtain self-diversion
	to improve self-image
7. Interpersonal	to imagine conversations with others
8. Intrapersonal	to talk to oneself

FIGURE 5.3 Differences found in the nature of inner speech during mental rehearsal of the second language among low, intermediate, and advanced proficiency ESL students.

SIGNIFICANT DIFFERENCES IN THE FREQUENCY OF:
+ experiencing inner speech
+ hearing the sounds of English in the mind
+ long-type syntactic and discourse structures
+ meaningful thoughts
− use of the native language within inner speech
+ mental correction of grammar errors
+ using inner speech for clarifying thought
+ imagining conversations with others
+ talking to oneself
+ class-unrelated inner speech
+ POSITIVE ASSOCIATION BETWEEN THESE VARIABLES AND PROFICIENCY
− NEGATIVE ASSOCIATION BETWEEN THIS VARIABLE AND PROFICIENCY

L2 inner speech with more proficiency in the L2 would indicate that inner speech is a developmental phenomenon, much as Vygotsky (1963, 1979) conceived of inner speech. As children grow and their egocentric speech turns into inner speech, Vygotsky (1963) speculated, this becomes an entirely different speech entity: "a distinct plane of verbal thought" (p. 148). As adult L2 learners receive greater doses of L2 input, as their stored knowledge of the L2 increases, and as the cognitive tasks in the L2 become more demanding, so may their inner speech develop into an increasingly indispensable and rich vehicle for thinking in the other language.

Several formal traits of adult L2 inner speech were discovered. In terms of sound, this study confirmed Sokolov's (1972) argument that although inner speech is soundless from the point of view of the hearer, it may not be so for the person experiencing it. The statistical data, as well as the students' retrospective self-reports, provided evidence that L2 inner speech has some kind of phonological representation in the mind that makes it predominantly sonorous. Exactly how inner speech is represented acoustically in the mind is a matter of speculation in the L1 literature. Some researchers (Hardyck & Petrinovich, 1970) believe that inner speech consists of auditory images in which there is no or minimal activity in the speech effectors. McGuigan (1970) and Sokolov (1972) claim that the auditory and visual perception of words is always accompanied by movements in the speech musculature. Trimbur (1987) stresses the polyphony of inner speech resulting from the internalization of other people's voices. Other researchers describe inner speech as a reconstruction of the prosody of language (Beggs & Howarth, 1985) or as a phonemically reduced code (Anan'ev, cited in Sokolov, 1972, p. 50). This study has provided evidence that students sometimes do attempt to overtly vocalize their inner speech, especially when rehearsing the pronunciation of difficult words, thus indicating the occasional need for unfolded phonemic articulation of inner speech. Moreover, L2 inner speech was reported as sometimes having a polyphonic quality, noticeably adopting the voice characteristics of professors and other sources of input (movies, classmates). The internalization and condensation of other people's voices that occurs during the acquisition of another language by adult learners thus closely parallels the social-to-the-individual movement proposed by Vygotsky (1962, 1979) as the typical ontogenetic trait of L1 inner speech. The social origin of L2 inner speech may also explain why to some of the participants the pronunciation they heard in their minds appeared to be better, more native-like, than their own overt pronunciations. It remains to be discerned, however, what production problems account for the discrepancy between what is heard in the mind and what is actually articulated.

As regards structure, the data revealed a tendency towards syntactic abbreviation and simplification in the inner speech used during mental rehearsal of the L2. Four types of syntactic and discourse patterns with increasing levels of complexity (words, phrases, sentences, and conversations or dialogues) as well as length of thoughts were tested through the questionnaire. The statistical analysis of the pertinent items (3, 4, 5, 6, 17, 18) showed that as the structures increased in length and complexity, their frequency decreased. These data, together with the students' interview reports about their experiencing "incomplete sentences," indicate a predominance of characteristically elliptical, fragmentary syntactic forms in L2 inner speech. On the basis of his observations, Vygotsky had made "predication"—the omission of the subject and the preservation of the predicate—"the basic syntactic form of inner speech" (1962, p. 139). This notion has been reformulated by other authors (Anan'ev, cited in Sokolov, 1972; Podolskii, cited in Sokolov, 1972; Wertsch, 1977) to accommodate the fact that either the subject or the predicate may be absent in inner speech structures. The reduced nature of inner speech may also respond to the presence of semantically loaded "key words." In Sokolov's (1972) view these "semantic points of reference...play the role of the principal structural element of inner speech" (p. 88). It is safe to assume then that the "predicativeness" of adult L2 inner speech entails not just the absence of either subject or predicate, but the presence of highly condensed semantic structures.

When the data were analyzed for differences among the three proficiency samples, an important discovery was made: as proficiency increased so did the length and complexity of the L2 inner speech structures. While the word-type structure (Item 3) showed no significant difference among the samples, suggesting that the abbreviated form of inner speech was common to all the participants, the sentence (Item 5) and conversation/dialogue (Item 6) types yielded significant group differences and a positive correlation with proficiency.

An analysis of the data indicates, then, that even though in general the participants tended to produce reduced forms in their inner speech, the more proficient ones were capable of generating lengthier constructions. This finding is supported by the data provided by Items 17 and 18, which measured respectively the frequency of short thoughts and long, elaborate thoughts in inner speech. While no significant difference was found in the frequency of short thoughts, a significant difference was found in the frequency of long, elaborate thoughts among the samples. Long thoughts were significantly more frequent as proficiency increased. The interview data confirmed this finding. The intermediate and the high proficiency students reported longer and more complex syntactic and discourse structures than the low ones.

The predominance of abbreviated structures among all the participants and the increased presence of expanded forms among the more proficient ones raise some apparently conflicting possibilities pertaining to the idiosyncratic nature of L2 inner speech. On the one hand, it is possible to argue that L2 inner speech usually has an abbreviated form because it is natural for the mind to work in reduced, condensed semantic complexes; on the other hand, it can also be contended that L2 learners think predominantly in words because they are not yet capable of constructing long structures. The answer to this enigma seems to lie in the developmental nature of L2 inner speech and in the fact that inner speech itself changes as it reflects stages of language development (Wertsch, 1977). While low proficiency students may find the simple, abbreviated forms of inner speech the only way to express their limited knowledge of the L2, more proficient ones can afford more variation and complexity in their inner speech structures. When verbal tasks in the L2 become automatic, for example, inner speech will tend to be reduced and highly condensed.[4] When confronted with difficult language input or demanding cognitive tasks, when rehearsing for tasks that require certain socially acceptable or formulaic utterances, or when leisurely engaged in diversionary self-talk, proficient learners may resort to expanded forms of L2 inner speech.

An interesting discovery in relation to structure and vocabulary was made through the students' retrospective reports, namely, the use of graphic images to substitute for words in their inner speech. This was particularly evident in the inner speech associated with Communicative Activity 2, which had a picture component. According to Sokolov (1972), this "mixed" or "verbal-pictorial" structure resulting from a combination of auditory word images and visual images of objects is very frequent in L1 inner speech. The use of graphic images suggests that inner speech, like overt speech, has a strong extralinguistic component. The visual images that occur in the students' L2 inner speech thus become a non-linguistic, yet integral and effective, component of intrapersonal communication.

No significant differences among the groups were apparent in their inner speech vocabulary. Both the quantitative and the qualitative data of the study showed that while the students were mentally rehearsing, a great deal of their mental lexicons was taken up by new words they wanted to learn, words whose pronunciation they wanted to imitate, words they tried to recall, and, less frequently, words with an unfamiliar meaning. From the types of lexicon reported by the students, it is possible to see inner speech as an ideal ground for the processing of what Krashen (1982) calls "optimal comprehensible input," which, in addition to language that is fully understood by the learner, introduces new material the learner needs to grapple with. Several strategies were reported to deal mentally with shortage of L2 lexicon. Students reported consulting outside sources (dictionaries, textbooks) or other people (relatives, classmates) to express meaning through words or to understand unfamiliar words. When no English words came to mind, Spanish—the students' vernacular—came to their aid or new words were coined.

In this study, L2 inner speech appeared to be highly meaningful for the most part. Item 13, which measured the extent to which

---

[4] Sokolov's (1972) L1 studies provide evidence that inner speech does not disappear but becomes structurally reduced as verbal tasks turn automatic.

inner speech in English made sense, had 95.30 percent of affirmative responses (100% in the high proficiency level). Furthermore, a strong urge to construct meaning through inner speech as the participants rehearsed for the communicative activities was reported. Even the students' lapse into Spanish or their coinage of nonexistent words may be seen as efforts to crystallize thought into coherent terms. As Vygotsky put it, "with syntax and sound reduced to a minimum, meaning is more than ever in the forefront" (1962, p. 145). Certainly, the findings related to vocabulary and meaning suggest that inner speech has an essential role in the process of understanding and expressing meaning in the L2. As has been suggested for L1 speakers (Sokolov, 1972), semantic hypotheses about the second language might be formed at the level of inner speech.

This study has provided evidence of the multifunctional nature of inner speech during mental rehearsal of a second language. Eight different functional roles were detected, each displaying various specific functions. Not surprisingly, the ideational role (in its thought-clarifying function) had one of highest percentages of affirmative responses in the questionnaire data (97.18%). The interview data confirmed the importance of L2 inner speech for the creation, analysis, and clarification of thought. Without doubt, inner speech emerged from this study as the necessary medium for verbal thought in the L2.

Outstanding, too, was the mnemonic role, both in its storing and retrieving functions. Item 8, which measured the use of repetition as a storage strategy, had 95.78 percent affirmative responses, while Item 11, which measured use of inner speech as a language retrieving tool, had 97.65 percent. In addition, the interview data indicated that inner speech was involved in several mnemonic techniques: silent repetition, spontaneous recall, deliberate recall, repeating the text aloud, jotting down key words, and writing down the ideas. It was also found that inner speech sometimes followed a circular pattern of memorization (storage-retrieval-storage) or presented a series of memorization attempts. These findings agree with the well-established view within psychology that "elaborative" rehearsal (as opposed to "rote" rehearsal) is crucial for storage of information in long-term memory (Bjork, 1970; Bransford, 1979; Donahoe & Wessells, 1980; Lindsay & Norman, 1977). Sokolov's (1972) experiments also demonstrated that interference or disruption of inner speech activity strongly affects memorization, a finding which led him to pose "semantic memorization" as one of the main functions of inner speech. It follows, then, that inner speech, as the vehicle in which rehearsal is conducted, is of utmost importance for the long-term retention of L2 input and consequently for permanent and successful learning of the L2.

Very frequent, too, were some instructional, evaluative, and textual functions. For instance, the use of inner speech to imitate pronunciation (Item 9), an instructional function, had 96.48 percent of affirmative responses. Another very highly rated function was the use of inner speech to answer questions in the mind (Item 33), a self-evaluative function which called for 96 percent of affirmative responses. Particularly striking, however, is the use of inner speech in rehearsing texts for future oral production. Item 19, which measured this function, had 92.25 percent of affirmative responses and a median of five (always), the highest median yielded by the questionnaire data.

The findings on the inter- and intrapersonal roles of inner speech during mental rehearsal of the L2 have interesting implications in terms of self-development. The fact that both functions were not rated as highly as the other functions and that, at the same time, both showed a positive correlation with proficiency suggests a possible inadequacy for "decentering" (Johnson, 1984; McFarland, 1984; Murphy, 1989; Streff, 1984) through inner speech among the less proficient students. Decentering presupposes an ability to adopt the interlocutor's perspective. For inner speech to perform the inter- and intrapersonal functions, it is necessary for the person to entertain two different points of view simultaneously, the self and another version of the self in the intrapersonal function, and the self and an interlocutor in the interpersonal function. It has been suggested (Murphy, 1989) that inner speech can help L2 students achieve decentering.

The affective role, which was not measured by the questionnaire but which appeared consistently in the students' verbal reports, also shows potential for the learner's self-development. It was demonstrated that through inner speech, adult L2 learners can derive self-satisfaction (feel good about the possibility of thinking in another language), develop self-confidence in language tasks, lose some of their communicative apprehension and nervousness, find a means for self-diversion, and generally improve their self-image as L2 learners. Adult L2 learners could benefit from a discussion of the affective impact of inner speech, though they should be forewarned about the possibility of negative, counterproductive self-talk (Helmstetter, 1982).

This study has begun to discern the shape of L2 inner speech and the role it plays in learning a second language. The model presented below (based on Bransford's information processing model of memory, 1979) tries of offer, admittedly in an oversimplified fashion and obviously in want of further elaboration by future research, a possible explanation of how inner speech works in the reception and production of an L2 (see Figure 5.4).

As can be seen in Figure 5.4, after being processed by the corresponding sensory channels, L2 input—obtained through listening or reading—is transformed into inner speech. Subsequently, after active rehearsal in short-term (ST) memory, processed input is transferred to long-term (LT) memory, where knowledge of the L2 is stored. ST memory thus emerges as the main locus of inner speech activity. Prior knowledge activation as well as a cyclical memorization strategy of storage-retrieval-storage are characteristic processes during rehearsal (both being depicted in the model by a broken curved arrow within the ST memory system). Inner speech is also involved in L2 oral and written production. With the retrieval of L2 language information from LT memory and its rehearsal in ST memory, inner speech unfolds into external language, manifested through speaking or writing. Sometimes the learner's own production may become input for inner speech

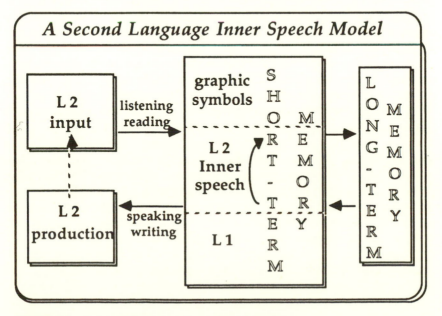

FIGURE 5.4   A second language inner speech model.

activity, usually for purposes of self-evaluation (see arrow going from L2 production to L2 input in Figure 5.4). Also possible is an integration of graphic symbols and the native language with L2 inner speech. Although this model seems to emphasize the mnemonic role of inner speech, it is important to note that while the second language is being rehearsed in ST memory, several ideational, textual, affective, evaluative, instructional, interpersonal, and intrapersonal functions may also be performed.

CONCLUSION

An exploration into the nature of adult L2 inner speech during mental rehearsal of the L2 has revealed several characteristics of form—phonological, syntactic, semantic, and lexical—as well as a rich gamut of roles and functions. On the basis of the evidence provided by the study, adult L2 inner speech does not emerge as a static, uniform entity among learners of all proficiency levels. Some aspects of form and function vary with proficiency. L2 inner speech seems to be a developmental phenomenon characterized by low levels of structural complexity among low-proficiency students and by highly condensed, but expandable, syntactic/semantic complexes among high-proficiency learners. Indeed, in its richness and complexity among adult high-proficiency learners, L2 inner speech appears tantamount to verbal thought, much in the same way as Vygotsky (1962) regarded L1 inner speech.

As has been suggested here, the study of L2 inner speech has powerful implications for L2 acquisition. Inner speech may provide researchers with one of the most effective means of finding out what goes on in the learners' minds as they are learning a second language. Beyond inner speech lies what Vygotsky called "the next plane of verbal thought, the one still more inward than inner speech" (1962, p. 149), the plane of pure thought, where hidden unconscious processes inaccessible even to self-examination take place. Inner speech constitutes an excellent bridge for the study of these processes in the L2. In general, it is expected that further research continues to exploit L2 inner speech for clues to how an L2 is acquired. It is also expected that research on L2 inner speech will in turn contribute to an overall understanding of inner speech, as an inherently human thought/language mechanism.

APPENDIX A

Questionnaire on Inner Speech and Mental
Rehearsal of the Second Language
(English translation)

The purpose of this questionnaire is to explore the "inner speech" that students of English as a second language experience as they are mentally rehearsing in English.

The following definitions will help you understand the questionnaire better:

> *Inner speech* is any type of language in English that occurs in your mind and that is not vocalized (spoken). Inner speech may include sounds, words, phrases, sentences, dialogues, and even conversations in English.
>
> *Mental rehearsal* is a voluntary or involuntary activity by means of which students practice in their minds the language they have learned, heard, or read, or the language they will have to use in a future oral or written activity. When mentally rehearsing, the students may simply be recalling, repeating, or imitating words in the second language. Sometimes, mental rehearsal is more creative, as, for example, when the students imagine dialogues, plan what they are going to say or write, mentally self-correct, evaluate other students' language, or engage in conversations with themselves.

If you do not recognize these definitions, or you have never mentally rehearsed in English, do not worry. Answer the questions, anyway; your answers will be equally valuable.

The questionnaire has two parts. Part I will help the researcher determine what kind of contact with English you have had. Part II has questions on inner speech and mental rehearsal of the English language.

Try to answer as truthfully and precisely as possible and do not leave questions unanswered. You will have to write your name. This is only to enable the researcher to identify some students that may participate in a second phase of the study. The results of this questionnaire will only be used for research purposes and will be kept strictly confidential.

Thank you very much for cooperating with this study.

PART I

1. Student name: _____
2. Age: _____
3. Sex: Female ____ Male ____
4. Place of birth: _____
5. English courses that you have taken in this
    university: _____
6. English course that you are taking now: _____
    Section _____ Professor _____
7. What elementary school(s) did you attend?
    School(s): _____
    Place: _____
8. What intermediate school(s) did you attend?
    School(s): _____
    Place: _____
9. What high school(s) did you attend?
    School(s): _____
    Place: _____
10. Have you lived in the United States or in some other place
    where English is spoken?
    Yes ____ No ____
    How long? _____
11. Which do you consider your first language?
    ____ Spanish
    ____ English
    ____ other (specify) _____
12. Which language is spoken in your home?
    ____ mostly Spanish
    ____ mostly English
    ____ both Spanish and English
    ____ other (specify) _____

PART II

Instructions.   Choose the alternative that you prefer and darken
the corresponding space on the answer sheet.

1. Have you had inner speech in English? (You can read the
    definition again.)
2. Is your inner speech in English mingled with Spanish?
    Is your inner speech in English made up of

3.   words?

4.   phrases?

5.   sentences?

6.   conversations or dialogues?

7.   Can you "hear" the sounds of English in your mind? When you mentally rehearse,

8.   do you repeat words you want to learn?

9.   do you try to imitate the pronunciation of words you have learned?

10.   do you try to make sentences with certain words?

11.   do you try to recall words you have learned?

12.   do words with meanings you do not know well come to your mind?

13.   do your thoughts in English make sense?

14.   Do you hear in your mind voices of other people in English?

15.   Do you repeat aloud any of the words of that inner speech when you are alone?

16.   Do you look up in a book or dictionary the meaning of English words that come to your mind?
When you mentally rehearse in English,

17.   does your inner speech consist of short thoughts?

18.   is your inner speech expressed in long, elaborate thoughts?

19.   If you have to talk to someone in English or you have an oral presentation, do you mentally rehearse what you are going to say?

20.   If you have to write something in English, do you rehearse first in your mind what you are going to write?

21.   Do you mentally rehearse how you are going to say something in English before speaking?

22.   Do you plan in your mind the sequence in which you are going to present your ideas orally?

23.   Do you mentally rehearse how you are going to write something in English before writing it?

24.   Do you plan in your mind the sequence in which you are going to write your ideas?

25.   Do you ever think how you would write or say something in English, even if you are not going to use it?

26.   Do you try to correct the pronunciation of words in your mind?

27. Do you try to correct grammar errors when you mentally rehearse?

28. Do you try to apply the grammar rules you have learned to your inner speech in English?

29. When you hear other people speaking English, do you mentally evaluate how those people use the language?

30. Do you try to put your thoughts in English in order so that they are clear in their message?

31. Do you catch yourself thinking in English about things not related to your English class?

32. Is your inner speech in English related to your English class?

33. When the English teacher asks a question in class, do you answer it in your mind even though you are not called to answer?

34. Do you imagine dialogues or conversations with other people in English?

35. Do you talk to yourself in English?

If you want to comment about your inner speech or mental rehearsal in English or about this questionnaire, you can do it here.

_____

_____

_____

_____

APPENDIX B

Interview Form
(English translation)

Instructions.   (read aloud by the researcher) The purpose of this interview is that you describe the inner speech that you had in relation to the activity that was recently conducted in class. Let me remind you of two concepts we will be using:

Inner speech is any type of language in English that occurs in your mind and that is not vocalized (spoken). Inner speech may include sounds, words, phrases, sentences, dialogues, and even conversations in English.

Mental rehearsal is a voluntary or involuntary activity by means of which students practice in their minds the language they have learned, heard, or read, or the language they will have to use in a future oral or written activity. When mentally rehearsing, the students may simply be recalling, repeating, or imitating words in the second language. Sometimes, mental rehearsal is more creative, as, for example, when the students imagine dialogues, plan what they are going to say or write, mentally self-correct, evaluate other students' language, or engage in conversations with themselves.

Try to remember as much as possible, but if you do not remember, do not fabricate your responses just to please me. Answer as sincerely as possible. The questions that I am going to ask you have to do with the nature of inner speech, in other words, what it is like and what it is used for. The interview will be recorded so that I can analyze the information later. Your answers will be kept strictly confidential. Do you have any question before starting?

Questions.

1. Did you mentally rehearse in English before the activity? When?
2. Try to remember your mental rehearsal before the activity. Can you describe it?
3. What specific language came to your mind? Do you remember it?
4. What was that inner speech like in its sound?
5. What was that inner speech like in its structure? Was it made up of words, phrases, sentences, or conversations?
6. What was that inner speech like in its meaning?
7. What was that inner speech like in its vocabulary?
8. Did you go to any person, book, or dictionary to get help in expressing that inner speech?
9. Can you tell me if that inner speech was fast or slow?
10. Did that language come spontaneously to your mind or did you deliberately set to rehearse it mentally?
11. What was the use of that mental rehearsal? Did it help you learn or memorize the English that you were rehearsing?

12. Did you mentally plan the language that you were going to use in the activity? How?

13. Did you try to "correct" yourself or to think which was the best way to say something? In relation to grammar, pronunciation, vocabulary, or the message?

14. Were you paying more attention to the formal aspect of what you were going to say or to the message?

15. Did you imagine what the others would say in the activity?

16. During the activity, were you mentally rehearsing in English? Try to describe that language.

17. What was the use of that mental rehearsal during the activity? To be well-prepared? To express clearly what you wanted to say?

18. Did you mentally correct or evaluate the language of those that were speaking?

19. After the activity, did you have any type of inner speech? Can you describe it?

20. Did you try to evaluate the language that you used or that the others used during the activity?

21. Did new, useful, or interesting words that you heard during the activity come to your mind?

22. Tell me everything else you remember about the inner speech related to the activity that has not been mentioned yet.

Specific questions for Interview 2.

23. Have you had any type of inner speech since our first interview?

24. Which of the two activities generated more inner speech?

25. Are you more conscious now of your inner speech in English? Do you think it is important?

APPENDIX C

Sample of Interview Protocol Analysis

Amarilis (real first name used with participant's permission) was one of the high-proficiency rehearsers selected for Phase II. (The interviews were held in Spanish, but quotations from them are reported here in English. Words that were used in English during the interview have been underlined.) The following linguistic characteristics were observed in Amarilis's report concerning the inner speech related to Communicative Activity 1.

Phonologically, her inner speech sounded in her mind as if she "were saying it, exactly with [her] own voice." Structurally, her inner speech consisted of a conversation, in which turn-taking was important: "I imagined what I was going to say and what the person was going to answer." Her lines were in complete sentences, but her interlocutor's questions were not. "They were not perfect sentences, just ideas. I knew they were going to ask me about benefits, salary, *training.* But I did think my part in complete sentences because I had to say it." Lexically, Amarilis's inner speech confronted problems dealing with some words which were "too difficult" in the job ad. Amarilis consulted the meaning of these words in the dictionary. She also obtained some vocabulary from the supplementary material the teacher had distributed. Semantically, her inner speech did not always make sense to her. For example, the term *"benefit package,"* which she didn't understand, kept coming up to her mind.

Amarilis's inner speech had six functional roles: the ideational, the interpersonal, the textual, the evaluative, the mnemonic, and the affective. Ideationally, Amarilis's inner speech had two major functions: to create verbal ideas and to clarify thought. Amarilis started creating ideas for the activity since the moment she had handed the instructions. She also used her inner speech for clarification purposes. Because she had difficulty understanding the job ad, she analyzed it "back and forth" trying to make some sense out of it.

Amarilis's inner speech performed an important interpersonal role as she imagined the conversation with her interlocutor: "I prepared everything, even the answers that the person would give me...That's exactly how my mind worked...what the person answered and what I answered."

Textually, Amarilis was concerned with giving a structure to the text and organizing it in a sequence. To give a structure to her inner speech, Amarilis set herself to write it. She gave her inner speech the shape of a conversation, composed of her own questions and answers and her interlocutor's. Amarilis planned a sequence for her thoughts. She rehearsed an introduction, including a greeting and a description of the company. Then she was ready to answer questions as they came. For the ending she planned a handshake and the phrase *"good luck."*

The evaluative role emerged as Amarilis self-evaluated her text mainly after the activity. As she was going home on the bus, she "was thinking what [she] should have said and how [she] should have said it." She also other-evaluated the text as she recalled the language used by her classmate and her difficulty in understanding what this person had said.

Mnemonically, Amarilis's inner speech had two functions: to retrieve language related to the activity and to store it for later use. Amarilis experienced deliberate language retrieval as she set herself to prepare the activity, but she also had spontaneous retrieval as words came to her mind while watching television, and after the activity as she was riding on the bus home. To store the language for later recall, Amarilis covered the paper she had written and repeated what she had to say in her mind. Unfortunately, Amarilis reported suffering a memory lapse during the activity, during which her mind "went blank."

Affectively, Amarilis's inner speech had an important function, especially after the activity. Because her performance was impaired by her memory loss and because she received a grade of 44 out of 50, Amarilis felt extremely disappointed with herself. Amarilis used her inner speech to boost her self-image: "On the bus...I did it all over again to see if I was so stupid that I would forget everything. And I gave myself a 50 [the highest grade]."

REFERENCES

Bedford, D.A. (1985). Spontaneous playback of the second language: A descriptive study. *Foreign Language Annals, 18,* 279–287.

Beggs, W.D.A., & Howarth, P.N. (1985). Inner speech as a learned skill. *Journal of Experimental Child Psychology, 39,* 396–411.

Bjork, R.A. (1970). Repetition and rehearsal mechanisms in models for short-term memory. In D.A. Norman (Ed.), *Models of human memory* (pp. 307–33). New York: Academic Press.

Bransford, J.D. (1979). *Human cognition.* Belmont, CA: Wadsworth.

Chamot, A.U. (1987). The learning strategies of ESL students. In A. Wenden & J. Rubin (Eds.), *Learner strategies in language learning* (pp. 71–83). Englewood Cliffs, NJ: Prentice Hall.

Chapman, P., & Krashen, S. (1986). Involuntary rehearsal of second languages in beginning and advanced performers. *System, 14,* 275–278.

Cohen, A.D. (1991). Feedback on writing. The use of verbal report. *Studies in Second Language Acquisition, 13,* 133–159.

Cohen, A., & Hosenfeld, C. (1981). Some uses of mentalistic data in second language research. *Language Learning, 31,* 285–313.

de Guerrero, M.C.M. (1987). The din phenomenon: Mental rehearsal in the second language. *Foreign Language Annals, 20,* 537–548.

de Guerrero, M.C.M. (1991). Nature of inner speech in mental rehearsal of the second language (Doctoral dissertation, Inter American University of Puerto Rico, 1990). *Dissertation Abstracts International, 51,* 4044A.

Donahoe, J.W., & Wessells, M.G. (1980). *Learning, language, and memory.* New York: Harper & Row.

Faerch, C., & Kasper, G. (1987). From product to process—Introspective methods in second language research. In C. Faerch & G. Kasper (Eds.), *Introspection in second language research* (pp. 5–23). Clevendon, England: Multilingual Matters.

Grotjahn, R. (1987). On the methodological basis of introspective methods. In C. Faerch & G. Kasper (Eds.), *Introspection in second language research* (pp. 54–82). Clevendon, England: Multilingual Matters.

Grotjahn, R. (1991). The research programme subjective theories. A new approach in second language research. *Studies in Second Language Acquisition, 13,* 187–214.

Halliday, M.A.K. (1973). *Explorations in the functions of language.* New York: Elsevier North-Holland.

Hardyck, L.V., & Petrinovich, L.R. (1970). Sub-vocal speech and comprehension level as a function of difficulty level of reading material. *Journal of Verbal Learning and Verbal Behavior, 9,* 647–652.

Hellmich, H., & Esser, U. (1975). Innere Sprache, inneres Sprechen und ihre Wirksamkeit im Fremdsprachenunterricht [Inner speech, inner language, and their effect on foreign language teaching]. *Deutsch als Fremdsprache, 12,* 128–142.

Helmstetter, S. (1982). *What to say when you talk to yourself.* New York: Pocket Books.

Honeycutt, J.M., Zagacki, K.S., & Edwards, R. (1989). Intrapersonal communication, social cognition, and imagined interactions. In C.V. Roberts & K.W. Watson (Eds.), *Intrapersonal Communication Processes* (pp. 166–184). New Orleans, LA: Spectra.

Johnson, J.R. (1984). The role of inner speech in human communication. *Communication Education, 33,* 211–222.

Kerlinger, F.N. (1973). *Foundations of behavioral research* (2nd ed.). New York: Holt, Rinehart, & Winston.

Korba, R.J. (1987). The rate of inner speech. (Doctoral dissertation, University of Denver, 1986.) *Dissertation Abstracts International, 47,* 3239A–3240A.

Korba, R.J. (1989). The cognitive psychophysiology of inner speech. In C.V. Roberts & K.W. Watson (Eds.), *Intrapersonal communication processes* (pp. 217–242). New Orleans, LA: Spectra.

Krashen, S.D. (1982). *Principles and practice in second language acquisition.* Oxford: Pergamon.

Lindsay, P.H., & Norman, D.A. (1977). *Human information processing.* New York: Academic Press.

Littlewood, W. (1981). *Communicative language teaching.* Cambridge: Cambridge University Press.

Luria, A.R. (1982). *Language and cognition.* New York: John Wiley & Sons.

McFarland, J.L. (1984). The role of speech in self development, self-concept, and decentration. *Communication Education, 33,* 231–236.

McGuigan, F.J. (1970). Covert oral behavior during the silent performance of language tasks. *Psychological Bulletin, 74,* 309–326.

McGuigan, F.J. (1978). *Cognitive psychophysiology: Principles of covert behavior.* Englewood Cliffs, NJ: Prentice Hall.

McNeill, D. (1987). *Psycholinguistics: A new approach.* New York: Harper & Row.

Moffet, J. (1982). Writing, inner speech, and meditation. *College English, 44,* 231–246.

Moffet, J. (1985). Liberating inner speech. *College Composition and Communication, 36,* 304–308.

Murphy, J.M. (1989). Listening in a second language: Hermeneutics and inner speech. *TESL Canada Journal, 6*(2), 27–44.

Murphy, J.M. (1991). Oral communication in TESOL: Integrating Speaking, Listening, and Pronunciation. *TESOL Quarterly, 25,* 51–75.

O'Malley, J.M., Chamot, A.U., Stewner-Manzanares, G., Russo, R.P., & Küpper, L. (1985). Learning strategy applications with students of English as a second language. *TESOL Quarterly, 19,* 557–584.

Rohrer, J. (1987). Inner speech. Implications for foreign language learning. *Die Neueren Sprachen, 86,* 92–101.

Rosenblatt, P.C., & Meyer, C. (1986). Imagined interactions and the family. *Family Relations, 35,* 319–324.

Rubin, J. (1987). Learner strategies: Theoretical assumptions, research history and typology. In A. Wenden & J. Rubin (Eds.), *Learner strategies in language learning* (pp. 15–30). Englewood Cliffs, NJ: Prentice Hall.

Smith, F. (1983). *Essays into literacy.* London: Heinemann Educational Books.

Sokolov, A.N. (1972). *Inner speech and thought.* New York: Plenum.

Streff, C. (1984). The concept of inner speech and its implications for an integrated language arts curriculum. *Communication Education, 33,* 223–230.

Trimbur, J. (1987). Beyond cognition: The voices of inner speech. *Rhetoric Review, 5,* 211–221.

Vygotsky, L.S. (1962). *Thought and language.* Cambridge, MA: MIT Press.

Vygotsky, L.S. (1979). *El desarrollo de los procesos psicológicos superiores [Mind in society. The development of higher psychological processes]* (S. Furió, Trans.). Barcelona: Editorial Crítica.

Wenden, A.L. (1987). How to be a successful language learner: Insights and prescriptions from L2 learners. In A. Wenden & J. Rubin (Eds.), *Learner strategies in language learning* (pp. 103–107). Englewood Cliffs, NJ: Prentice Hall.

Wertsch, J.V. (1977). *Inner speech revisited.* Chicago: Center for Psychosocial Studies. (ERIC Document Reproduction Service No. ED 139 500)

Wertsch, J.V. (1980). The significance of dialogue in Vygotsky's account of social, egocentric, and inner speech. *Contemporary Educational Psychology, 5,* 150–162.

Yaden, D.B., Jr. (1984). Inner speech, oral language, and reading: Huey and Vygotsky revisited. *Reading Psychology, 5*(1–2), 155–166.

6

The Use of Private Speech by Adult ESL Learners at Different Levels of Proficiency*

Steven G. McCafferty

Department of Modern Languages and
*   Linguistics*
Cornell University
Ithaca, NY

INTRODUCTION

In his investigations of psychological development, L.S. Vygotsky found that children, when faced with difficulties encountered during the course of goal-directed activities, used forms of *private speech* ("thinking aloud") for gaining control over task performance. When it was employed in this capacity, Vygotsky considered private speech to be the convergence of thought and language and

* I would like to thank Jean Newman for her valuable help and advice.

moreover, to play a critical role in promoting intellectual growth and eventual psychological independence or *self-regulation.*

Although for the most part private speech has gone "underground" by the time of adulthood as *inner speech*, vocalized forms do resurface in times of cognitive stress. Soskin and John (1963), in a naturalistic study that recorded adult subjects' vocalizations by use of a radio transmitter over a period of days at a summer resort, found that when they were involved in the unfamiliar task of making leather sandals, participants engaged in the use of private speech for the same functional purpose as identified by Vygotsky in his work with children: "How do I do this?" and "The needle may be too thin to get through" are two examples from this study cited in John-Steiner (1991).

When operating as a problem-solving or mediational "tool" as in the examples above, private speech functions metacognitively, being involved with planning, guiding, and monitoring the course of an activity. It is not, however, unifunctional, and serves affective purposes as well. Expressions such as "I did it" show relief or pleasure (John-Steiner & Tatter, 1983, p. 92), and examples such as "I can't do it" display uncertainty or anxiety about being able to perform some element of a task (McCafferty, 1992).

In their application of Vygotskian theory to second language (L2) learning, Frawley and Lantolf (1985) contend that adult L2 learners revert to the use of private speech, in all its functional roles, to help them in their efforts to gain control in communicative tasks over the task, over themselves, and over the task situation. In their attempts to become self-regulated, it is suggested that learners use strategies that derive from the development of self-regulation during childhood, which through *continuous access* remain available throughout ontogenesis.

Vygotsky claimed that cognitive development is first a product of social interaction; in other words, the child, born into a sociocultural environment, is dependent on those around him or her for coming to know and learn about the world beyond features of the immediate environment. With maturation, the child beings to internalize what has been gained through interaction at the interpsychological plane and to assimilate that knowledge at an intrapsychological level, moving progressively toward psychological autonomy. As a model for this process, Frawley and Lantolf adopt the framework for self-regulation in childhood provided by Wertsch (1979), who identifies three important periods of development. Furthermore, Frawley and Lantolf use these periods to devise a classification scheme for forms of private speech that they apply to results of a picture narration task used in their investigations.

Wertsch's first level, *object-regulation*, comes before the development of self-regulatory private speech, and is characterized by an inability to channel behavior toward specific goals, the child not yet able to exercise control over competing stimuli in the environment through selective attention. Wertsch (1979) suggests that early forms of private speech also reflect this orientation as they are concerned with "describing and naming aspects of the environment" (p. 93). In both Lantolf and Frawley (1984) and Frawley and Lantolf (1985), L2 learners at intermediate levels of proficiency were found to "externalize" various aspects of the discourse macrostructure in their efforts to gain control of the task such as by naming the characters in the pictures: "What's that? Let me just call *John*. *John* is standing on the road"; or by concretizing aspects of the pictures: "He's a boy!" (Frawley & Lantolf, 1985, p. 26).

As they mature, although again before the onset of self-regulatory private speech, Wertsch suggests that children are led through goal-directed activities by adults, a point at which they are heavily dependent on others for guidance. Wertsch's term for this stage, *other-regulation*, is adopted by Frawley and Lantolf and applied to private speech taking the form of self-directed questions, as in "this road—*what's this*? Let me..." (Frawley & Lantolf, 1985, p. 26). Because of their dialogic form, these instances are considered to derive from the interaction that took place when adults provided the primary source of mediation, and, again, are functionally involved with gaining control over aspects of the task.

At Wertsch's third level, *self-regulation*, the individual has progressed to the point where he or she can resolve task-related difficulties independently, no longer distracted by irrelevant features in the environment, and no longer overly dependent on the assistance of others. Private speech forms that indicate mastery over a particular source of confusion are designated as belonging to this category. The second "OK" in the following protocol from a native-speaking child is an example (Frawley & Lantolf, 1985, p. 28): "Where? On what? And tell this? OK. But I don't know how! Oh! *OK*. Now I know. Now I know."

It is Lantolf and Frawley's belief that too little attention has been paid in the field of second language acquisition to learners' intrapsychological strategies. In contrast to the notion that "communication" is basically the passing back and forth of information—a pervasive view in the L2 literature—they claim that much of what goes on in supposedly communicative situations actually relates to the individual needs of the learners and their efforts to become self-regulated in the situation: to understand what is going on around then and to present themselves in a manner in which they wish to be regarded by others.

USE OF PRIVATE SPEECH AS RELATED TO L2 PROFICIENCY

As described above, forms of private speech are produced in times of cognitive stress, and conversely, when an individual is self-regulated in a task, he or she is not expected to engage in the use of these forms to any great extent. Therefore, it seems reasonable to assume that private speech aids in the mastery over task-related difficulties; and of course, this is a main reason for Vygotsky's interest in the phenomenon. L2 studies have not yet investigated this relationship, but a number of child studies have, and despite mixed results in the past, recently Bivens and Berk (1990), in a longitudinal study of elementary school students' use of task-relevant private speech, found significant correlations with its use and eventual academic achievement. The production of task-related subvocal forms ("mutterings") by students identified as higher achievers from the beginning of the study was also found to be positively correlated with long-term gains in academic achievement. These findings are relevant to L2 learning as they hold forth the possibility that as adults, learners may continue to benefit from the strategic role of private speech in cognitively demanding situations, and thus the possibility that these strategies may contribute to the process of second language acquisition.

In an effort to establish parallels between Vygotsky's observations of the use of private speech by children and its use by adult L2 learners, Frawley and Lantolf (1985) compared the private speech of learners of English as a second language (ESL) at intermediate and advanced levels of proficiency with child and adult native speakers of English. Subjects were asked to narrate a series of six sequential drawings illustrating the adventures of a little boy and his ice cream cone. Each frame was shown one at a time sequentially, forcing participants to create their narratives "online." Many similarities between the intermediate learners and the native-speaking children's use of private speech were found. However, the source of difficulty experienced by participants in the two groups proved quite different. The ESL learners were primarily hampered by their limited ability to express themselves in English and the native-speaking children by their inability to "unpack" the narrative, that is, structure the discourse within an appropriate framework.

The narratives of the advanced ESL learners were found to compare favorably to those of the adult native speakers. Neither of these groups had any particular difficulty with the task and produced few instances of private speech. This relative scarcity of forms on the part of the advanced learners is considered a consequence of an increase in their facility in using the language for communicative purposes.

In a related study (Lantolf & Frawley, 1984), the same narration task was given to intermediate and advanced students of Spanish as a second language and adult native speakers of the language. Again, the advanced learners were comparatively more self-regulated in the task, their narrations proving more like the adult native speakers than the intermediate learners. This study also compared the private speech of the intermediate and advanced Spanish students with two similar groups of ESL students. The narratives of the intermediate Spanish learners are characterized as "a series of unconnected episodes"; furthermore, these subjects displayed no "sustained attempt at gaining self-regulation in the task" (Lantolf & Frawley, 1984, pp. 434-435). The intermediate ESL group also produced "unconnected" sounding discourse, but in contrast, were relatively prolific in their efforts to become self-regulated.

This disparity between the learners of the two languages is attributed to a difference in language learning contexts. The Spanish learners had received little opportunity to communicate in Spanish due to exposure to *classroom-only contexts* while the ESL learners, who were living in the United States, had, besides receiving classroom instruction, also been able to communicate with native speakers of the L2 daily *(mixed contexts)*. This aspect of their findings suggests the importance of naturalistic interaction to the development of self-regulation—a condition that is said to "speed up" the process.

In both these studies (Frawley & Lantolf, 1985; Lantolf & Frawley, 1984), increased L2 proficiency was accompanied by a decrease in the use of private speech,suggesting similarities to Vygotsky's findings for children's use and development of private speech. However, at the same time, it is important to point out that the researchers argue against the idea of assigning significance to group behavior in evaluating the use of private speech, and also disparage the notion of attempting to determine L2 proficiency on the basis of private speech production alone. Instead, they focus on the individual, believing that variation at this level far outweighs its homogeneity of use: "we cannot properly speak of stable variables for a population since a population is only a collection of individuals. It is the individuals who are important, not the population. It is thus the individual discourses, as they stand in themselves, which are of primary relevance" (Frawley & Lantolf, 1984, p. 149). And indeed, subsequent research has born out that factors such as a subject's background affect production.[1] As a result of this point of view, no attempt was made in either of the studies cited above to establish the level of L2 proficiency of participants beyond the impressionistic designation of being "intermediate" or "advanced."

Because of their emphasis on the individual, the value of statistical methods of analysis is also brought into question: "Western statistical rhetoric is based on the concept of the mean, which by definition excludes the individual" (Frawley & Lantolf, 1985, p. 24). However, in both studies observations are made about group dynamics, a form of investigation for which statistical measures have proven useful. In fact, the majority of private speech studies to date are child studies, and of these, most have adopted statistical designs (see Diaz & Berk, 1992, for an overview of this research; and Diaz, 1986, for a discussion of the usefulness of statistical methods, in exploring private speech).

McCafferty (1992), in a study concerning possible cross-cultural differences in the use of private speech by ESL learners, established three proficiency levels based on empirical evaluation. Overall production was found to decrease with an increase in proficiency, although no attempt was made to find out if these differences were in fact significant, or to analyze the data further for possible effects related to proficiency as this was not the focus of the research.

THE STUDY

Purpose

This study was an attempt to examine through empirical means the relationship between L2 proficiency level and the use of private speech in an effort to explore further the hypothesis that with

---

[1] See Ahmed (1988), Appel (1986), and Donato (1988). These studies have included private speech production for adult L2 learners as found in a number of different tasks and situations that include individual, dyadic, and group activities.

increased proficiency learners' use of these forms diminishes; and as such, to further substantiate the link between Vygotsky's observations for the use of private speech by children and its mediational role in the course of acquiring a second language.

Given the nonspecific nature of the task (below), it was expected that learners at low levels of proficiency, because of their greater difficulty in expressing themselves in the target language, would resort to the use of private speech to a greater extent than more advanced learners. Therefore, all three levels of self-regulatory private speech (object-, other-, and self-regulation) were expected to be produced at higher levels by low intermediate as opposed to advanced learners.

Another concern of the investigation related to the designation by Lantolf and Frawley of use of the tense as a form of object-regulation. Although not tested, McCafferty (1992) found this tense to be more prevalent in the narratives of advanced as opposed to low-intermediate and intermediate L2 learners, a finding that seemingly contradicts the suggestion that it is used by learners to gain self-regulation.

Subjects

All 39 participants in the study were ESL students attending the University of New Mexico. Two groups of 15 subjects each were formed, one consisting of learners of low-intermediate proficiency and the other of high-intermediate to advanced proficiency. Subjects' inclusion in each group was first determined through consultation with instructors familiar with their work as ESL students. Since standardized test scores, such as for the TOEFL test, are primarily based on discrete point questions (Oller, 1979), their use for establishing proficiency in this study was considered inappropriate because it primarily involved active communication in the L2. Therefore, in order to determine proficiency, two native speakers (both ESL instructors—one man and one woman) each listened separately to each subject's recorded performance of the task (described below) in conjunction with a written transcript, and in random order. Each subject was rated on a 1 to 10 scale—a designation of 1 indicating little or no facility and 10 native-like proficiency. Scores were based on a list of criteria that included such elements as grammatical correctness, fluency, vocabulary use, and sentence complexity.

Raters reached an interrater reliability of $r = .92$ (Pearson product-moment correlation coefficient) as to agreement on individual performance, and 100 percent concurrence concerning group designation—that is, neither rater judged a subject to belong to the group other than the one predetermined by the researcher. The mean rating for the low intermediates was 2.9 and the advanced group received a mean rating of 6.4. Thus, overall, raters found considerable difference between the two groups' proficiency levels.

All subjects were from either Hispanic or Asian backgrounds. McCafferty, (1992) found that levels of private speech production for learners from these two backgrounds significantly differed on two of the comparisons undertaken in the study. Therefore, an attempt was made to balance the two groups with regard to cultural background although matters related to proficiency took priority. The lower proficiency group consisted of 8 Asians and 7 Hispanics and the more advanced group of 9 Asians and 6 Hispanics.

The two groups were also relatively balanced with regard to gender. The low-intermediate group consisted of 10 women and 5 men, and 8 women and 7 men were included in the advanced group. The range in the age of the subjects was also similar, the low intermediates ranging from 18 to 41 years of age, and the advanced participants from 18 to 36. The average age for the low intermediates was 24, and 26 for the advanced subjects.

As an earlier study indicated that differences in exposure to language contexts resulted indifferences in the use of private speech, exposure to mixed contexts "speeding up" the process of self-regulation (Lantolf & Frawley, 1984), an effort was made to insure that the language-learning backgrounds for the two groups were not too dissimilar. Participants at both levels of proficiency had received about the same amount of exposure to English instruction in their native countries: the range was 0 to 10 years for both groups, and the mean number of years of exposure was 4.7 for the low intermediates and 5.7 for the advanced participants. The mean number of years of study in the U.S. (which in all cases was also equivalent to the total amount of time spent in mixed contexts) was, however, quite different—the advanced subjects having received an average of 3.1 years as compared to 1.0 years for the low intermediates. This difference in exposure, although not desired, became unavoidable as efforts to locate subjects with advanced proficiency but without extensive experience in mixed contexts proved very difficult.

Materials

A picture narration task was used for data collection. All subjects were asked to construct a narrative based on a series of six consecutive drawings shown one at a time in sequence:

1. A hat seller sits beneath a tree in which there are five playful monkeys.
2. As the hat seller sleeps, the monkeys each take a hat from one of two baskets next to the tree.
3. The hat seller awakens and is startled to see his hats on the heads of the monkeys—now back up in the tree.
4. The hat seller shakes his fist at the monkeys and they imitate him.
5. The hat seller holds his hat in his hand and scratches his head—the monkeys imitate him.
6. The hat seller smiles and throws his hat downward; the monkeys do the same.

All responses were tape recorded and later transcribed and coded. This same task had been found accessible to learners at lower levels of English proficiency in McCafferty (1992); equally important, the method of presenting the pictures one frame at a time made the task difficult enough to elicit private speech from more advanced learners as well. Also of importance in choosing this particular task was the fact that results for a previous study (Ahmed, 1988) found that learners' background knowledge influenced private speech production. The subject matter of this narrative did not involve any specialized areas of knowledge that would distinguish one participant from another in this aspect.

Data Analysis

It was necessary to define self-regulatory private speech fully and to establish criteria for each of the three forms (object-, other-, and self-regulation) included in the analysis. Any utterance considered to be an instance of self-regulatory private speech had to meet three basic requirements: (a) it had to be essentially tangential to the narrative, (b) it had to be self-directed in the sense of being basically and effort to seek self-guidance, and (c) it had to be concerned with mastering some task-relevant difficulty. For example, upon seeing the first picture in the series one of the low-intermediate subjects responded: "I watching monkeys in the tree, and they are...I think this man is a farmer, or I don't know—farmer, or he's a seller." virtually all of this response is outside the bounds of normal narrative discourse, primarily directed to the self as opposed to a listener, and, finally, represents an attempt to master the task through understanding the nature of the central character in the picture.

Most of the criteria established in Frawley and Lantolf (1985) and McCafferty (1992) for determining the function–form relationship for each of the three private speech categories was adopted for use in this study as well. An explanation with examples follows.

Object-Regulation

All instances in this category essentially displayed learners' attempts to gain self-regulation through objectifying aspects of the task. According to Frawley and Lantolf, this primarily involves externalizing the macrostructure of the discourse, and stems, psychologically, from a known or internalized structure appearing in contexts that in effect renders it unfamiliar. Externalization provides a vantage point from which the component parts can again be assimilated into a known entity. Object-regulation was subdivided into three categories.

Category 1. (Attempts to impose inappropriate schema on the task.) Although there is certainly a sense of "story" involved in the narrative (in fact, directions called for subjects to "tell the story"), in their efforts to provide structure, participants sometimes attempted to relate the narrative in the form of a children's story. For example, upon seeing the first frame one subject responded with "Once upon a time," initially providing a "fairytale-ish" framework to the discourse. Other examples come from learners' efforts to provide storylike background information: "Oh, um—John is in the park—um—he's in the, in the break time. He, he think of his life and a proceed...um—the trees, animals...and he's thinking about his awful job because he needs to sell hats to live."

Efforts to "quote" the hat seller (provide dialogue—or, as in the case of this task, monologue) were also considered to be an aspect of discourse belonging to this category. Some of these forms were much like what might take place with an adult reading a story to a child. For example, in response to the last frame, when the hat seller discovers that he can take advantage of the fact that the monkeys imitate him, a subject responded: "Oh, they are imitating me. So, if I drop the hat they might drop the hat."

Category 2. (Labeling, counting, or commenting on some aspect of the narrative.) Participants sometimes labeled aspects of the pictures or characteristics of the hat seller (as in previous examples). Also, the various component parts of a picture were sometimes counted out, as if the subject were taking mental inventory of its particular features. For instance, one of the low intermediates continued to refer to the hat seller as "one man" for the first two frames of the story and to "count" the monkeys until the fifth frame:

1. Here are *one* man sit, sit down in the ground, um sit down, sit down on the ground so, um, and next to him are many hats.

2. Um, *two* house are behind the wood, behind the tree, *one* man is sleeping, so, *one* monkey is, is a, um, oh, *one* monkey is looking a sky, the sky.

3. the man wake up, call himself—oh, he looks like thinking some, surprise, while *five* monkey he's talking.

4. Oh, *five* monkeys are playing with a man. No, the man is angry because of, because the *five* monkeys make a noise.

5. So, *five* monkeys are sorry about the noise, so he looks like "that's okay, no problem."

6. So, the monkeys are playing with the man. That's it.

There were also a number of comments either about some aspect of the pictures or concerning task performance.When commenting on the pictures, learners produced examples such as "This is in summer" or "The monkeys are cute." Comments on task perform-ance were more prolific, "I *don't know* what to say" and "I *think* he wants to put the hats on the monkeys" are typical of these expressions. Perspectival markers such as "now," as found in "*Now*, the old man is watching the monkeys" were also included as "comments" as essentially they relate to the picture as it appears within the learner's immediate frame of reference and not to the temporal framework of the narrative.

Category 3.   (Sigh, laughter, and exclamations when indicating that the learner felt he or she did not have a complete grasp of some element of the task, or in response to stimuli found in the picture.) For example, "Um, he, he thought its better he—do you know—have fun...don't worry about—be happy!" *(laughs)*. The laughter in this case signifies the subject's amusement at how she had expressed herself through use of the refrain from a then popular song ("Don't worry, be happy!").

Other-Regulation

These forms consisted of questions directed either to the self, as in "He fall asleep and the monkeys fell down—*how do you say*—fell down to catch the hats"; or to the researcher, as in "Oh, should I talk about this?" Questions to the researcher were included as in essence there was no interaction between a subject and the researcher once the task had started. Linguistically, questions of both types often took the form of a statement given rising intonation, as in "the man is sleeping," in which the subject, unsure of the correctness of her statement, made eye contact with the researcher and produced a rise in intonation on the word "sleeping," It should be noted, however, that it was not always clear to whom this type of question was being addressed as eye contact was not always sought, and even in cases as in the example above, the addressee could still be hard to determine—eye contact not being able to serve as a completely definitive criterion.

Self-Regulation

Utterances comprising this category were basically demonstrations by the learner concerning his or her mastery over a particular source of confusion, as with the use of "oh" in the following protocol: "The man wake up—call himself... *oh*, he's thinking some surprise." Consideration was given to the contexts in which these utterances were found. In this case, immediately following the exclamation the subject's thinking became redirected as she had changed her mind about her interpretation of events.

Tense and Aspect

Frawley and Lantolf (1985) also believe that use of the past tense and progressive aspect constitutes a form of object-regulation and that these forms are employed to exercise control when learners encounter difficulties with the temporal framework of events in the narrative. With use of the past tense the learner "distances" the events of the story, turning them into "completed facts" as opposed to on-going events. With use of the progressive, the learner, unable to manage the larger task, attempts to exercise control over the events of each separate frame, as in the following: "There are lots of monkeys on the tree and they are *playing* around. Some of them are *hanging* over—and I don't know—*climbing* up and down and play around. and there is and old man *selling*—who is *selling* hats under the tree."

Native speakers, outside occasional use of both the past tense and progressive aspect, were found by Frawley and Lantolf to rely primarily on the historical present tense to relate their narratives, as did McCafferty (1992) as in the following example: "When he wakes up, he realizes that the monkeys are wearing all of the hats that he wants to sell...and he's pretty surprised."

RESULTS

The total number of forms of private speech recorded in the study was 351. Of these, the low intermediates produced 236, or over twice the number as the advanced subjects (115). This relationship also held true for each of the three self-regulatory categories, more than twice the number of forms being produced by the low intermediates than the advanced subjects in each category (Table 6.1). By far, the most productive category for both groups proved to be object-regulation. This finding is not surprising given the inherent difficulty of the task and the fact that this category contained the greatest linguistic diversity.

The mean production of forms for each of the three types of private speech (object-, other-, and self-regulation) was compared for each of the two proficiency levels (low intermediate and advanced) through the use of separate t tests. One of the three comparisons showed significant results. The low-intermediate group was found to produce a significantly higher incidence of object-regulation than the advanced group (t (28) = 3.57; p <.005). Also, marginally significant results were found for the comparison of forms of self-regulation, the low intermediates showing a trend toward the greater use of these forms (t (28) = 1.46; .05 < p <.10). Findings for the comparison of other-regulation did not reach significance.

A further analysis of forms of object-regulation revealed that in all three subcategories the low-intermediate learners produced more forms than the advanced learners (Table 6.2). Separate t tests were performed for each of the three subcategories (Category 1:

TABLE 6.1
Distribution of Private Speech Utterances.

Proficiency Level	Object	Other	Self
Low Intermediate	185	38	13
Advanced	92	17	6
Total	277	55	19

TABLE 6.2.
Distribution of Forms of Object Regulation.

Proficiency Level	Schema	Labeling Counting Commenting	Sighs Laughter Exclamations
Low Intermediate	21	129	35
Advanced	7	68	17
Total	28	197	52

discourse structures appropriate to children's stories; Category 2: labeling, counting, or commenting on some aspect of the story or task performance; Category 3: sighs, laughter, and exclamations when in response to either the story or something said) in relation to each of the two proficiency levels (low intermediate and advanced).

Results for this analysis found significantly greater use on the part of the low intermediates for both Categories 2 (t (28) = 2.10; p <.025) and 3 (t (28) = 2.34; p <.025). Findings for Category 1 were marginally significant (t(28) = 1.62; .05 < p <.10), indicating a trend toward the greater use of these forms by the low-intermediate subjects.

Results for the two temporal forms of object-regulation found the advanced learners producing more instances of both the past tense and progressive aspect (Table 6.3). Separate t tests for each of the two temporal forms (past tense and progressive aspect) were undertaken for each of the two proficiency levels (low intermediate and advanced). Results found that use of the past tense was significantly greater for the more advanced learners (t (28) = 1.79; p <.05). The comparison for use of the progressive aspect did not reach significance ($t = p$ >.10).

TABLE 6.3
Distribution of forms of Past Tense Verbs and Progressive Aspect.

Proficiency Level	Past Tense	Progressive Aspect
Low Intermediate	70	74
Advanced	112	91
Total	182	165

DISCUSSION AND CONCLUSION

Findings that the low-intermediate group produced significantly more object-regulatory utterances (two of the three subcategories reaching significance and the third marginal significance), together with findings showing a trend toward the greater use of forms of self-regulation for this group, support the hypothesis that with increased proficiency learners' use of private speech diminishes. As such, these results are considered to provide evidence for a link to Vygotsky's ideas concerning the mediational function of private speech in the process of self-regulation as applied to L2 learning.

However, it needs to be kept in mind that the content of the task, task modality (spoken or written), the type of task (tasks other than picture narration), number of participants, and the motivational level and cultural background of subjects have all been found to effect L2 learners' use of private speech. Any one of these factors could possibly outweigh matters of proficiency; and indeed,cultural background may be one such element in this study.

The fact that no significant difference between the two proficiency groups was found for either forms of other-regulation or the progressive aspect is possibly related to the findings of McCafferty (1992), in which significantly greater use of both these forms was found for Hispanic subjects as compared to Asians at the same levels of proficiency. This supposition is based on the fact that although the present study included fewer Hispanic participants (13) than Asian (17), most of whom were in the advanced group (9), the Hispanics still produced far more forms of both other-regulation (47 of a total of 55) and the progressive (Hispanics with 104 forms and Asians with 61).

Because of the importance he accorded cultural-historical contexts on the process of cognitive development as well as other sources of influence, Vygotsky did not view development as linear; rather, he considered it as: "...a complex dialectical process characterized by periodicity, unevenness in the development of different functions, metamorphosis or qualitative transformation of one form into another, intertwining of external and internal factors, and adaptive processes than overcome impediments that the child encounters" (Vygotsky, 1978, p. 71). Given this perspective, it is not surprising that learners exhibit cultural diversity in the use of forms of private speech.

The further analysis of forms of object-regulation indicates a comparatively heavy reliance on the externalization of various aspects of the task by the low-intermediate learners. The subjects labeled and named elements in the pictures more often than the advanced subjects, were more hesitant in committing themselves to their understanding of both the narrative and their expression of it in the L2 (Category 2), showed a tendency toward the greater use of "storyish" discourse elements (Category 1), and also used more affective forms of object-regulation (Category 3).

Results for the use of past tense forms found that the advanced group used this tense significantly more often than did the low-intermediate group, despite Frawley and Lantolf's (1985) claim that it represents a form of object-regulation. This seeming contradiction can perhaps be explained by discourse continuity and coherence. While it may be true, as Frawley and Lantolf suggest, that the past tense allows for a "distancing" of events, it is also true that it can provide a sense of continuity and coherence to the narrative, preventing the kind of fragmentation that occurs when learners fail to establish and hold to a temporal framework, as often happened in the case of the low intermediates. This finding is also supported by Ahmed (1988), who observed that use of the past tense sometimes is simply associated with the relation of one event to another and need not represent a form of object-regulation.

The fact that the advanced group had spent, collectively, a good deal more time in mixed contexts than the low intermediates needs to be addressed due to the notion that mixed contexts contribute to hastening the development of self-regulation. Of the subject variables included in the investigation, length of exposure to the L2 in mixed contexts proved to be the most defining of differences between the two groups outside of proficiency. The additional time spent in these circumstances by the advanced subjects could at least in part be responsible for their being more self-regulated, and thus judged as more proficient by the two raters. However, as mixed contexts also allow for additional instruction, it is of course possible that this factor could have influenced communicative proficiency as well; although, as described in the L2 literature, most classroom approaches emphasized the structural nature of the target language and thus do not promote the kind of activities thought beneficial to developing self-regulation.

At the individual level, however, language learning contexts may not prove to be predictive of the degree to which an individual is self-regulated. As pointed out by John-Steiner (1985), the active involvement of the learner in trying to acquire a second language, especially under less than ideal conditions, can play a critical role in facilitating acquisition. In support of this perspective, the findings of Bialystok (1978) are cited in which outside activities such as going to films and reading books were found to be important sources of input for motivated learners—activities that could possibly be positively associated with the development of self-regulation, despite a lack of opportunity to use the L2 for communicative purposes.

In conclusion, although further research is needed, this study is considered to provide evidence that, comparatively, learners at lower levels of proficiency, because they experience more difficulty communicating in the L2, produce more forms of self-regulatory private speech than more advanced learners—a finding that offers general support for the Vygotskian theoretical framework of self-regulation. However, this claim is modified to the extent that a number of other factors have been shown to influence private speech production as well, and may, as in the case of cultural background in this study, possibly prove to override elements related to proficiency. Also, use of the past tense does not appear to be a particularly robust form of object-regulation, as in addition to acting as a form of self-regulation, it is also associated with providing a consistent and coherent temporal framework in narrative discourse.

REFERENCES

Ahmed, M. (1988). *Speaking as cognitive regulation: A study of L1 and L2 dyadic problem-solving activity.* Unpublished doctoral dissertation, University of Delaware, Newark.

Appel, G. (1986). *L1 and L2 narrative and expository discourse production: A Vygotskian analysis.* Unpublished doctoral dissertation, University of Delaware, Newark.

Bialystok, E. (1978). *The role of conscious strategies in second language proficiency.* Unpublished manuscript. Ontario Institute for Studies in Education.

Bivens, J.A., & Berk, L.E. (1990). A longitudinal study of the development of elementary school children's private speech. *Merrill-Palmer Quarterly, 36,* 443–463.

Diaz, R.M., & Berk, L.E. (1992). *Private speech: from social interaction to self-regulation,* Hillsdale, NJ: Erlbaum.

Diaz, R.M. (1986). Issues in the empirical study of private speech: A response to Frawley and Lantolf's commentary. *Developmental Psychology, 22,* 709–711.

Donato, R. (1988). *Beyond group: A psycholinguistic rationale for collective activity in second language learning.* Unpublished doctoral dissertation, University of Delaware, Newark.

Frawley, W., & Lantolf, J.P. (1984). Speaking and self-order: A critique of orthodox L2 research. *Studies in Second Language Acquisition, 6,* 143–59.

Frawley, W., & Lantolf, J.P. (1985). Second language discourse: A Vygotskian perspective. *Applied Linguistics, 6,* 19–44.

John-Steiner, V.P. (1985). The road to competence in an alien land: A Vygotskian perspective on bilingualism. In J. Wertsch (Ed.), *Cognition: Vygotskian perspectives* (pp. 348–371). Cambridge: Cambridge University Press.

John-Steiner, V.P. (1991). Private speech among adults. In R.M. Diaz & L.E. Berk (Eds.), *Private speech: From social interaction to self-regulation* (pp. 285–296). Hillsdale, NJ: Erlbaum.

John-Steiner, V., & Tatter, P. (1983). An interactionist model of language development. In B. Bain (Ed.), *The sociogenesis of language and human conduct* (pp. 79–97). New York: Plenum.

Lantolf, J.P., & Frawley, W. (1984). Second language performance, and Vygotskian psycholinguistics: Implications for L2 instruction. In A. Manning, P. Martin, & K. McCalla (Eds.), *The tenth Lacus forum, 1983* (pp. 235–440). Columbia, SC: Hornbeam.

Oller, J.W., Jr. (1979). *Language tests at school.* London: Longman.

McCafferty, S.G. (1992). The use of private speech by adult second language learners: A cross-cultural study. *Modern Language Journal, 76,* 179–189.

Soskin, W.F., & John, V.P. (1963). The study of spontaneous talk. In G. Baker (Ed.), *The stream of behavior: Explorations of its structure and context* (pp. 228–281). New York: MIT Press.

Vygotsky, L.S. (1978) *Mind in society: The development of higher psychological processes.* Cambridge, MA: Harvard University Press.

Wertsch, J.V. (1979). The regulation of human action and the given-new organization of private speech. In G. Ziven (Ed.), *The development of self-regulation through private speech* (pp. 79–98). New York: John Wiley & Sons.

7

Inner Speech and Second Language Acquisition: An Experimental-Theoretical Approach*

Tatiana N. Ushakova

Institute of Psychology
Russian Academy of Sciences
Moscow, Russia

INTRODUCTION

The concepts that appear in the title of this chapter are not related accidentally. The connection between them occurs at a deep level. The concept of inner speech is interpreted as the mechanism hidden from direct observation, comprising functional structures for word storage, relations between words, semantic fields, grammatical rules, and rules for discourse production. The processes

---

* This chapter was translated from Russian by Vladimir Sedov.

that take part in those structures result in the individual's ability to express thoughts by speaking and to understand the speech directed at him or her. The structures and processes of inner speech in a child are formed on the basis of influence of the speech of others and are manifested in first language acquisition. Second language acquisition takes place in the form of plugging into the inner speech mechanisms that have been worked out with respect to the first language, the influence of which on the second language can rarely, if ever, be completely eliminated.

If one wants to penetrate the very essence of second language acquisition, one should attend to the processes that participate in the mechanism of inner speech: take into account structures and processes related to first language functioning, reveal the rules of interaction of the first and second language, understand the meaning of the second language structure. This is a very complex problem. The group working on it in my laboratory managed to solve it only after years of theoretical and experimental studies on the mechanisms of inner speech.

The research materials dealing with second language acquisition from the perspective of inner speech mechanisms should be preceded by clarifying our positions as to what we consider to be inner speech. This concept, as is well known, is the crucial one in Vygotsky's theory. Since it has been considerably developed and modified since the time of Vygotsky, we believe it necessary to address the first part of this chapter to the problem of inner speech.

THE PROBLEM OF INNER SPEECH

The initial formulation of the inner speech problem is apparently connected with philosophical and ethical investigations: Ethics first addressed the notion of inner monologue in the theories of conscience and duty. Descriptions of inner speech in literature are quite common as well. There the object of consideration is ordinarily presented in the form of thought in language or of a latent monologue or dialogue within the subject. We find this technique used in the works of such masters of *belle lettre* as Tolstoy and Chekhov, among others. Such literary descriptions of inner speech served as direct material for psychological analysis. One can hardly agree with it, since inner speech is no more than a technique used to introduce the reader into the hidden world of a particular character in the book. Neither Tolstoy nor Chekhov studied inner speech per se and neither knew more about it than professional psychologists. The description of internal discourse is quite an arbitrary literary technique.

The concept of inner speech in scientific psychology is interpreted differently by various authors. One term serves to denote different objects. Frequently one may come across a situation when no explanation at all is provided. Undifferentiated use of the term inner speech may be found in classic authors, such as A. Binet, A. Lemaitre, Fr. Poland, and Fr. Kaints. Various hypotheses explaining the origin and nature of inner speech have been discussed. According to the auditory hypothesis, for example, inner speech is formed on the basis of auditory images: It functions through the activation and the internal activity of these images. R. Dodge, A. Thorson, and E. Jacobson, among other scholars, advocated the motor-kinesthetic hypothesis, according to which inner speech is based on incomplete inhibition of the movements of the articulatory organs. Accordingly, it is exhausted by "motor models of words." Lemaitre proposed the so-called ideographic hypothesis, according to which visual images of words constitute the basis of inner speech in an educated human being.

Vygotsky's (1956) views on inner speech have dominated Soviet psychology. His approach was based on bringing together the concepts of inner speech and egocentric speech. He believed that these two phenomena were genetically related, the former replacing the latter. According to Piaget, at the beginning of school age, egocentric speech diminishes and eventually dies away. Vygotsky, on the other hand, believed that it was exactly at this point that inner speech was born. The two types of speech are similar in structure and both carry out intellectual functions. The affinity between egocentric speech and inner speech is based on the fact that egocentric speech is a transitional form from interpsychic to intrapsychic functions—that is, from social collective activity to individual activity. The structural features of egocentric speech are reorganized in accordance with a new purpose, transforming it into the phenomenon that Vygotsky called inner speech, "speech for oneself" (Vygotsky, 1956, p. 327).

In developing his argument about the relationship between these two types of speech, Vygotsky concluded that the structural features of egocentric speech and, especially, the tendency for these features to evolve, may also be applied to characterize inner speech, inaccessible to observation by other means. Properly speaking, this line of reasoning came to be called the Vygotsky method of studying inner speech.

The first, and principal, feature discriminated by means of this approach deals with the syntax of inner speech. Compared with external speech, inner speech is fragmented and contracted. Inner speech is incomprehensible without reference to a particular situation. This characteristic is also noticeable in the egocentric speech of early childhood and becomes even more conspicuous as the child approaches school age. The contraction of inner speech is hardly accidental and concerns mainly the subject and the words linked to it, whereas the predicate and the words related to it are mostly retained. This observation led to the conclusion that inner speech was predicative "within the limits of absolute predicativeness" (Vygotsky, 1956, p. 237). The omission of the subject in inner speech and its operation mainly with predicates can be explained by the fact that the subject of an utterance is well-known to the speaker and does not require special naming.

The contraction of inner speech is also evident, according to Vygotsky, in the truncated aspect of its phonetic aspect. There is no need to pronounce full words in inner speech, they are understood by the very intention to utter them: "Inner speech is speech almost without words in the precise meaning of the term" (Vygotsky, 1956, p. 368).

The contraction of inner speech means that its syntax and phonetics are reduced to a minimum, and word meaning acquires primary significance. This makes the semantics of inner speech unique, since in this case sense dominates over meaning. Sense is understood as the broad range of impressions associated with a word, whereas meaning is one of the most stable and unified areas of sense. According to Vygotsky, in inner speech words are enriched with sense, and the predominance of sense over meaning reaches its limit.

The very same circumstance results in the joining together and fusion of words. Words form a kind of agglutinated unities. In these structures the principal concepts or word roots carry maximum semantic load, so that agglutinations become easily understandable. What is being described is the phenomenon in which word senses, as they are, flow into one another. In explicating this description, Vygotsky draws an analogy with works of literature where the title carries the sense of the entire work (*Don Quixote, Hamlet, Eugene Onegin, Dead Souls*). In all these cases titles are treated as if they were "agglutinations of sense." Words play the same role in inner speech.

It seems absolutely necessary to be quite clear about the psychological phenomenon behind the term inner speech in Vygotsky.

When considering this problem he expresses his emphatic disagreement with the authors who relate the term inner speech to
verbal memory or the process of preparing for speaking.

Vygotsky (1956) wrote:

> In a certain sense we can say that inner speech not only is not that
> which precedes external speech or reproduces it in memory but is
> opposed to external speech. External speech is a process of trans-
> forming a thought into words, its materialization and objectivization.
> Inner speech proceeds in the opposite direction, from outside to
> within, a process of absorbing speech into thought. (p. 340–341)

Vygotsky identifies three levels of the speech and thought process: semantic (the initial, first level of all internal levels of speech),
the level of inner speech, and the level of external speech. In
speaking, the transition takes place from the internal to the
external level, whereas in understanding the reverse movement
takes place. On the whole, this three-level construct may be used to
explain the transition from non-material thought to a material
word in which the elements of the inner (lower) level are semantics,
meaning and sense; those of the external (upper) level are words;
and those of the intermediate level are certain hybrid structures.

One cannot help but notice the multilevel nature of the concepts
used by Vygotsky (sense and meaning at one level, material forms of
the words at another level). Given these different levels, it is
impossible to imagine how different elements (semantic, on the one
hand, and material—acoustic—on the other) are able to interact.
This problem continues to be of major importance nowadays; it is
actively debated in psychology and computer science. Recently,
theories about the structure of semantic memory have also been
taken into consideration. Vygotsky was the one who drew attention
to the discussion of this extremely important topic in psychology.

These views of Vygotsky's have been discussed in the literature.
Galperin (1957) called attention to the fact that the idea of "pure
thought," although popular at the turn of the century, is now
obsolete; today we do not recognize the existence of "bare" thoughts
that are to be conjoined with speech by some means or other.
Anan'ev (1960) points out the dubious nature of the statement
about "the absorption of words into thought" (p. 345). He believed
that, in this case, inner speech can be interpreted as a structure
artificially concocted out of reality and consciousness (Anan'ev,
1960, p. 356).

In Blonskij's (1935) opinion, inner speech could not be derived from the spoken word. The question rather should be: where does any speech come from? The child's inner speech develops from listening to others. Listening involves repeating what a person hears. Repetition is a form of imitation characteristic of humans in general and, in particular, involves the functioning of the speech organs (coughing, laughing, yawning, singing). For children and primitive humans, with their highly developed imitative abilities, the repetition of heard speech should be a powerful source of the development of inner speech. Speech as a means of communication is a two-way process. Two partners speak at the same time, except that one speaks aloud and the other speaks to the self: "To speak in this case means to think aloud, and to listen means to think to oneself" (Blonskij, 1935, p. 291). Thought, along with internal and external speech, develop simultaneously. The origin of inner speech is to be found where the origin of speech in general is to be found, and that is communication.

Anan'ev (1960) observed that the concepts of inner speech and inner talking were not identical. He called the former an undifferentiable and incompletely recognizable verbal state from which talking evolves: "It is only natural, therefore, to study talking as the inner phase of the entire integral process of inner speech" (p. 355). As for the nature of inner speech, Anan'ev's position was a synthesis of the hypothesis mentioned above. In his view, inner speech is based on various sensorimotor mechanisms: processes taking place during listening and perception of the speech of others and participating in its formation, processes occurring while the speaker talks (the motor component is the essential one), and visual impressions occurring in an educated human being. One might want to notice that the rules of these components are different. Inner speech develops onto genetically from listening (not from egocentric speech). Its source at preschool age is the oral speech of others; beginning with school age, it is written speech.

Anan'ev (1960) described in three phases of inner speech:

1. orientation towards verbalizing or denoting a cognizable content (here he supports D.N. Uznadze's view, according to which inner speech is oriented towards objectification);
2. a process of inner verbalization, in which nominal and verbal structures are present;
3. ostensive definition of the place of verbalized thought in judgments and conclusions (in connection with which spatial definitions of the type "here" and "there" arise).

With regard to the qualitative elements of inner speech, Anan'ev thought that they could be nouns, verbs, and even indicators of location. Patients with sensory aphasia exhibit the predicative nature of speech, and those with motor aphasia display its nominal nature. In sensory aphasia, speech comprehension is disrupted; and according to Anan'ev's hypothesis, this is associated with the decomposition of "nominal structures." Predicative forms are related to the activity of talking, and hence they are disrupted in motor aphasia. The general peculiarities of this stage of speech are, according to Anan'ev, that inner speech processes take place soundlessly, they are compact, contracted, and dependent on the external speech, whereas inner speech has a processual character and is variable, depending on its readiness for transition into external speech.

Other students of inner speech, for example, Baev (1967), mention another aspect of inner speech besides its nominal and predicative qualities—its demonstrative pronouns. The words "this" and "these" often accompany the activity of singling out in thought different parts of an object and establishing relations between them (Baev, 1967, p. 11).

A. A. Leont'ev considered the subject, the predicate, and the object as the principal components of inner speech. He maintained that "a program is made up of all the semantic markers, i.e., it includes correlates of particular, especially important, components such as the subject, the predicate and the object, since their interaction is essential for a future utterance" (Leont'ev, 1969, p. 159).

Sokolov (1968), following a series of experiments, managed to identify the concrete forms of relationships between inner speech and the process of thinking. Agreeing with the idea that kinesthetic impulses are the basic components of thinking, he discovered, during experiments on the detection of hidden movements of the articulatory organs, that the more complex the intellectual activity is, the more active articulatory movements are. There exists an optimal level on which intellectual work can be performed with optimal results.

Zhinkin dealt with the problem of inner speech in a highly original fashion. The peculiarity of his approach consists in the fact that he posed the problem of inner speech within the broader contexts of the problems of forming and exchanging information. Inner speech is treated as part of the structure of integral "communicative circuits," embracing a large number of people (Zhinkin, 1982, p. 147). Generation, retrieval, reception, and processing of information are linked to ways of reflecting reality, shaping meaning in human consciousness, control over linguistic activity, and the formation of a system of linguistic tools.

For Zhinkin, there is no doubt that "internal and external speech" constitute a binary pair. "A person is not able to say anything if the composition of units to be uttered has not been already anticipated" (Zhinkin, 1982, p. 150) "...no one doubts that inner speech takes place in the process of communication (Zachesova, 1984, p. 142). However, a shift occurs in the concept of inner speech when it is asserted that it is more correct to speak of two languages, internal and external (cf. Zhinkin, 1982). Inner "silent" speech helps a person to think over and control his practical movements in a group. It develops and is reinforced together with collective acts, especially labor. Strengthening of inner speech results in the formation of a new, stable, internal language (Zhinkin, 1982, p. 120). Internal "silent" language exists for the purpose of understanding the environment, it reflects the sensory continuum of reality, it portrays the attributes of things, phenomena and events, and it is a servant of thought. External language provides communication between people, it is formal and it merely sets the rules of speech without touching upon its content (Zhinkin, 1982, p. 147).

The difference between external and internal speech is manifested in the fact that the dynamics of the signs serving as their vehicle differ, although identity of meaning is preserved. Both external and internal speech are used in dialogue between people. The listener hears the conveyed text and, at the same time, compresses its sense and develops a compressed thought (Zhinkin, 1982, p. 144). Dialogue presupposes a link between the participants: what is identified and differentiated by one participant is also identified and differentiated by the other (Zhinkin, 1982, p. 136).

This concept repeatedly emphasizes the relationship between internal language and reality. Internal language is formed as a result of revealing attributes and phenomena latent in a sensory continuum. To acquire a language one must be able to understand the objective structure hidden behind a term (Zhinkin, 1982, p. 132). Texts are constructed in such a way that object references of an utterance can be understood. The concept of inner speech, according to Zhinkin, is closely related to the concept of a universal objective code "that serves as a mediator not only between language and intelligence, and between oral and written speech, but also between national languages" (Zhinkin, 1982, pp. 18–19). An objective code requires that what is being spoken about and what precisely is being said be discernible from any intelligible speech segment. This code is inherent in all human languages, and hence can be called universal (Zhinkin, 1982, p. 145).

The semantic aspect of speech is closely related to operations in the objective code. Sense is that which reflects the reality at hand (Zhinkin, 1982, p. 131). Sense is formed in inner speech, it registers the sensory configuration of the situational dynamics (Zhinkin, 1982, p. 127). Only that which fits in with reality can be clad in sense.

In our studies of the inner speech problem, we proceeded from the assumption that it will be possible to understand this phenomenon only if inner speech is examined within the context of speech communication and the structure of the speech mechanism. The overall contours of the speech mechanism are defined with regard to the fundamental fact that, being an act of communication, speech is always addressed to someone. Communication requires a minimum of two participants, one sending and the other receiving a message. This situation may be represented schematically as a closed circuit as depicted in Figure 7.1. In Figure 7.1 the ovals stand for the communicating partners, the arrows between the ovals show the direction of speech from one partner (A) to the other (B).

This general schema can be differentiated and extended according to the accumulation of empirical data. Three fundamentally different parts are identifiable in the speech mechanism of each participant. These parts may be called stages, or units, in the speech mechanism: the first is the unit for speech perception, the second is the unit for pronunciation, and the third is a special unit with respect to the other two. It does not have direct output into the external world, and hence may be referred to as inner speech. The first two units of the speech mechanism have a direct link to the external world, translating speech into the objectively existing speech product or receiving that product. These components of the speech mechanism can be singled out by virtue of the simple fact that the stages of perception and pronunciation of speech are variable and mutually exchangeable (which reveals their subordinate position with respect to the inner speech stage). Each one of the peripheral stages has its own variants. Thus, a person can technically reproduce speech in various ways: with sounds produced by the articulatory organs (regular spoken speech), as written speech (by the hand, foot or mouth), as gestural speech (for example, sign language), and by touch (as blind and deaf people do). The speech perception stage varies in strict accordance with the

FIGURE 7.1 Schema of speech communication

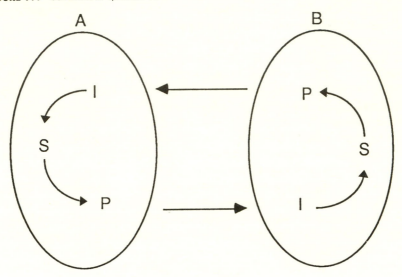

A/B — Communicating Partners

S — Central Stage of Speech

P — Stage of Pronounciation

I — Inner Speech

speech production stage: as many ways of producing speech physically can be used as there are ways of perceiving it.

Let us emphasize once again that the main purpose of the speech mechanism is to transmit contents from one communicator to another. The content of an utterance is formed in one participant and perceived by others during the inner speech stage essential for every communicator. Hence, it is clear that this stage is sense forming and may be central in the structuring of speech communication.

If one chooses to look at the inner speech stage from a more naturalistic point of view, it can be characterized as a psychophysiological process consisting of the activation of speech mechanisms without the visible manifestations of speech (external speech). Inner speech processes are qualitatively different from external speech and, under normal conditions, are a necessary foundation for it. This results from the fact that human speech, as usually uttered, expresses sense and uses a previously acquired language with its system of rules. A special integrative process is necessary to organize external speech according to the rules of the language and in conformity with the sense a person wishes to express. This process takes place in the neurophysiological structures formed in the human brain as the person acquires language and speech experience (speech mechanisms).

The characteristics of inner speech discovered by physiological analysis closely parallel Pavlov's notion of the second-signal system of humans (Pavlov, 1949). Indeed, Pavlov related the second-signal system to the functioning of speech mechanisms, believed that it constituted a basis for speech and abstract thought in language, and regarded the analysis and synthesis of speech signals as constituents of second-signal activity in the broadest physiological sense. Thus, psychology and physiology examine the same object, though from different perspectives.

Based on the results of experiments conducted in our laboratory, we have developed a general "mechanismic" description of inner speech. Several functional levels can be identified here. These levels differ according to the specific function each of them carries out. Note that all these functions are important in the act of speech communication taken as a whole. The hierarchy of levels is defined according to the ordering where a higher level is constructed on the basis of using the organization of the preceding level.

Certain structures corresponding to words with concrete semantics are formed on the relatively lower level (the level of "base elements"). These structures are complex in nature and include, at least, the following types of components: (a) fixing impressions from the objects of the objective world (referents) which receive their names, (b) forming conceptual structures which generalize and classify these impressions, (c) specific patterns corresponding to the sound characteristic of a word and its motor program for pronunciation. The components mentioned above are integrated and form the whole units—"base elements," stored in long-term memory and serving as the foundation for the construction of the next level of inner speech. This notion parallels the idea of "logogene" developed by Morton (1980).

Many findings of different authors indicate that the base elements of inner speech do not remain isolated, but are integrated, joined together by multiple temporary connections, forming an extensive system of interrelated structures (Kintsch & Buschke, 1979; Razran, 1949; Ushakova, 1979; von Wright, Anderson, &

Stenman, 1975). In psychophysiology this system has been labeled "a verbal network," which may be regarded as the second level of inner speech structures. The connections in the verbal network, though numerous, are nevertheless selective. Functional structures corresponding to words similar in meaning and sound are the most closely linked. Essentially, all the segments of a verbal network are connected with one another, at least in an indirect fashion. This structure, however, is complex and irregular, and there are some clusters and gaps, as well as multiple overlappings.

Traces of verbal stimuli are organized in inner speech mechanisms on the basis of speech perceived from outside (verbal signals often act as repetitive verbal sequences) and, in this respect, are one form of accumulation of speech experience and a materialization of language. Concepts of how the traces of verbal signals are organized in inner speech mechanisms, constructed on the basis of psychophysiological findings, coincide with new psychological views on the network organization of long-term speech memory.

The organization of traces of verbal stimuli into a network has an adaptive function: The development of connections between verbal signals creates a new level of generalization and abstraction through words. Words appear whose meaning is determined not by their connections with immediate impressions, but by their connection with other words; that is, a basis is created for the formation of verbal concepts.

There is research that supports the hypothesis that a network of grammatical structures is hierarchically a higher level of inner speech as compared to the verbal network level. The former resembles something like the grammatical classification of the material stored at the preceding level. This classification is complex in nature: all grammatical rules that we intuitively use (note that we start using them in early childhood) are based on such a classification. Dynamic processes that participate in the structures of the third level provide for the generation of grammatically well-formed sentences. As these processes unfold, some structures of the verbal network are activated and others are inhibited, and various types of mosaics of activity are formed. Activation of any particular verbal structure is connected with the recognition of their semantics on the part of the speaker or the hearer. The systematic ordering of their activation can be regarded from the physiological point of view as a form of dynamic stereotyping (Ushakova, 1979, pp. 189–194). In linguistics this phenomenon is described as syntactic structuring.

This concept explains why speech mechanisms become the

instrument of human communication and how the content of thought is conveyed from one person to another by means of conventional physical signals. People can communicate when they have something in common. The verbal network (the natural matrix of verbal experience) and the mosaic of activity emerging in it in the process of verbal communication constitute this common aspect of verbal communication. The speaker transmits the pattern of activity in his verbal network to the listener by means of uttered speech, thereby eliciting an analogous pattern in an analogous verbal network in the listener. This is possible because the verbal matrix serves as the common alphabet to both of them, as is described in theories of communication.

It has been observed that the formation of the consecutively organized structures of the elements of inner speech (that is, of sentence formation in linguistic terms) occurs on the level at which dynamic patterns emerge. However, the processes on this level cannot be used to explain away the activation of the semantically loaded inner speech elements. To be able to explain this, one should examine the highest level, the communicative level, which provides an answer to the question of why and how a person might want to say something.

Paying attention to the communicative level is relevant because the circulation of speech production inside the closed speech circuit is not an end in itself (see Figure 7.1). The speech mechanism should be open to the outside world because one person always conveys to another information about the world, his or her ideas, feelings, attitudes, evaluations. This aspect is treated on the communicative level, which is connected not with the formation of sentences but with the formation of discourses. The organization of the communicative or discourse level also has its own peculiarities.

If one person wants to convey to another person a certain discourse, he or she must be concerned in advance with the availability of common background knowledge (context, presupposition). The speaker needs to introduce an object of description (topic), and then, keeping it in the consciousness of the hearer through periodic reminding and modification, the speaker has to predicate something of it. If the description is extended enough, the speaker proceeds from one topic to another. This transition has to have logically well-grounded forms, and the accumulation of information—the degree of productivity of the message—must vary according to how well the speaker or the audience are prepared for it. There are some typical forms for the description of events, places, and introductions into conversation (Lakoff, 1973; Linde &

Labov, 1975; Sinclair & Coulthard, 1975; van Dijk & Kintsch, 1983). Besides realizing this or that descriptive form for the topic, the speaker organizes a personal communicative perspective on the conversation: the speaker uses the technique of attracting and keeping the hearer's attention, forms an opinion about the character and the social status of the partner or the audience, expresses and evaluation with respect to another communicator, assumes a formal, friendly, or even condescending manner of speaking.

Facts show that the discourse level directly provides for the central, communicative function of speech. This level possesses relative independence, since it is connected with specific organization and specific problems. At the same time it cannot function in complete isolation, since it necessarily has to rely on the work of all lower levels: syntactic, conceptual-verbal, lexical.

Several words should be said about the semantics of speech.When we considered the levels of inner speech organization, we touched upon this problem in passing. It should be noted that all levels of the speech mechanism are structured according to the semantic principle; that is, they provide storing, recognition, and reproduction of meaning. Different elements of speech, however, have a different "semantic load." Distinctive features contain an elementary meaning that helps to distinguish one phoneme from another. The semantics of words cannot be described as elementary, since it makes it possible to characterize the objects of thought, and sometimes it is the equivalent of an entire utterance (for example, "fire!"). Semantics receives its ultimate, and perhaps most difficult, manifestation in discourse which we interpret as the means to communicate any idea related to the outside world, the human psyche, and speech itself.

The model being developed here has been tested by a number of experiments carried out in our laboratory. The following phenomena have been studied: dynamics of sentence formation (Baitikova & Kokoreva, as cited in Ushakova, 1979), the mechanism of understanding polysemantic words (Pavlova, 1986), verbal association formation, the structure of the verbal network (Zachesova & Sokolova, as cited in Ushakova, 1979), the inner structure of a word trace in long-term memory (the case of child's word creation), the organization of discourse level of speech (Ushakova, Pavlov, & Zachesova, 1989), and the relationship between the speech process and brain structures based on the studies using the distance synchronization technique proposed by Shustova (1985).

No reference has been made in our works to the stages of speech production and speech perception, although they are undoubtedly essential for spoken communication. Concentration solely on inner speech can be explained by the fact that the organization and functioning of this stage largely determines the main psychological characteristics of speech and communication, in particular. We hope that the accuracy of the last statement and the productivity of the model described here will find further confirmation in studies dealing with the semantics of speech, verbal memory, and discourse analysis.

SECOND LANGUAGE ACQUISITION AND INNER SPEECH MECHANISMS

Based on the notions of inner speech described above, Zachesova (1984) conducted a series of experiments aimed at the identification of second language acquisition mechanisms. The material we used in the experiments can be classified as an articifical language. The respondents learned 20 artificial sound combinations containing two open syllables, including *muba, vema,* and *gochi.* Every "word" took its meaning from one of three grammatical categories: nouns denoting animals and food (wolf, bear, cat, dog, animal; milk, meat, honey, sugar, food), verbs denoting a way of eating (to nibble, to chew, to lap up, to swallow, to feed on) and adjectives denoting colors (black, white, gray, multi-colored). Although the material was, in some sense, artificial, it conforms to the organization of natural language systems.

The experiments were organized in the following way. At the preliminary stage of the experiment, the respondents were given sufficient instruction in the phonological form of the speech material so as to be able to recognize 20 main words and distinguish these from similar sound combinations. The main series of experiments begin once the respondents showed that they could indeed discriminate the necessary sound patterns. Each respondent was then given the meanings of the acquired words and was asked to learn them. For this purpose an audiotape with the Russian equivalent was played to the respondent, who had to furnish the corresponding artificial word as rapidly as possible. Irrespective of the respondent's answer, the corresponding artificial word was pronounced three seconds after the Russian word had been presented. One experiment contained 200 presentations. It usually took three experiments to learn the list of words completely.

Judgments about how well the acquisition of the artificial language was taking place were based on response time—the interval between the moment of presentation of the Russian equivalent and the respondent's articulation of the memorized word. We assumed that, all things being equal, the stronger and more active the connection between the word structures, the more rapidly and stable it could be reproduced.

The experimental results revealed dramatic differences in the processes of memorizing the meaning of a word depending on the category to which the word belonged. For clarity of discussion, we mention again that the process of memorizing began when the respondents could accurately and rapidly recognize all 20 words according to their phonological form. (Their meaning remained unknown.) As soon as the process of associating form with meaning began, the stratification of the initially homogeneous field containing 20 words became increasingly apparent. It turns out that even at the first stage of instruction (up to 220 presentations) the groups of words denoting nouns—animals and food—could be more easily identified than those denoting verbs (for example, ways of eating) and attributes denoting color (black, white, gray). Although after the first stage of instruction (between 1 and 220 presentations), the reaction time differences were not statistically significant, subjects responded faster to nouns of both types than to verbs and attributes (food nouns = 1940 ms, animal nouns = 1820 ms, verbs = 1960 ms, attributes = 2200 ms). At the second stage of instruction (from 220 to 420 presentations) the response differences between the respective indices increased statistically significantly in favor of the nominal categories (food nouns = 1380 ms, animals nouns = 1340 ms, verbs = 1880 ms, attributes = 1740 ms). The error margin calculated using the Wilcoxon–Mann––Whitney criterion is .01–.05. Words denoting actions and attributes were reproduced with longer delay and less stability during the entire period of instruction, although after the third stage of presentation, the differences between these and the nominal groups were not significant (food nouns = 880 ms, animal nouns = 980 ms, verbs = 1060 ms, attributes = 1042 ms).

This fact we interpret to mean that the differences registered in the course of instruction reveal the inner grouping of the experimental words. This claim is supported by an analysis of the nature of the respondents' erroneous answers, which shows that they confused words according to phonological form as well as meaning. Mistakes of the second type, constituting the majority, reveal that respondents confuse only words belonging to the same semantic category: dog (*pogu*) and animal (*tevu*), honey (*choni*) and sugar (*ziru*), food (*visa*) and to devour (*rega*).

On the basis of the above argument, we have come to the conclusion that the grouping of memorized words is subject to the semantic foundation realized in the system of the earlier acquired (first) language. Acquisition of the second (and other) language(s) occurs as a "plugging" of the new lexicon into the already established linguistic structures, which allows for categorization and linking of structures when necessary, and, most importantly, interpretation. This is the fundamental way in which the first language influences the second.

Another form of correspondence between first and second languages has been discovered as the result of our experiments (Zachesova, 1984). This can be described as the incorporation of additional associations, consonances, mental images, and situations representing the formation verbal links. This circumstance came to light during the individual reports of our respondents. Two mediating associations were observed, one based on the consonance of two words (for example, both *vema* and *moloko* "milk" contain the letter m), and another based on use of semantic inclusions (*choni—med* "honey"). Thus, for example, one respondent created a phrase in order to remember the meaning of the nonsense word *choni*—"honey." Through the phrase, *cheln, vezshchij bochki s medom*— "a boat carrying barrels of honey"— the respondent linked *choni* to *cheln*—"boat"—because of their phonological similarity, which, in turn, created a link to the real word for "honey," *med*.

To further understand the process of "incorporation" of the second language into the first, an additional series of experiments was carried out using the same technique of teaching an artificial language. This time, however, we paid special attention to the selection of respondents. Only those with a high level of linguistic ability were selected to participate in this experiment. The respondents were chosen form among senior students of M. Torez Institute of Modern Languages (six people) and from among philologists who had speaking knowledge of several foreign languages (three people). As with the initial experiment, any age difference among the respondents was considered irrelevant.

The additional series of experiments demonstrated approximately the same picture as the initial series with regard to acquisition of the words of the artificial language. The homogenous "field" containing 20 words that had to be memorized underwent immediate stratification as soon as an attempt was made to connect each word with a certain meaning. The group of words denoting animals and food was the first one to have been formed.

Two additional groups, denoting actions and attributes, were formed shortly thereafter. Besides being able to reproduce the general dynamics of the acquisition process, we also achieved a high degree of success in the instruction process. This was manifested by the fact that the instruction process was considerably faster, the latent time for associating a given word with a meaning from the beginning of work was much shorter, and the grouping of "words" was also quicker and far less mistake-prone.

In an attempt to penetrate into the essence of the phenomenon under observation, we turned once again to the reports of individual respondents, who demonstrated a great deal of effort, as well as variety, in deploying mediation techniques with respect to the memorized words. For example, some artificial words were interpreted as proper names of relevant animals (a cat's name, *Muba*); there were also cases in which the memorized words were interpreted within the structure of sentences composed in the first language (*Koshka lakaet moloko*—"A cat laps some milk"—and then *Muba—siba—vema*). Use of the phonological form of the word was very revealing in this respect. Associations based on similarity of phonological form were included in more than 60 percent of the mediation techniques. This figure is considerably higher than the corresponding one in the main experimental series. Consonances of the first as well as other languages acquired prior to the experiment were also actively used.

The results of the additional experimental series revealed that success in acquiring words of the artificial language depends on the intensity of their incorporation into the structure of the earlier acquired languages. The newly acquired aggregate of words is classified according to the classification of the first language. The similarity in the phonological composition of semantic equivalents is established. Some cognitive structures are formed, making connections between verbal equivalents more complex and thus much stronger. Associations are diverse in nature and are oriented toward different parts of the sound system of both the first and the second languages.

Let us try to identify and compare the main features of child first, and any non-primary, language acquisition as it was represented in the experiments described above. In our previous work we addressed the ontogenetic aspect of inner speech structures identified by Blonskij (1935). Speech ontogeny has a number of specific characteristics, the description of which is repeated from one work into another. It has been shown that a child's first words have an extended and diffuse meaning. They are often classified as one word sentences. Thus, the word *mama*, "mother," can mean that the child registers his or her mother's presence, asks her for help and many other things. As the number of these early words grows, the relationships between them start developing (a child begins to use word sequences) and the generalization of words takes place. One of the most remarkable features of speech ontogeny, as our research has demonstrated, is the powerful and spontaneous inner processing of speech material. It is most vividly manifested when a child creates new words. The child utters words constructed according to the rules of the language, but that nevertheless are not used in this language and have not been acquired from the people surrounding the child.

The analysis of word creation by Russian children led us to the conclusion that it is based on spontaneous analytic and synthetic processes. The analytic nature of these processes is manifested in the fact that words with recurrent partials are subdivided into constituents (roots and affixes in the case of Russian) as the result of their automatic comparison. This subdivision gives rise to future grammatical generalizations. The semantics of a word is analyzed and modified together with its form. Synthetic processes, connected mainly with the functioning of speech stereotypes, form new combinations of the earlier divided constituents, resulting in neologisms in the child's language patterns. Such words can be actively used by the child for a rather long time. However, under the pressure of adult language and constant corrections from people in the child's social environment, they become extremely rare by school age and are inevitably eliminated altogether. This is irrelevant for our purposes.

What is relevant, however, is that one notices the same analytic and synthetic operations mentioned above at work in the formation of children's words. The action of these operations, explicitly perceived, must be much wider. This means that many words in child speech that have the correct form can also be the result of the child's invention rather than borrowings from the surrounding environment. Furthermore, if this is really the case, then we must recognize the important role played by spontaneous processing of perceived speech material extending outward from the child and the formation of inner speech structures in ontogeny.

On the whole, first language ontogeny is an extremely complex procedure of forming inner speech structures and processes, including perception and imprinting in memory of speech material produced by speakers in the child's environment, "self development" of numerous word forms, cognition of the external and internal world by means of language, and many other phenomena. This procedure moves from initially diffuse and relatively primitive structures toward specialization, with their taking on of increased complexity in both form and meaning.

As for second language acquisition, our findings show that interaction of new speech material and the earlier developed inner speech structures turns out to be very strong. The second language is incorporated into the classification system already available in the first language, relies on the previously developed semantic system, and actively deploys first language phonology. This all means that the main driving force is not so much inner self-development as it is use of first language development. To put it figuratively, second language is looking into the windows cut out by the first language.

CONCLUSION

The role that humans play in direct communication, in different forms of creating and exchanging speech information, in literature, and in other spheres of life is worked out and perceived by a special functional device that we call inner speech. The inner speech mechanism includes special verbal structures capable of storing and reproducing lexical elements of the language being used. These structures reveal their multiple interrelationships and systematic organization into a "verbal network."

Inner speech structures are included in the dynamic processes connected with the generation and perception of external speech. The activation of a particular verbal structure results in the emergence in the human mind of the corresponding word, concept, image, or situation and also in the possibility of translating this word into external speech. There exist different forms of activation of verbal network structures: global, differentiated, "mosiac," consecutive, simultaneous, long-term, and short-term. For example, the consecutive, short-term activation of verbal structures, according to the developed stereotype, constitutes the basis for generating grammatically well-formed sentences. The long-term activation of verbal structures enables one to generate discourses expressing a pre-existing idea and realizing a certain plan.

Inner speech structures and processes are worked out during first language acquisition based on the borrowing of verbal material from the speech of other people and based on some inner, apparently genetically stipulated, driving forces. The general path of linguistic development and development of the self proceeds from primitive and diffuse organization to increasingly differentiated and complex structures. Second language acquisition reveals essentially different specific features. It primarily consists of incorporating and plugging the newly established structures into the ones worked out earlier, as well as in employing already existing verbal skills.

REFERENCES

Anan'ev, B.G. (1960). Teorii vnutrennej rechi v psikhologii. V kn. psikhologija chuvstvennogo poznanija [On the theory of inner speech in psychology]. *The Psychology of Perception.*

Baev, B.F. (1967). *Psikhologija vnutrennej rechi [The psychology of inner speech].* Author's abstract of dissertation for the degree of doctor of Psychological Sciences. Leningrad University.

Blonskij, P.P. (1935). *Pamjat i myshlenie [Memory and thought].* Moscow.

Galperin, P.J. (1957). Vnutrennjaja rech [Inner speech]. *Dokl. APN RSFSR,* 4, 55–60.

Kintsch, W., & Buschke, H. (1969). Homophones and synonyms in short-term memory. *Journal of Experimental Psychology, 80,* 403–407.

Lakoff, R.T. (1973). The logic of politeness; Or, minding your P's and Q's. In C. Corum, T.C. Smith-Stark, & A. Weiser (Eds.), *Papers from the ninth regional meeting Chicago linguistic society* (pp. 292–305). Chicago: Chicago Linguistic Society.

Leont'ev, A.A. (1969). *Psikholingvisticheskie edinitsy i porozhdenie rechevogo vyskazyvanija [Psycholinguistic units and the generation of a verbal utterance].* Moscow.

Linde, C., & Labov, W. (1975). Spatial networks as a site for the study of language and thought. *Language, 51,* 924–939.

Morton, J. (1980). The logogen model and orthographic structure. In U. Frith (Ed.), *Cognitive processes in spelling.* London: Academic Press.

Pavlova, N.D. (1986). Semantika rechi v razlichnykh uslovijakh obshchenija [The semantics of speech in different communication conditions]. *Psikhologicheskie i psikhofisiologicheskie issledovanija rechi [Psychological and Psychophysiological Studies of Speech],* 66–82.

Pavlov, I.P. (1949). *Polnoe sobranie trudov [Complete collected works],* Vol. 3. Moscow.

Razran, G.H. (1949). Stimulus generation. *Psychological Bulletin, 46,* 337–366.

Shustova, L.A. (1985). *Osobennosti prostranstvennoj organizatsii bioielektricheskoj aktivnosti mozga vo vremja rechevykh aktov [On some peculiarities of spatial organization of bioelectric brain activity during speech acts].* Unpublished doctoral dissertation. Moscow.

Sinclair, J.M., & Coulthard, B.M. (1975). *Towards an analysis of discourse: The English used by teachers and pupils.* London: Oxford University Press.

Sokolov, A.N. (1968). *Vnutrennjaja rech i myshlenie [Inner speech and thought].* Moscow.

van Dijk, T.A., & Kintsch, W. (1983). *Strategies of discourse comprehension.* New York: Academic Press.

von Wright, J.M., Anderson, K., & Stenman, U. (1975). Generalization of conditioned GSRs in dichotic listening. In P.M.A. Rabbitt & S. Dornic (Eds.), *Attention and performance* (pp. 194–204). London: Academic Press.

Ushakova, T.N. (1979). *Funktsionalnye struktury vtoroj signalnoj sistemy. Psikhofisiologicheskie mekhanismy vnutrennej rechi [Functional structures of the second signal system. Psychophysiological mechanisms of inner speech].* Moscow.

Ushakova, T.N., Pavlova, N.D., & Zachesova, I.A. (1989). *Rech cheloveka v obshchenii [Human speech in communication].* Moscow.

Vygotsky, L.S. (1956). *Myshlenie i rech [Thought and language].* Moscow.

Zachesova, I.A. (1984). O strukture slovesnoj pamjati i ee roli v usvoenii jazyka [The structure of word memory and its role in second language acquisition]. *Psikhologicheskij Zjhurnal [Journal of Psychology],* 4, 138–142.

Zhinkin, N.I. (1982). *Rech kak provodknik informatsii [Speech as the information medium].* Moscow.

Part III

8

Speaking As Cognitive Regulation: A Vygotskian Perspective on Dialogic Communication

Mohammed K. Ahmed

English Language Program
International University of Japan
Niigata
Japan

INTRODUCTION

Vygotskian psycholinguistic theory has gained considerable attention among a number of Western researchers within the last two decades. These researchers have been deeply interested in sociocultural theory for its unified perspective on cognitive development and its emphasis on the relevance of societal context and interpersonal relationships in the development of individual cognition. The present chapter utilizes Vygotskian concepts for understanding a specific area of second language research, namely, dialogic communication, or dyadic conversational interaction, which has emerged as an important factor in research on second language processes. The chapter analyzes selected linguistic data in task-based dyadic interactions involving native and nonnative speakers of English.

LANGUAGE AS FUNCTION

Since the research reported on here is motivated by a specific theoretical perspective, it is important to explain briefly the Vygotskian point of view on language use and dialogic communication. Vygotskian psycholinguistic theory holds a functional view of language that focuses on language as a means for engaging in social and cognitive activity. This functional view, however, is to be understood in specific terms. According to Vygotsky, language is a symbolic "tool." Humans use tools to interact with their external environment. In this interaction, tools mediate between the subjects (humans) and the objects (material world). Tools aid humans in controlling and changing the external environment. Thus, tools function as mediators in goal-directed activities. Similarly, language is simultaneously seen as a "psychological tool," the most sophisticated mediational mechanism in human sociocultural history. While physical tools are used to control the external environment, symbolic tools, or linguistic signs, serve not only to control and organize the social world and to mediate interpersonal activity but also to control and organize the psychological world and to mediate intrapersonal cognitive activity.

It is in these terms of control that language serves as the most important means of human cognitive development and behavior. Development proceeds from interindividual social activity to intrahuman mental functioning; from the social to the individual or from the dialogic to the monologic. Language, as the most advanced mediational mechanism, mediates the basic processes of perception, attention, memory, thinking, and even emotion. In short, cognitive development and functioning, for Vygotskian theory, is linguistically constituted.

Underlying cognitive development and behavior is the notion of *regulation*, whereby natural or elementary mental functions are subordinated to higher, socially derived mental functions. Regulation is a linguistically constituted process of "internalization" and "decontextualization," through which the locus of control of mental activity shifts from the external context (both physical environment and social relations) to the internal mind. Thus, a cognitively developed individual is one who has become independent of the external context in his or her mental functioning. Language is the driving force behind such independence.

A simple example will help clarify the point. Vygostky, in his account of quantitative operations, argues that the ability to see "two" as a combination of "one and one" is a relatively sophisticated mental function in that it shows the individual cognizing the numbers as abstract categories (Wertsch, 1985, p. 33). The numbers stand on their own without being tied to any external objects. On the other hand, as Vygotsky argues, in early times humans heavily depended on concrete objects and settings while doing any kind of counting. They lacked the ability to use numbers in a decontextualized manner. They were at a level of mental functioning in which counting was dependent on external stimuli in the physical environment. In this context, decontextualization is the result of the emergence of the number system in language. Such decontextualization shifts the locus of control from the external environment to the mind of the individual with the help of language.

Regulatory Functions of Language

Vygotsky's functional view of language, then, is explicable in terms of regulation or control. In this context, the function of language is "the reguraltion of self, others, and objects in the social environment" (Frawley, 1987, pp. 147). Language thus assumes three major regulatory functions: object-regulation, other-regulation, and self-regulation. It is worthwhile quoting at length Frawley's description of these three regulatory functions:

> Language serves to regulate, first, objects where "objects" means anything in the environment which is non-human and has ontological status. Thus objects are such things as tables, chairs, dogs, and even facts. The object-regulation function is the most elemental operation of language: naming is a classic example of object-regulation through language. Second, language functions to regulate other people. This other-regulation function can be either other-regulating (when speech functions from the point of view of the speaker to control other people) or other-regulated (when speech is produced because other people control the situation in which the speaker utters the language). Typical examples of language with other-regulation function are speech acts, or methods by which individuals attempt to control verbally the behavior of other individuals. Third, language serves to regulate the self...self-regulation is, in fact, the highest and most critical function of speech (since it is how the individual

ultimately controls himself and his mind...). All self-directed, mono-
logical utterances have this function. (Frawley, 1987, pp. 147–148)

Accordingly, researchers subscribing to Vygotskian theory adopt a
functional analysis of linguistic data in which linguistic forms are
analyzed in their regulatory functions in any kind of speech
activity.

Speaking in Dialogic Communication

Given the above functional view of language, the Vygotskian perspective on dialogic communication maintains that in a communicative situation involving two or more individuals interacting
face-to-face within a given task-setting, the focus of investigation is
on discovering the locus of control. In other words, it becomes
important to determine if the locus of control resides in one
interlocutor, is distributed between the two, or lies in the external
context of the task itself. The task of the researcher is to discover if
the speech of the individual interlocutors shows evidence of object-
regulation, other-regulation, or self-regulation. This is achieved
through careful analysis of the relationship between task factors
and specific linguistic forms manifested in the speech of the
interlocutors.

The activity of speaking is then to be seen in terms of behavioral
control on the part of an individual. The relationship between the
interlocutors in dialogic communication is often not of equal
exchange but "asymmetric" (Rommetveit; 1985). In asymmetric
patterns of dialogic communication, interlocutors enter into variable power relationships and their mutual behaviors are other-
regulating or other-regulated. Thus, focus is on the directionality of
control between the two interlocutors.

THE STUDY

Task and Subjects

The data to be analyzed in this chapter were taken from a larger
study (Ahmed, 1988) on task-based dyadic conversations. Here we
concern ourself with two dyads only, one comprised of a native
speaker (NS) and a non native speaker (NNS) of English and one
constituted by two English native speakers. The dyads were given a

visual puzzle (taken from Ur, 1981, p. 62) and a set of written instructions on how to solve the puzzle. The puzzle contained a sequence of seven pictures, each describing an event that represented one step in the solution to the puzzle. The subjects were expected to arrange the randomly ordered pictures into the proper sequence. In Figure 8.1 below, I present the instructions and a prose description of the pictures ordered as they were in the original task.

After providing the visual puzzle and the set of written instructions, the researcher left subjects alone to carry out the task. The conversation of each dyad was videotaped for analysis.

Instructions

You and your partner will see seven pictures. These pictures are on a single page in front of you. In each picture, you will see a goat, a wolf, a cabbage, and a man in a boat. The man is carrying the goat, the wolf, and the cabbage across a river. In the pictures, he is carrying them from the left to the right. However, the man faces a serious problem. The problem is *the wolf will eat the goat, and the goat will eat the cabbage, if given the chance.* You and your partner look at the pictures carefully, then both of you discuss and decide how the man is able to carry the wolf, the goat, and the cabbage across the river. You and your partner need to rearrange the pictures into the proper order. Each picture has the letter a,b,c,d,e,f, or g. You both must agree on how to rearrange the pictures. You have ten minutes to rearrange the pictures. If you do not finish this task in ten minutes, I will come in and stop you.

Pictures

a) goat is on left bank; man and wolf are in boat moving toward right bank; cabbage is on right bank.
b) wolf is on left bank; man and goat are in boat moving toward left bank; cabbage is on right bank.
c) goat is on left bank; man is in boat alone moving toward left bank; cabbage and wolf on right bank.
d) cabbage and wolf on left bank; man and goat in boat moving toward right bank; right bank is vacant.
e) left is vacant; goat is exiting from boat onto right bank; cabbage and wolf on right bank.
f) cabbage and wolf on left bank; man in boat moving toward left bank; goat on right bank.
g) wolf on left bank; man and cabbage in boat moving toward right bank; goat on right bank.

FIGURE 8.1   Visual puzzle task (Ur, 1981, p. 62)

Focus of Data Analysis

This chapter analyzes a specific linguistic feature in the conversations of the dyads: tense/aspect marking. This feature provides relevant evidence on the regulatory functions of speech as they were presented above. The analysis reported here was carried out at the microlevel to the extent that it interprets instances of tense/aspect marking in terms of its regulatory function in problem-solving dyadic discourse.

Regulatory Functions of Tense/Aspect in Narrative Discourse

This chapter extends the findings of an earlier study on the regulatory functions of tense/aspect use in narrative discourse presented in Frawley and Lantolf (1985). In their study, Frawley and Lantolf asked their subjects to relate a simple picture story orally. The subjects were intermediate and advanced ESL speakers, as well as English native-speaking adults and children. Among other things, Frawley and Lantolf report that in relating the story the historical present, the typical tense of oral narratives in English, was used less by the intermediate level NNSs and the NS children than it was by the advanced NNSs and the adult NSs. The two former groups relied more on the progressive and the simple past in relating their stories. Frawley and Lantolf (1985, p. 34) propose the regulatory schema given in Figure 8.2 to account for the difference in performance among the groups.

The above temporal distinctions are deictic in that they are based on a sense of remoteness versus proximity in the mind of a speaker. The ability to perceive a referent as remote is an ability to distance oneself cognitively from the specific stimulus and thereby gain some control over it. Frawley and Lantolf (1985) argue that in the task of narrative discourse, use of the past tense indicates that an

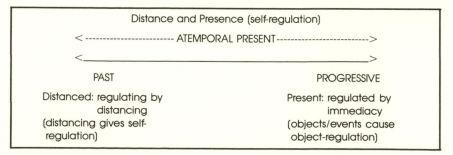

FIGURE 8.2. Tense-aspect functions in discourse (Frawley & Lantolf, 1985, p. 34)

individual tries to gain self-regulation through distancing an event as object. Conversely, they argue that use of the progressive indicates that the individual is caught by the immediacy of the stimuli that forces a reactive response. In this context, maximal self-regulation is shown by means of the atemporal present that indicates that the narrator controls the task by being able to express a sense of both immediacy and distance simultaneously in response to ask stimuli: "A self-regulated narrator can both control the events through distancing himself from them and relate the events as they actually are" (Frawley & Lantolf, 1985, p. 34). Thus, in narrative discourse, the past shows a speaker's attempt to achieve self-regulation, the progressive reveals object-regulation (that is the regulation of the individual by the events as objects in the task), and the atemporal present indicates the achievement of self-regulation.

In this context, the present chapter also deals with a task related to narrative discourse. To comply with the goal of arranging pictures in their proper order in the puzzle, the interlocutors needed to describe a series of events taking place in a chronological, event-based sequence. In order to narrate the series of events in the proper sequence, the speakers had to gain a macrolevel understanding of the arrangement of the pictures; that is, they had to understand how the events in the pictures related to one another, given the constraints of the puzzle. In their verbal response to the visual stimuli, they had to transcend the arrangement of pictures in terms of events as isolated frames and to visualize, instead, the connection among the pictures in terms of properly sequenced events. Mere description of the events as single frames in isolation would have been a reactive response to the events as objects, hence an instance of object-regulation. Control in this task (self-regulation) is thus expressed in the ability to narrate the events at the macrolevel of understanding of the properly sequenced events. Given this framework, the analysis that follows provides additional evidence for, and also extends, the claims made by Frawley and Lantolf regarding the regulatory functions of tense/aspect marking in narrative discourse.

ANALYSIS

In the NS–NNS conversation, given in [1] below, the atemporal present occurs in the speech of the NS, who attempts to explain to his nonnative speaking counterpart how the man in the puzzle solves his problem.

[1] a. NS: so he leaves those two on one side

    b. NNS: Side [NS points to the instruction sheet]

    c. NS: right...he takes the goat across first and the...he

    d.   comes back and he gets the cabbage...uh...and he

    e.   ...uh Is that right? [Very low tone] Yeah [Stressed]

    f.   he gets the cabbage and he takes it across but then he

    g.   picks...the goat...so he [Hand simultaneously

    h.   moves away from the instruction sheet. Waves hand

    i.   in the air]

    j. NNS: Uh...um

    k. NS: now he leaves the cabbage on one side

The NS in [1] formulates some macrolevel understanding of the problem from his own perspective. His use of the atemporal present indicates that he understands the solution to the puzzle and that his speaking is intended to relate the solution to his partner. It thus shows his control over the task of *narrating* the solution to the problem rather than *discovering* the solution.

On the other hand, in the dyad presented in [2], comprised of two NSs, we observe a proliferation of verbs marked for progressive and only an occasional use of the atemporal present.

[2] a. NS1: What's he...he's bringing the goat...right?

    b. NS2: uh...um

    c. NS1: so...he's bringing the goat there...the...he

    d.   brings the cabbage...that one's no good because if

    e.   he's bringing the goat...first...right? If he

    f.   brings the wolf...the wolf eats the goat...

    g. NS2: yeah

    h. NS1: he brings the cabbage...you can cross that one. I

    i.   think next one...I suppose wouldn't you say?

Use of the progressive occurs at points when the interlocutors respond to an event as it takes place at that moment in the picture as if they were viewing a photograph. Thus, in line (a), NS1 apparently intends to ask a question, pauses, shifts into a declarative statement in the progressive, and ends with a confirmation check. The utterance indicates his attempt to respond to the immediate context of the picture as object rather than as an episode in the story. In lines (c-d), he repeats his description of the event as it is. The repetition, however, contains clues to his attempt to gain some control over the event. In other words, "so" and "there" operate as distancing mechanisms—the first functioning as an orientation strategy and the second locating the event at some distance. Thus, in the next utterance he uses the atemporal present ("he brings the cabbage"), apparently having concluded in his mind that this step in the puzzle has been resolved. The use of the atemporal present thus shows the speaker's achievement of self-regulation by means of his ability to express both distance and immediacy simultaneously.

We note a return to the progressive in line (e). Significantly, however, this follows some cognitive interruption, as indicated by the speaker's evaluation ("that one's no good") in line (d). The interruption generates the shift from the atemporal present to the progressive. It indicates a realization that his previous solution was incorrect and that he must develop an alternative one, which immediately triggers a return to the progressive.

The excerpt given in [3], taken from a later portion of the same protocol produced by the speakers considered in [2], shows a shift between the past and the progressive.

[3] a. NS1: uh...um...so I don't see how that can work. I don't

   b.   understand this [Looks at NS2 and smiles]

   c. NS2: he's the only one...that's the only one though

   d. NS1: OK...he brought the goat...right? OK...he brought

   e.   the goat. Then he's bringing the cabbage. That won't

   f.   do [Looks at the final picture in the display]

   g. NS2: no

   h. NS1: OK...so he's bringing [Looks at another picture]

   i. NS2: [Interrupts] He already brought the cabbage. Now...he's

   j.   bringing the goat [Looks at picture a]

As shown by Frawley and Lantolf (1985), the past tense appears to serve as a means for a speaker to gain control over a difficult task by distancing the event as an object. In [3], however, the regulatory function of the past turns out to be rather complex. The past is not consistently used for distancing: it may also reflect immediacy, as shown by the visual stimuli in the specific picture referred to. In lines (d-e), NS1 refers to a single picture that shows the goat on the right bank. The man is depicted rowing his boat towards the left bank, away from the goat. The wolf and the cabbage are on the left bank (see Figure 8.1, line (f)). In this context, use of the past tense ("he brought the goat") describes the event as it is. In his description, speaker NS1 simply reacts to the visual stimuli of the picture as an isolated frame. Furthermore, the very next utterance ("then he's bringing the cabbage") refers to another picture that immediately follows the previous one. This utterance serves the same regulatory function (see Figure 8.1, line (g)). Thus, both the past and the progressive, in this instance, show object-regulation. They form part of the same functional system in which the speaker is controlled by the events as objects, indicating that the individual does not understand the situation—that is he has not resolved the problem.

NS1's evaluation "that won't do" in lines (e-f) is also significant. It reflects awareness that his proposal was incorrect—an understanding of the task in that he recognizes a constraint imposed by the instruction. More importantly, however, he lacks control of the solution to the problem. In fact, the next picture (see line (g) in Figure 8.1) is the correct choice to the proper sequence. In other words, the speaker's visual perspective is tied to these two pictures only and does not take into account the other pictures in the set. Had he considered all of the pictures and their connection, he might have evaluated his choice positively. Furthermore, the fact that he alternated between the past and the progressive shows clearly that he had no control of the task, and, in an important sense, could not have selected the correct next frame, other than by chance.

NS2 also exhibits features of object-regulation. She, in fact, responds to two different stimuli in the same picture as an isolated frame. In the given set of pictures, only one shows the cabbage already situated on the right bank and the man transporting the goat toward this bank (see (a) in Figure 8.1). Thus, her utterance "he already brought the cabbage" in line (i) focuses on the cabbage, while "now...he's bringing the goat" in lines (i-j) describes the activity of the man. Thus, the two utterances are focused on two different stimuli in the same picture. They are descriptions of events as they are depicted in the frame. Both are instances of object-regulation. In short, in these instances, both NSs show object-regulated behavior.

A bit further on in the same protocol, NS2 reconginzes the principle underlying the solution to the problem—the idea of replacing or switching. We notice, at this point, a shift to the atemporal present, as illustrated in excerpt [4].

[4] a. NS2: this is it...look [stressed]

    b.   'cause then...he brings the...he puts the cabbage

    c.   down...and brings the wolf...the goat back and

    d.   then...switches the goat

    e. NS1: Oh...I see...we've been

    f. NS2: and then brings...the...that back

    g. NS1: all right

    h. NS2: all right?...so

    i. NS1: so

    j. NS2: so the first one

    k. NS1: [interrupts] we've been making mistakes

    l. NS2: yeah

From this point on, the interaction transpires exclusively in the atemporal present, indicating that the interlocutors now understand the solution to the puzzle and have control over the discourse, which now becomes not so much a *working out* of the solution as it is a *relating* of the solution. The remainder of the protocol is given in [5].

[5] a. NS1: and then...so he switches the cabbage for the goat...

    b.   which is four

    c. NS2: uh...um

    d. NS1: and then...he switches...the wolf...for the goat

    e. NS2: what's left?

    f. NS1: what ? [low tone]

    g. NS2: how many're left?

    h. NS1: all right...wait [low tone] that's the last one we

    i.   have...so

    j. NS2: that's five

k. NS1: he switches the wolf and the goat...so that is five

l.   ...am I right about it?

m. NS2: yeah...that's it

n. NS1: no...but...is that all?

o. NS2: OK...let's see...he goes with the goat...all

p.   right? He leaves the goat there. Goes back to the

q.   cabbage...brings the cabbage back . . .

r. NS1: brings the cabbage back [low tone]

s. NS2: realizes it's no good. Leaves the cabbage here and takes

t.   the goat...all right?

u. NS1: Yeah

v. NS2: goes back to the wolf...brings the wolf back and gets

w.   that so I guess.

x. NS1: that's it

Returning to the NS–NNS dyad, some additional evidence of the more complex regulatory functions of the past is provided in the speech of the NNS, as shown in [6].

[6] a. NNS: this will be two...A...B...because he left...

b.   first he took the go...goat [points out a picture]

c. NS: all right

d. NNS: put on one side. He left the goat and he is returning

e.   here

f. NS: right

g. NNS: it will be B

As the excerpt in [6] shows, the NNS identifies what is, in fact, the correct picture (B in her referential perspective). In utterances (a-b) and (d-e) she explains the reason for her identification. Her utterance, "and he is returning here," in (d-e) describes the event as it is, showing that she is trying to find a solution through a strategy that simply labels the event depicted rather than integrating it into a narrative (a solution). Similarly, her use of past "left" in lines (a) and (d) serves the function of object regulation. It describes the event as it is in picture (f) (see Figure 8.1). However, when the other verbs in (a) and (d) are taken into consideration, our understanding of the NNS's use of the past becomes more complicated. After her identification of picture (f), at which point she begins to explain the reason for her selection, she first uses the verb "left." At this juncture, her focus is evidently on the right side of picture (f), which shows the goat. As already mentioned, the man is shown rowing his boat away from the goat in this picture. Thus, her explanation begins with a direct reaction to the stimuli in the picture–object regulation. Her next utterance, however, ("first he took the goat") indicates a potential shift in focus. She could now be looking at picture (d) in the given set, which happens to be the first picture in the correct solution to the puzzle. That this picture could be the focus of her attention is evidenced by her mentioning of the picture as soon as she identifies the second picture in the correct sequence ("this will be two...A...B") in line (a). The first picture is included in her referential perspective. In this context, her use of the past is not directly influenced by the stimuli in the first picture which shows the wolf and the cabbage on the left bank. The man is shown transporting the goat toward the right bank. An object-regulated utterance would thus be something like "the man is taking the goat."

Given the above context, it seems plausible to argue that when the NNS utters "first he took the goat," she is referring to the first event in the sequence of events—a sequence in which the proper location of the picture is based. At this point, she may be actually attempting to narrate the solution to the problem. Her use of the past instead of the atemporal present, however, indicates that she has not achieved maximal control over the solution. The past tense in this context does not show object-regulation but an attempt to gain self-regulation through distancing. Her subsequent use of "put" and "left" is ambiguous. It may be that both instances of the past continue the cognitive distancing mode initiated with "took" in line (b), or it may show her return to object-regulation in that both verbs refer, once again, to the visual stimuli in picture (f) in the given set and describe the events as they are and not as they form part of the solution. In short, the NNS's speech at least expresses a momentary attempt towards self-regulation by means of distancing.

The final occurrence of the verb in the progressive "is returning" in line (d) shows the subject's return to the sense of immediacy in the stimuli. In this context, her use of "this" and "here" in lines (a) and (e) respectively frame a macrostructure, showing lack of spatial distance between the nonlinguistic referents and the speaker. They reinforce the overall sense of object-regulation. Within this framework, "took" in line (b) expresses a momentary attempt at distancing in order to gain self-regulation. Thus, the locative "there" may be implied in "first he took the goat" in line (b).

The interlocutors in both dyads, whether NS or NNS, use the past and the progressive in similar ways. The progressive, reflecting the immediacy of the events in the individual frames of the puzzle, shows lack of control over the task. The past tense, indicating distance from the events of the puzzle as facts, shows an attempt by the speakers to regain self-regulation. Moreover, the shifts in use of the atemporal present, the past, and the progressive reveal that regulatory behaviors vary during the carrying out of a task.

CONCLUSION

Frawley and Lantolf (1985) show that in the specific task they presented to their subjects the NNSs of English resemble the native-speaking children in their use of the progressive. Thus, the adult NNSs and the children form a behavioral continuum rather than a categorical distinction. Both showed object-regulation in their speech. This study extends the continuum to include adult native speakers as well. In other words, if a task proves to be sufficiently difficult, whatever the source of the difficulty may be, even a native speaker may exhibit object-regulation as reflected through deployment of specific features of his or her linguistic system. Thus, in terms of regulatory behavior, there is no absolute distinction between a NS and a NNS.

Furthermore, this study shows that the same individual in the same task may display both object- and self-regulation, hence demonstrating that task performance is dynamic. An individual speaker, in his or her performance across tasks or within a task, may access different modes of regularity behavior depending on how easy or difficult the task is. A completely self-regulated individual is at best an ideal. Similarly, the form function relationship is dynamic. The discussion in this chapter has shown that two different linguistic features (the present progressive and the past tense) can have the same cognitive function. On the other hand, the same linguistic feature in the speech of the same person can serve more than one function (the use of the past tense by the NNS in the NS–NNS dyad). Thus the schema for the regulatory functions of tense-aspect provided by Frawley and Lantolf must be seen as based on data drawn from a specific task-based activity. It is not an absolute model for all tasks, even within the mode of narrative discourse. The form-function relationship arises as a result of the way a specific individual interacts with a specific task in a specific environment and is therefore dynamic.

REFERENCES

Ahmed, M. (1988). *Speaking as cognitive regulation: A study of L1 and L2 dyadic problem-solving activity.* Unpublished doctoral dissertation. University of Delaware, Newark.

Frawley, W. (1987). *Text and Epistemology. Norwood, NJ: Ablex*

Frawley, W., & Lantolf, J.P. (1985). Second language discourse: A Vygotskyan perspective. *Applied Linguistics*, 6, 19–44.

Rommetveit, R. (1985). Language acquisition as increasing linguistic structuring of experience and symbolic behavior control. In J.V. Wertsch (Ed.), *Culture, communication, and cognition: Vygotskian perspectives.* (pp. 183–204). Cambridge: Cambridge University Press.

Ur, P. (1981). *Discussions that work: Task-centered fluency.* New York: Cambridge University Press.

Wertsch, J.V. (1985). *Vygotsky and the social formation of mind.* Cambridge, MA: Harvard University Press.

9

Same Task, Different Activities: Analysis of SLA Task from an Activity Theory Perspective*

Peter Coughlan

Department of TESL/Applied Linguistics
University of California at Los Angeles
Los Angeles, CA

Patricia A. Duff

University of British Columbia
Vancouver, Canada

Researchers in second language acquisition, like many of their counterparts in other human sciences, frequently employ experimental tasks in order to elicit a particular behavior from a subject or group of subjects. Underlying such experimental research is the belief that these tasks, and their resulting behavior, are scien-

* This chapter was first presented at the Conference on Theory Construction and Methodology in Second Language Research, Michigan State University, October, 1991. We are indebted to Roger Andersen, James Lantolf, Elinor Ochs, and John Schumann for comments on various version of this chapter.

tifically controllable and measurable,[1]—if the same task can be repeatedly performed with the same materials, tools, or instructions, then the activity resulting from repeat performances can be compared, either over time or across subjects. Since many facets of the research task's implementation are subject to the control of the researcher, tasks earn the status of *constants* in the research design.

In this chapter, we would like to question the assumption that research tasks are indeed constants in research design. Through close examination of some L2 data, elicited by means of a commonly used SLA research task, we wish to illustrate that what is often conceived of a fixed "task" is really quite variable, not only across subjects but within the same subject at different times.

Our findings reflect fundamental ideas underlying Vygotsky's (and more recent activity theorists') understanding of human interaction, in which world knowledge is a product of one's interaction with that world (Wertsch, 1981, 1991). This interaction can be symbolic (for example, with a text), physical (with an object), or it can involve relations between human beings. It is understood that the tasks in which humans engage exist within a larger, multi-level segment of human activity,[2] and that there is a dialectic relationship between humans and the interaction in which they are engaged. We propose that such a dynamic perspective should be considered when we analyze linguistic data collected through use of a research task. This entails shifting from a focus on linguistic production alone to a more comprehensive consideration of the activities in which such linguistic production occurs.

DIFFERENTIATING "TASK" FROM "ACTIVITY" IN SLA RESEARCH

For the purpose of the present discussion, it is important to make a distinction between "task" and "activity," since these terms are often employed interchangeably both in vernacular use and in SLA

---

[1] A belief borrowed from the physical and biological sciences, where "controlled" experiments are set up to allow for measurement of certain physical or chemical variables, such as heat, light, or oxygen. Lynch (1991) examines the way in which even "scientific" measurement can be viewed as ethnomethodological phenomena, or agree-upon norms within a given community of scholars.

[2] Leont'ev (1981) understands such levels to consist in "operations," or "actions" (how the activity is physically carried out), "goals" (why participants behave the way they do), and "motives" (why the activity is undertaken). None of these levels exists on its own, but reflects (and is a reflection of) other levels of interaction.

research.[3] A task, we propose, is a kind of "behavioral blueprint" provided to subjects in order to elicit linguistic data. In the realm of SLA, these blueprints, or research tasks, are motivated by a set of research objectives (for example, in order to get long, uninterrupted passages of speech containing instances of the past tense or nominal reference), and their selection is usually constrained by several practice considerations (including time; availability, number and proficiency of subjects; and transcription requirements).

An activity, by comparison, comprises the behavior that is actually produced when an individual (or group) performs a task. It is the process, as well as the outcome, of a task, examined in its sociocultural context.[4] Unlike a task, an activity has no set of objectives in and of itself—rather, participants have their own objectives, and act according to these and the researchers' objectives, all of which are negotiated (either implicitly or explicitly) over the course of the interaction. Furthermore, activities have no inherent parameters or boundaries, except imposed those by the task and by the interpretations and expectations of the individuals involved in a given task. In a language-based activity, constraints on task performance might include the level of knowledge (cultural, linguistic) shared by the interactants, or the time and interest they are willing, or able, to invest in order to complete the task at hand.

We will now examine some data that were originally collected by one of the authors for the purpose of analyzing L2 development, and are re-examined here to illustrate the relationship between task and activity. One dataset comes from a case study conducted in Canada, and the other from a larger-scale study conducted in Hungary. Through a look at L2 discourse generated by a commonly employed picture description task, we will show how the "same task" does not yield comparable results when performed by several individuals, or even when performed by the same individual on two different occasions.[5]

---

[3] See Crookes (1986) for an early review of literature on task.

[4] The heightened awareness of the role of context has perhaps led to the frequent use of the terms "setting" and "situation" or "context" as synonymous with "activity," in contradistinction to task, in much of the L2 literature.

[5] This consideration of the potential sameness of tasks does not originate with us, although it is an issue in need of greater attention in our field. Newman, Griffin, and Cole (1984), for example, faced much the same quandary regarding tasks in a study comparing children's performance on certain cognitive tasks in laboratory and nonlaboratory settings: "The term 'same task' has been placed in quotes because the sense in which two tasks can ever be considered the 'same' is a central question. A cognitive task cannot be specified independently of its social context. Cognitive tasks are always social constructions. Transformations of the social organization of the tasks in the study drastically changed the constraints

EXAMPLE OF DIFFERENT SUBJECTS DOING THE
SAME TASK

In the data being analyzed, five different subjects—one Cambodian and four Hungarians—were asked to describe a picture from a commonly used source (see Figure 9.1, "Beach Scene.") The subject in Example 1, a Cambodian man, "JDB," was a recent immigrant to Canada, enrolled in intensive government-sponsored ESL courses. He was meeting the interviewer for the third in a series of meetings, as part of a longitudinal study (Duff, in press). JDB was told from the outset that he was being interviewed in order for the researcher to study his language development and to learn more about his native culture and his experiences in Cambodia and Canada. He was paid for each hour-long meeting. Interviews took place roughly every week for the first six months, but for the next year occurred every few weeks. The final interview (from which one of our examples is taken) took place one year after regular meetings had stopped.

The data collected from the subjects in Examples 2 through 5 come from a 15- to 20-minute structured interview conducted with students learning EFL at secondary schools in Hungary.[6] The purpose behind these interviews was to gather information about Hungarian dual-language students' background and experiences, their attitudes toward their EFL and content area learning situation at school, and especially their English language ability, which was monitored longitudinally for several dozen subjects as part of a larger evaluation of dual-language school education in that country (Duff, 1991).

As we hope the examples will illustrate, the activity (or rather, that portion of the activity that is observable through the discourse) produced a number of different forms in response to the so-called same task. To explain these diverse results, we will look at

---

on behavior, thereby rendering the tasks instantly different according to widely shared ideas of what constitutes a task in cognitive psychology. It was hoped that highlighting the way in which efforts failed to make the 'same task' occur in different settings would lead to a clearer specification of the class of social constructions represented by such activities as tests and experiment" (LCHC 1978, 1979, p. 175). While these researchers are concerned with differences in subjects' conceptualization and implementation of tasks in rather different settings, our own research suggests that even in what appears to be a similar setting (laboratory-like, face-to-face interviews with a researcher), subjects may vary considerably in their interaction with the researcher and with the task.

[6] All subjects were third year secondary school girls.

FIGURE 9.1   Prompt used for picture description task

In Heaton (1966) Composition Through Pictures. London: Longman.

the way the picture description task is introduced by the interviewer into the larger activity in which it is embedded, and how the
subjects' linguistic production reflects (or fails to reflect) their
apparent attitudes toward, or interpretation of, the picture description task.

The meeting the JDB from which Example 1 comes began with
some general conversation, followed by this picture description:

Example 1[7]

```
01  I:  Okay, now—what I'm going to ask you is (4.0) ((looks
02      through notes)) to describe—a picture, (2.0)
03      ((speaking softly)) which one? yeah this one. I
04      want you to tell me—or make a story, (0.6) about
05      this picture? (0.3) Anything.
06      (11.0)
07  S:  This picture as ((=at)) the: seaside—sea, ((@))
08      seaside? (1.4) At the seaside. (1.0) uh s—maybe this
09      uh hotel, hotel oh no? (2.0) I think this—it is a—
10      hotel and—restaurant (0.4) for—holy-holiday—days
11      people to visits at the seaside and they play
12      something thats they like. ((S is playing with
13      paper which crackles next to microphone))
14      (4.0)
15  I:  Maybe you can put it here. ((referring to paper))
16  S:  Oh yes. (3.0) The old man is—the old man whoo: (1.4)
17      has the glasses and with (2.6) and with hat, they
```

---

[7] Transcription conventions can be found in Appendix A.

18		sitting on the—chair. (3.6) They read-ing a—
19		newspaper, (0.4) and—behinds him has the three
20		children, (2.0) one girl and—two s—two boy. Maybe
21		they dancing because the—radio turn on? ((@))
22		turn ons about music. And they happy. They
23		dancing. (2.4) An:d over:—his head has a (1.4)
24		ball? (@) Maybe ball yes. (1.4) And behind(s) far
25		away (1.4) him, has a (4.0) alot os peo-ple. Some
26		peo—uh some people they sitting, (2.0) on the chair,
27		and—some people they standing, and some people
28		they sitting on the (1.0) on the: (1.0) sam.
29		((end of the cassette tape; I turns tape over))
30	I:	Oka:y? (1.0) Sorry.
31	S:	xx
32	I:	Which one? Same?
33		((referring to S's last discernible word))
34	S:	S(w)aeme.
35	I:	Oh swim yeah. [Swim
36		[Y'know?
37	I:	Yeah
38	S:	Same (1.0) near the sea?
39	I:	Yeah.
40	S:	Seaside has same.
41		(2.0)
42	I:	Yeah. Swimming? (0.6) Like this?
43		((I demonstrates))
44	S:	No swimming.
45	I:	On the ground?
46	S:	Yes ground!
47	I:	Oh sand.
48	S:	Sand?
49	I:	Yeah
50	S:	Yes sand.
51	I:	Mhm,
52		(8.0)
53	S:	And (1.0) righthishand beside—at the: (0.6) at the
54		sea, has the: (0.4) six bot. Yeah six bot, (0.8) and
55		(3.0) a big boat has people sitting alot of and some
56		people they—jum—uh they jum (0.4) into- the water
57		and [swimming.
58	I:	[Mhm,
59	S:	Maybe they very happy. (0.4) And over the sea has
60		(1.0) of bird—flying on the sky. ((S clears throat))
61		(1.0) And he is uh—cameraman, (0.8) they take un:
62		potograss to (a/the) strongman ((@)) (.4) run into
63		the sea. And one lady, he: (4.5) and one lady, they
64		gries about (3.0) about the strongman runs

65   into the sea. And they happy. And some people,
66   and one old man who with the camera, (2.0) they
67   laugh-uh he laughing, and they take his potograss
68   also. Behind him has—one boy—and maybe his
69   wi(fe). (1.0) And behind his wi(fe) maybe (2.5)
70   grindmother or grindfather. (2.0) Altogether, they
71   happy about that. (4.0) An:d (1.0) he is the—
72   sleeping?, sleeping on the—on the sand, near, on
73   the sam—and the children he has the—oh I dunno.
74   (4.0) What's this?
75 I: This one? Shovel?
76 S: Yeah.
77 I: Sho[vel
78 S: [Sovel. (0.4) And one boy's (.6) he: (1.0) s- he has
79   sovvor, (3.0) take the groun(d)—through the: (1.0)
80   through his leg. And the man, (0.6) they don't
81   know everything. Because they sleeping. His head
82   (0.4) on the rokt. (1.4) And behind- and behind the
83   boy has—small basket. (5.5) I think this picture-
84   nnear—uh close the s—seasides.
85 I: Mhm?
86 S: Yeah.
87   (1.5)
88 I: In Cambodia do you have—beach or—near the
89   seaside?
90 S: I never, I never to visit at seaside.
91 I: Just—you're in the [city?
92 S: [Yes because my home (0.4)
93   faraway from seaside.
94 I: Mmm.
    ((continues with discussion about Cambodia))

The picture description task in this example comes as the first task in an hour-long meeting held at the researcher's home, after a few minutes of informal discussion. This is the third consecutive meeting in which a picture-description task has been presented to JDB. The interviewer introduces the task after pausing to look through her notebook for the appropriate materials. She tells JDB that she wants him to "describe—a picture," and after a two-second pause, she adds "tell me—or make a story, about this picture." After another three-second pause, she adds the word "anything." This is followed by a very long pause (interactionally speaking), after which JDB begins to describe the picture in front of him.

Juding from his linguistic output, JDB opts for the first of the options presented by the researcher (that is, to "describe a picture" rather than "make a story"), since his output is surely more descriptive than storylike in nature. At any point in his description where he must draw inferences from the limited information available in the picture—for example, the exact function of a building (lines 1: 08-09) or the motivation behind the characters' dancing (lines 1: 20-21)—he qualifies his observations with the phrases "I think" or "maybe." JDB adheres closely to a straightforward description of the picture, and, except when his description breaks down due to interaction with the interviewer, he produces what most researchers would consider a model picture description, rich with detail. Through this task, one of the interviewer's underlying objectives—eliciting existential constructions—was successfully met.

Because we cannot conduct a retrospective interview with JDB about this session, which took place more than five years ago, we have no way of knowing exactly how he conceived of the task, except through the recorded discourse. Though JDB appears to perform the task as desired, and produces certain types of existential constructions, he also frequently strays from the "ideal form" (Labov, 1984) of the task by engaging the interviewer during its execution. For example, he ends certain statements with rising intonation, to elicit confirmation of the interviewer's understanding (Example 1: lines 08, 09, 21). At one point in this description (1: 74) he asks the interviewer for help with a vocabulary word, "shovel," which she supplies (compromisingly so, in view of her interest in his vocabulary development, circumlocution, and so on). There is also an extended sequence (1: 28-51) referred to above, in which the interviewer and JDB together attempt to clarify one of JDB's utterances, pivoting on the interviewer's misunderstanding of the word "sand." (This extended clarification sequence appears to result from JDB's pronunciation /sæm/ and the interviewer's shifting her attention away from JDB's speech and toward the task of turning over the cassette tape.) The intended monologue thus occasionally becomes a dialogue between subject and interviewer, and this interaction has a discernible effect on the subject's linguistic output. The closer we examine the discourse produced by this task, the more difficult it becomes to attribute specific aspects of the discourse to the subject or to the researcher, since both were doing the task, not just the subject.

Examples 2 through 5, though elicited by the same picture description task used in Example 1, yield quite different results from those above. The task in these examples comes as one in a series given during a 20-minute interview with subjects whom the interviewer is meeting for the first time at their school. The picture description task is preceded by a discussion of the student's family life (prompted by a cartoon), which was frequently protracted and emotional. The description is in turn followed by a number of other tasks, ranging from elicited imitation to personal narrative.

Example 2

```
01  S:  and uh we uh: don't go on an excursion,
02  I:  Mmm. They are too busy?
03  S:  Yes.
04  I:  Gee. Okay good. Now I'd like you to tell me about
05      that scene. (2.0)
06  S:  I think uh uh it's uh a seaside ((@)) and un—I saw-I
07      saw a man uh who—uh who is uh lying on the—who
08      is lying on the beach, and uh I think his uh son uh
09      put—uh some—uh some—uh (3.0) put some—uh
10      (2.0) stones—on him, ((@)) and I saw a man uh who
11      uh who is reading a newspaper, and (2.0) uh I saw—
12      and I see un—three children, who are playing ((@))
13      and shouting ((@)), and uh mm—I—uh I see uh a
14      man—((@)) and I can see a man uh who uh who is
15      running, uh because uh he-uhm (1.0) he saw a
16      woman—uh who can't swim ((@)) and uh uh this
17      woman uh perhaps uh say uh "help help" ((smiles))
18  I:  Mhm, Okay great. You see a lot of things in that
19      picture. Tch. Now what I'm going to have you do is
20      listen to this tape, and you're gonna hear eighteen
21      sentences...
```

Example 3

```
01  I:  Okay the next thing is—could you describe this
02      picture to me, in as much detail as possible.
03  S:  Yeah. (3.5) Maybee: (1.0) I think it's a beach ((@))
04      and the people here are recording maybe a film?
05      ((@)) It's something like (0.4) uhh: the Jaw. Do you
06      know the Jaws?
07  I:  Oh Jaws, uhhuh,
08  S:  Jaws?
09  I:  Yea:h.
10  S:  Because (0.2) uhh (4.0) maybe this girl (0.6) will get
11      drown ((@)) or killed by a jaw—((@)) by a shark,
12      ((@)) if this man won't—(2.0) if this man will be
13      late. ((@)) Then there are some s—uh children—who
14      are really happy ((@)) because (1.5) really—maybe
15      it's just a vacation, ((@)) a holiday, ((@)) and uh:
16      this boy wanna cover—(1.0) wants to cover his
17      father, ((@)) and uhh: everybody is very happy and
```

18   very (1.0) ca:lm ((@)) And (2.0) here's a city ((@))
19   and (1.0) maybe it can be in Greece because the:
20   houses are all white ((Mmm)), then (1.0) What else
21   can I say? Mmm.
22 I: Oh that—that's good. That's plenty. Thanks.
23 S: Yes?
24 I: I have to give you so many things. Now the next
25   thing...

Example 4
01 I: Now I'm going to show you an other picture, (1.0)
02   and (1.0) I'd like you to describe it in as much detail
03   as you can, please?
04 S: yeah so let's say it is in America, California,
05 I: Mhm x guess [so
06 S: [in the beach, uh this is July, ((@)) uh-
07   these people have vacation here, ((@)) and uh (2.0) they are
08   enjoying their time ((@)) as I see, they are reading,
09   playing and (1.4) uh there are some men who- who
10   are making film, ((@)) maybe the shark, ((@))
11   because I see somebody who's shouting, ((@)) and
12   uh (2.0) what else?
13   (3.0)
14 I: Why do you think it's California.
15 S: Because—((little laugh)) well I don't think but that-
16   that is my favorite place,
17 I: Why?
18 S: Um (0.6) I don't know I like that place and ((@))
19   because Michael Jackson lives there—somewhere
20   there ((smiles)).
21 I: Well I live there too.
22 S: Really?
23 I: Yeah: Okay good thanks. Next, I'm going to have
24   you listen...to some sentences—and after...

Example 5
01 I: Mm. That's too bad. Okay I'm gonna show you a—
02   more cheerful scene here, ((referring to prior
03   discussion on theme of divorce among parents)) of—
04   something with—lots of things are going on in it,
05   ((I pulls out picture)) and I wonder if you can
06   describe to me—what's happening there.
07 S: Mm yes. This is a ((clears throat)) summer picture
08   ((@)) (1.4) uh:m it could be in Hungary—by Lake
09   Balaton, (0.8) why not. an:d (1.4) some tourists
10   taking pictures, and (1.0) and the man (2.0) uhm:
11   (2.0) with the video camera, ((@)) and the girl who

```
12      cannot swim and (4.0) ((@)) what else? children
13      (1.0) playing with sand and (4.0) [mm
14 I:                                     [Okay—that's good thank
15      you. Now I'm going to ask you to listen to some sentences
16      on this machine...
```

Many of the differences between Example 1 and Examples 2 through 5 may be explained by looking at the context in which the task was introduced. In Example 1, there is abundant time for the interviewer and subject to go about their business: They have agreed to meet on a regular basis for an unspecified number of meetings, and the picture description is one of just a few tasks scheduled to take place in one hour. (Sometimes these tasks were abandoned if more urgent topics presented themselves—again a reflection of ongoing negotiation of the activity by researcher and subject.) Thus, the interviewer can afford to allow the picture description task to drift back into informal conversation (from which it originated), with no pressing need to introduce the next task. Indeed, the researcher later reflected that it was her intention to make transitions from task to task as smooth and as informal as possible, and also would be most likely to personally engage JDB. This is not true in the latter four examples, where there is a 20 minute maximum period allotted for many different tasks (and where students often arrived late or had classes to return to immediately after). The transcripts consequently reveal very little transition time between the tasks, since the interviewer, usually after receiving a cue from the subjects that they had no more to say (especially 3: 20-21, "What else can I say?"; 4: 12, and 5: 12, "what else?"), quickly and formulaically ends the task with an assessment (2: 18, "Okay great"; 3: 22, "that's good"; 4: 23, "That's plenty"; 5: 14, "Thanks") and introduces the next task, an elicited imitation task. By giving the subjects limited opportunity to produce talk that might expand on the picture description task, the interviewer attempts to control the amount of time allotted to each task.

While expansion on topics such as Michael Jackson (4: 19), *Jaws* (3: 5-7), or Greece (3: 19) might have been welcomed in an interview setting similar to that found in Example 1, here the interviewer gives what appear to be minimal responses to expansion. In one exception, (4:14 -17), the interviewer does appear to elicit "off-task" talk from the subject (similar to line 1: 88, when she asks JDB about the beaches in Cambodia), but soon cuts this elicited talk short in order to move on to the next task (4: 23).

Examples 2 through 5 are quite varied, in spite of the relatively uniform conditions under which the task is introduced to the subjects,[8] and the relatively little time subjects are engaged in the task. The subject in Example 2, through her frequent use of "I saw" and "I see," appears to interpret the task as an exercise in visual acuity, the object of which is to notice (and name) as many things in the picture as possible.[9] In Example 3, the subject sees it as her task (or her right) to relate the picture to personal experience, trying perhaps to engage the interviewer through introduction of possible shared knowledge (a film and a popular tourist spot), and to increase the cognitive and social sophistication of the activity. Rather than give a simple description, she couches her observations in hypothetical statements (3: 05, "It's something like (0.4) uhh: the Jaw"; 3: 19, "maybe it can be in Greece"). In Example 4, the subject also invokes experience in the form of cultural knowledge, by providing the scene with a hypothetical setting (California).[10] The subject in Example 5 begins by suggesting a setting closer to home (based on personal experience) and proceeds to simply list the people in the picture and the activities they are engaged in. Although she was later discovered to be one of the most advanced subjects of the group and one who had spent time in the United States, her discourse on this task provided a minimum of inflected verbs and a maximum of noun phrases (that is, a list) illustrative of talk traditionally attributed to less advanced speakers. Perhaps one could infer from her performance on this task, juxtaposed with her earlier expansive discussion of social issues, that the picture-description task seemed so unnatural and devoid of communicative interest or import that it did not warrant further elaboration.

The variety of task interpretations seen above, and the language that subjects use to express such interpretations, offers contradictory evidence to researchers' beliefs that if they control for task in their research, they will be able to elicit "a single discourse type," or that by using a variety of tasks, it is possible to "prevent their results being attributable to the task itself" (Crookes, p. 125, 1991).

---

[8] With less proficient students, instructions were at times necessarily paraphrased to facilitate comprehension of tasks.

[9] The subject in Example 2 does not attend a dual-language school, but is in an English-track at a normal Hungarian high school; thus, a possible source of difference from those in Examples 3 through 5. That is, she has had less exposure to such tasks, to English input, and to English-speaking interlocutors than her counterparts at the neighboring dual-language school.

[10] In later informal talk with the researcher, the subject retracts her original hypothetical setting of the picture.

Even with a single, relatively controlled task, a range of discourse types may result from subjects' multiple interpretations of that task, their desire (as well as that of the researcher) to establish interpersonal bonds with their interlocutor, their attempt to make the picture description task a more interesting one by evaluating events, making comparisons to personal experience, playing language games, and so on.

EXAMPLE OF A REPEATED "SAME TASK"

We have attempted to illustrate that the same basic task can be conceptualized differently by different people, though the contexts surrounding such a task appear to be quite similar. We would now like to show that the "same task" also becomes a different entity over time when repeated by the same person—as it changes from a picture description to a picture *re*-description.

Test-retest procedures are common in the L2 literature, though some linguists have reported problems with such methods. Clancy (n.d.), Erbaugh (1990), and Tannen (1980), for example, have shown that, with respect to first language task-related discourse, the same task may be interpreted in different ways by different subjects, for example, as a memory test (in the case of video retelling task), and as a multiple single-picture description exercise (in the case of a picture sequence task). Subjects are often asked to perform the same task (such as a picture description or a video retelling) on two occasions, so that the data from the two events can be compared (Duff, in press).[11] In analyzing data collected from such test-retest procedures, it is assumed that differences in task performance can be attributed to learning (cognitive development) that has taken place in the interim.

The following example is a "retest" in which JDB (the subject from Example 1) is administered the same picture-description task two years and two months later, during the final interview in the longitudinal study. The task is introduced in the middle of what became a two-hour session, following an extended informal discussion between JDB and the interviewer, who had not met for one year. Example 6 is the second of three picture-description tasks re-

---

[11] Duff discusses the "inherent contradiction" (cf. Labov, 1984) in some retest procedures where authenticity and controllability are inversely related, the repeated task becoming increasingly contrived over time.

administered during that session. The interviewer's intention with this task was primarily to examine the development of JDB's production of existential constructions over the two years she had worked with him.

Example 6
```
01  I:  It's bad when you're driving on the highway or
02      something like that. Okay:, anything else about
03      that? (3.0) Then I'll give you this one which should
04      look familiar too.
05      (6.0)
06  S:  The picture on x on the beach, ((@)) (9.0) ((Laugh))
07      I don't know what's happen. ((S plays with
08      microphone)) Maybe the people they go to—on
09      vacation, ((@))
10      (4.0)
11  I:  Can you describe the scene?
12      (8.0)
13  S:  x cameraman?
14  I:  Yeah. This guy? ((I points))
15  S:  Oh he's
16      (2.0)
17  I:  You mean?
18  S:  Yeah. He's take—he::: he took a picture. I think
19      maybe the lady (4.0) she's going drown on- in the
20      water, ((@)) and he (1.0) he need(s)
21      some help ((@)).
22      (4.8)
23  I:  Okay what else? What about this picture?
24      (11.0)
25  S:  Ah this man I think he—he's not happy I think
26      because ah the children play (0.6) ((@)) to make a
27      noisy. ((@)) (e.0) @)) (3.0) Ah I dunno ((S sniggers))
28  I:  Kay what about this kid?
29  S:  Oh: he: (1.4) Maybe he- his father sleeping. ((@))
30      I'm not sure. ((@)) And he- (3.0) he put a sand (1.0)
31      on his leg.
32  I:  Yeah?
33  S:  Yeah.
34  I:  Okay, and then there's one more. Twenty four.
35      ((referring to picture number; interviewer takes
36      picture out)) (I want) to look at this one. You can
37      describe that situation...
```

In this example, the interviewer introduces the picture in the task as one that "should look familiar," yet JDB claims not to "know what's happen" (6: 07), and follows with a very general statement,

"Maybe the people they go to—on vacation" (6: 08 and 09). The interviewer then repeats that task instructions, and JDB labels one of the characters in the picture. The interviewer continues her prompting throughout the task (at 6: 14, 23, and 28), apparently to encourage a more detailed, elaborate, or syntactically complex response from JDB.

We would expect that, due to the intervening years of exposure to English (through work and ESL classes in an English-speaking country), JDB's response to this retelling would reflect progress at the linguistic level (it would be more "grammatical"), as well as at the discourse level (he would be more familiar with the "art" of doing picture descriptions and other classroom and research tasks.). Instead, his language production in this second exposure to the same task appears much less fluent, and his confidence in the ability to do the task appears to have diminished as well. An evaluation of his acquisition of extential constructions through a pre- and post-comparison based on the two passages suggests that JDB had not acquired target English constructions (*there BE NP*), but that he had lost his former "has a NP" existential, which was so productive in Example 1. The combination of unclearly introduced referents (6: 08, 13) and interviewer prompting/pointing (6: 11, 14, 17, 23) in the discourse makes an analysis of JDB's nominal reference problematic in this example. This leads us to seek an understanding of these anomalous findings at a different level of analysis: one that addresses the roles of the researcher and subject in their jointly constructed activity.

THE ROLES OF SUBJECT AND RESEARCHER DURING THE ACTIVITY

Data collection and analysis in SLA research (particularly L2 grammar-oriented studies) has traditionally focused on individual subjects' linguistic abilities, rather than on the interaction between interviewer and subject. While an implicit goal in SLA research is to design tasks that elicit linguistic output from the subject, it is clear in face-to-face interview situations that the interviewer plays a large role in shaping the subject's production.[12]

---

[12] This phenomenon has been noted in the other research as well. Marlaine (1990), for instance, discusses the "invisible collaboration" in the context of special education clinicians and children during diagnostic interviews. Brigg (1986) provides a detailed discussion of the practice and peril of interviewing from an anthropological perspective.

She does this by providing needed (or solicited) vocabulary, additional instructions about the task, questions or comments to focus the subject's attention, positive signals (verbal and nonverbal) when a task is going "correctly" or negative ones when it is not, pauses to allow (or compel) the subject to speak, and introductions or evaluations (cued by the subject's moves) to frame the task in its surrounding discourse. She is through her ostensibly "minimal" co-participation in the task, indicating what to her constitutes a proper "picture-description" activity. Surely this influences the outcome of a task, whether it is the subject's first or second exposure to it.

This interaction puts us at odds as to how to characterize "subject" or "researcher" in the activity. It is tempting to label the interviewer as the "expert," who is in control of the task, and the subject as the "novice," who follows instructions and performs according to the interviewer's wishes. In our data, however, we find numerous instances where (perhaps because we are looking at performance-oriented rather than learning-oriented interaction) the relationship of expert and novice is not the best way to characterize the interaction. In Example 3, for instance, the subject becomes the "expert" when she draws a connection between the picture in the task and the movie "The Jaw" (3: 05)—since it has not been overtly stated, the interviewer can only assume why such a connection has been made. One turn later, however, the interviewer becomes the expert when she provides the subject, who is linguistically and culturally (in this particular domain) less expert than she, with the correct movie title. In Example 4, the subject initially displays her knowledge of beach scenes by supplying the proposition that the picture could be a scene from California, but soon after invokes the interviewer's knowledge (expertise) about California by showing interest in the fact that she lives there, and by inviting expansion on it (4: 22). At the same time, she demonstrates expertise about (or at least familiarity with) a popular American musician, who also apparently resides in California (4: 19). In spite of the subject's interest in pursuing the topic, the researcher tables it (by means of her expert status as researcher, and the power thereby vested in her) due to time constraints imposed by the data collection objective (4: 23).

The interaction is thus constructed by both participants in a moment-by-moment fashion as they go about their task together, such that the attribution of a single role to each participant is misleading, in much the same way as it is erroneous to assume that subjects view the task itself in a single way. Certain factors about the participants do appear to shape the interaction (for example, researcher versus subject, first versus second-language speaker); these factors, however, are important not in and of themselves, but are made important due to their co-occurrence in this particular context, involving this particular task.

The question of subject and researcher roles is made more problematic because the task—to describe a picture—is not a naturally "communicative" activity. Because both participants have visual access to the picture being described, there is no need for information to flow from one participant to the other, except at a linguistic level, specifically for the purpose of data collection. Linguistic data collected through this research task therefore reflects the ambiguous and constrained interaction between the participants, whose primary task becomes speaking for the sake of speaking, listening for the sake of facilitating further speech, or, in other words, language production as an end in itself.

An instance of this can be found in Example 2, where the interviewer closes the task with the compliment "You see a lot of things in that picture." This utterance sounds like praise for the subject's ability to visually decode the picture (since this is how the subject appears to have chosen to approach the task) and is reminiscent of "motherese" or "teacherese" feedback. The interviewer's comment (probably an attempt to praise or compliment the subject for plentiful verbal production, and also as a way for the researcher to note, for future analysis, the subject's orientation to the task) appears in retrospect to be rather stilted or unnatural, though for the subject it may fall within the range of appropriate utterances, given the similarity of the research task to other language-learning contexts, or second language activities, the subject may be familiar with.

Another effect of such laboratory-like tasks is that participants may subvert the immediate goal (description of a picture) in their search for appropriate interactional roles during the course of a task. The numerous instances of interaction between the interviewer and subject presented in the previous section suggest that both subject and interviewer look for (or attempt to create) a communicative side to the picture-description task, or even a different communicative task altogether.[13]

---

[13] In another research task with JDB involving picture-sequence narration, we became acutely aware of the complexity of the interviewer–subject role relationship. In one such task, there was extensive collaboration by interviewer and subject in the narration, since JDB had difficulty constructing a plausible story for a number of reasons—for example, he could suggest neither a plausible setting for the story nor the relationship between the two characters who appeared in the story, partly because of his lack of cultural familiarity with the depicted setting.

The more reciprocal interaction that springs up through the completion of the task (and that resembles familiar forms of teaching and learning, or transfer of information from "expert" to "novice") interferes with the researcher's implicit goal of eliciting uninterrupted discourse. At the same time this bidirectional exchange forms the basis for more meaningful, interpersonal communication. Which interaction behavior—that planned by the researcher, or that arising spontaneously between researcher and subject—will supply us with more information about a particular learner's development or performance in a second language setting? While second language acquisition researchers' ideal subject may be one who produces language without recourse to the interviewer's knowledge or expertise, perhaps the more successful second language user (from a "real world" perspective) is one who uses interlocutors to help create meaning, despite limited linguistic resources.[14]

FUTURE DIRECTIONS AND ISSUES

The preceding analysis has, we hope, illustrated the notion that second language data cannot be neatly removed from the sociocultural context in which is was created or collected. A number of SLA researchers still believe that carefully designed linguistic data collection techniques (or tasks) can allow us to isolate and quantify "uncontaminated" interlanguage. This chapter serves as a reminder that any event that generates communicative language is unique—an activity born from a particular constellation of actors, settings, tasks, motivations, and histories. A linguistic event never duplicates a past one, and can never be truly replicated in the future. For these reasons, we must be careful when we assume that "task" is indeed a constant in our measurements: While the task or blueprint may be the same, the activity it generates will be unique. We must therefore exercise caution when attempting to generalize about data from similar, but distinct, activities.

We stand to learn a lot about what goes on in the minds and experiences of individual language learners by looking at the activity that emerges from interactive second language situations. Perhaps, through this kind of discourse-based investigation, we

---

[14] Hatch (1978, 1983) arrives at similar conclusions through her work on interactionism and SLA. See also Hatch and Hawkins (1985), and Hatch, Flashner, and Hunt (1986).

will discover that variation in second language acquisition is not entirely *intra*personal—rather, some answers must reside in the *inter*personal relationships among participants engaged in second language activities, and in subject–task relationships. In short, it would be useful for SLA researchers to look more closely at the activity that surrounds the data they have collected, and to use this information to shed light on otherwise anomalous results.

APPENDIX A
TRANSCRIPTION CONVENTIONS

Notation	Meaning
(0.5)	inter- or intraturn pauses, measured in tenths of seconds
(())	researcher comments/clarifications
((@))	interviewer backchanneling
?	rising intonation
,	slightly rising intonation
.	falling intonation
:	sound stretch
[	onset of overlap
xx	unclear utterance
( )	alternative hearings of utterance

REFERENCES

Brigg, C. (1986). *Learning how to ask: A sociolinguistic appraisal of the role of the interview in social science research.* New York: Cambridge University Press.

Clancy, P. (N.D.). *Referential strategies in the narratives of Japanese children.* Unpublished manuscript, University of California, Santa Barbara.

Crookes, G. (1986). *Task classification: A cross-disciplinary view.* (Tech. Rep. No. 4). Honolulu: University of Hawaii, Center for Second Language Classroom Research.

Crookes, G. (1991). Second language speech production research: A methodologically oriented review. *Studies in Second Language Acquisition, 13,* 113–132.

Duff, P. (1991): Innovations in foreign language education: An evaluation of three Hungarian-English dual-language programs. *Journal of Multilingual and Multicultural Development, 12,* 459–476.

Duff, P. (in press). Tasks and interlanguage performance: An SLA research perspective. In G. Crookes & S. Gass (Eds.), *Tasks in language learning: Integrating theory and practice.* Clevedon, English: Multilingual Matters.

Erbaugh, M.S. (1990). Mandarin oral narratives compared with English: The Pear/Guava stories. *Journal of the Chinese Language teachers Association, 25* (2), 21–42.

Hatch, E. (1978). *Second language acquisition: A book of readings.* Rowley, MA: Newbury House.

Hatch, E. (1983). *Psycholinguistics: A second language perspective.* Rowley, MA: Newbury House.

Hatch, E., & Hawkins, B. (1985). Second language acquisition: An experiential approach. In S. Rosenberg (Ed.), *Advances in Applied Psycholinguistics: Vol. 2* (pp. 241–283). New York: Cambridge University Press.

Hatch, E., Flashner, V., & Hunt, L. (1986). The experiential model and language teaching. In R. Day (Ed.), *Talking to learn: Conversation in second language acquisition* (pp. 5–22). Rowley, MA: Newbury House.

Heaton, J. (1966) *Composition through pictures.* London: Longman.

Labov, W. (1984). Field methods of the project on linguistic change and variation. In F. Baugh & J. Sherzer (Eds.), *Language in use: Readings in sociolinguistics* (pp. 28–53). Englewood Cliffs, NJ: Prentice Hall.

LCHC. (1978). Cognition as a residual category in anthropology. *Annual Review of Anthropology, 7,* 51–69.

LCHC. (1979). What's cultural about cross-cultural psychology? *Annual Review of Psychology, 30,* 145–172.

Leont'ev, A.N. (1981). The problem of activity in psychology. In J. Wertsch (Ed.), *The concept of activity in Soviet psychology* (pp. 37–71). Armonk, NY: M.E. Sharpe.

Lynch, M. (1991). Method: measurement—ordinary and scientific measurement as ethnomethodological phenomena. In G. Button (Ed.), *Ethnomethodology and the human sciences* (pp. 77–108). New York: Cambridge University Press.

Marlaine, C. (1990). On questions, communication and bias: Educational testing as "invisible" collaboration. *Perspectives on Social Problems, 2,* 231–258.

Newman, D., Griffin, P., & Cole, M. (1984). Social constraints in laboratory and classroom. In B. Rogoff & J. Lave (Eds.), *Everyday cognition: Its development in social context* (pp. 172–193). Cambridge, MA: Harvard University Press.

Tannen, D. (1980). A comparative analysis of oral narrative strategies: Athenian Greek and American English. In W. Chafe (Ed.), *The pear stories: Cognitive, cultural, and linguistic aspects of narrative production* (pp. 51–87). Norwood, NJ: Ablex.

Wertsch, J. (1981). The concept of activity in Soviet psychology: An introduction. In J. Wertsch (Ed.), *The concept of activity in Soviet psychology* (pp. 3–36). Armonk, NY: M.E. Sharpe.

Wertsch, J. (1991). *Voices of the mind: A sociocultural approach to mediated action.* Cambridge: MA: Harvard University Press.

10

The Role of Learner Goals in L2 Success

Barbara Gillette

Department of Modern Languages and
*   Literatures*
University of Delaware
Newark, DE

INTRODUCTION

This chapter addresses the issue of individual differences in L2 achievement. It reports on the results of a longitudinal study of three effective and three ineffective language learners in a required third-semester language course (Intermediate French I) at the University of Delaware. The six participants were chosen based on two neutral measures of their language skills, a cloze test (see Oller, 1979) and an oral imitation task (see Henning, 1983), as well as biodata, class observation, and writing samples. In an effort to include learner satisfaction as a criterion for success in SLA, self-ratings and essays describing the participants' experience as language learners were also used in the selection process.

After this initial screening by the author, who was also the instructor of the class, all six candidates identified through the above measures agreed to participate in the present study. The students kept a learner's diary for the remainder of the semester and were available for interviews concerning their language learning histories. They also completed questionnaires assessing attitude and motivation (see Gardner & Lambert, 1972). The observation of six students continued for a full semester and took account of as much of their learning behavior in and out of class as feasible.

Examining the whole person in a rich natural setting helped elaborate a more complete picture of each student's language learning effort and its relative success or failure than has been the case in quantitative studies of language learning. Instead of focusing only on aptitude, attitude, or some other casual variable presumed to drive SLA, this study views each learner as a motivated human being, whose existential experience, world view, and intentions all influence classroom behavior. The multiple data sources used clarify and corroborate each other, a factor particularly important where much of the data stem from self-reports. A further means to "validate" qualitative data, according to Chaudron (1988), is to apply an independent theory to the interpretation of such data.

The theoretical framework used in this investigation is that developed within the Vygotskian school of sociocultural theory (Vygotsky, 1978, 1986). According to this theory, the initial motive of an activity determines the character of that activity. Thus, for instance, if two students are asked to write an essay in a second language class, but one student's motive for being in the class is simply to fulfill a requirement, while the other genuinely desires to learn the language, they are not engaged in the same activity. The resulting essays may appear similar on the surface, but different learning outcomes can be expected when learners have such divergent orientations to the task (Galperin, 1980). In the analysis to be presented here, it will be demonstrated that individuals identified as effective and ineffective language learners by their test scores and overall performance did indeed have divergent reasons for engaging in second language study. This, in turn, determined their strategic approaches to language learning.

The three major data sources, which together elucidate each student's approach to second language learning, are language learning histories, language learning diaries, and class notes. While the analyses of diaries and class notes below focus on *how* learners go about tackling another language, the language learning histories, compiled as a result of interviews, biodata, and informal student comments, help explain *why* students behave the way they do.

LANGUAGE LEARNING HISTORIES

A thorough examination of each participant's background and values reveals that a learner's social environment is crucial in determining whether acquiring a second language is viewed as a worthwhile pursuit or not. This study traces how, based on this initial difference in orientation, learners form divergent goals in the language classroom. In one case, their behavior is geared towards genuine learning of the L2, and in the other, towards fulfilling an other-imposed requirement as efficiently as possible. Each student's approach to language learning reflects one of these basic orientations, which becomes particularly apparent in the analyses of learner diaries and class notes. The language learning histories discussed here shed light on how such goals are formed in the first place.

Two contrasting examples, students B. and J., illustrate how exposure to the world at large influences a learner's outlook and predisposition for foreign language success. B., a native speaker of Chinese, grew up in the bilingual community of Hong Kong, an international business center where language skills, particularly in English, carry high instrumental value. Foreign languages are a key to social mobility in this setting and are appreciated accordingly. Even though English was B.'s strongest subject in elementary school, her parents, themselves multilingual, thought language skills important enough to hire a conversational partner to tutor their daughter. From then on, and throughout her language learning history, B. not only saw foreign languages as clearly useful, but also as satisfying, interesting, and fun.

J., on the other hand, has always viewed foreign languages as "useless baggage" and, while in high school, would have preferred to spend the time allotted to foreign language study on a computer course instead. J., in his own words, "just saw NO PURPOSE in taking a language." The use value ascribed to a second language is a reflection of each learner's social environment, as illustrated by the example of student B., who grew up in Hong Kong. J. has never traveled more than two hours from his hometown to visit the nearest beach resort. The value of language study and of academic achievement in general is very low for this student, who views sports and earning money in a part-time position at a bank as more fulfilling than a college education.

J. and B.'s different orientations to language study are reflected in their actual language learning experience as well. Once in the United States, B. tackled high school Spanish with great enthusiasm and, once again, "did very well" (B.). She continues to find languages both useful and satisfying and is the only student who has enrolled in her current college French course without being required to do so. J. describes his attitude towards learning French as follows:

> I am not a big fan of learning French, or other foreign languages. The reason why I am in this class is to fulfill the language requirement for Arts and Science majors. I am actually very terrified about coming to French class each day. I got this way from taking FR 101 last year. The teacher I had was very tough and demanding. The way she taught the class turned me off from day one, and I have struggled with the language every since.

J. explicitly recognizes the importance of his language learning history in the formation of present attitudes, and explains his current behavior through his history. As was shown for B., however, this history beings prior to actual language study with the background factors determining her life goals and expectations. Ramsey (1980), Gardner and Lambert (1972), and Burstall (1975) all emphasize the importance of a learner's social environment in determining attitudes toward foreign language study. Students are likely to act and think in accordance with their milieu, as explained by Festinger (1957). Their life circumstances, therefore, cannot be excluded from investigations of L2 success.

In another pertinent example, M., an ineffective language learner, grew up in a family that encouraged only her younger sisters to succeed academically. M. herself was groomed to become a professional tennis player from a young age. In contrast to B., and other effective language learners, academic pursuits took a back seat to more and more tennis training in M.'s life. After a series of disappointing experiences with foreign languages in both high school and college, M. sums up how she feels about learning French as follows:

> I am taking French as a requirement. It's not that I hate French but I find learning a language very difficult no matter how hard I try. I think it is a silly requirement and that a foreign language should be started earlier than high school. After a certain age, it has been said, that a person cannot learn to speak.

The effective language learner P., on the other hand, is a returning adult student who considers his college education an "amazing opportunity" and has a very different view of language study:

Learning French, or any other language, makes me feel a greater scope of things in this world that I can appreciate. With each increment of language ability I feel a growth in my self. At times, after a period of quantitative accumulation, there is a qualitative shift, a pleasure akin to discovering harmony on fourth hearing where there seemed dissonance, as with a Bartok quartet. The artificial stammering of pronoun order, gender agreement, and inflection becomes the faculty of speech and finally the act of thinking and feeling in new ways.

In addition to appreciating his education in general, P., like B., has experienced the use value of foreign languages first hand at an early age. After having lived in France as a child for six months, P. never lost interest in languages and studied Italian and Spanish as well.

R., the third effective language learner in the group, never doubted the usefulness of studying French either, because she has relatives in a francophone region of Canada. Her first attempts at language study left her, too, with a positive outlook:

My earliest impression of another language goes back to about when I was seven or so. I was enrolled in Hebrew School... I remember doing well, learning and retaining the language, and used the language a bit when I went to Israel with my family in 1980.

R., convinced of the practical value of foreign languages, always attempts to "apply what she has learned," which then motivates her to go even further in her effort to acquire an L2. R.'s highly productive approach to French stems from a strong positive orientation towards learning languages in general:

I enjoy speaking in French. I really believe that there is so much that can be learned about communication in general through the study of more than one language. Although I am taking this class as a requirement, I appreciate the exposure to another language because I am a writer, and the more I learn about different languages, the better I can be as a writer.

All six language learning histories demonstrate that a learner's basic orientation, namely to value or not value foreign language study, does not necessarily change because of a positive or negative learning experience. R., for instance, reports that her first semester of university French was far from satisfactory:

Unfortunately, I didn't like the instructors I had for 102, and they didn't teach much (the lab instructor treated us like two-year olds!). I guess I was a bit ahead of the course material. I felt like I was wasting my time in that class. I tried to go on the trip to France over Winter Session, but only got on the waiting list. I was hoping to go so that I would be challenged to remember all the French I had learned in high school.

In this and similar episodes reported by other students, a learner's goal to acquire a specific language is shown to outweigh one disappointing learning experience. Ineffective learners, too, persist in their goal to do only the minimum required, even when they themselves judge an instructor or language class positively at a given point in their language learning experience. Thus, it is not primarily schooling but life goals that may influence the effort a learner makes in learning an L2 and the success he or she may enjoy as a result. An analysis of the six language learning histories shows that in the course of his or her life experience, each learner has come to regard foreign languages either as useful and desirable, or as a "useless requirement" that is "extremely tedious" to fulfill, according to J. The use value the participants ascribe to the L2 appears to be proportional to each student's exposure to the world at large. Learners such as J. simply lack concrete evidence of the utility of foreign languages, while others, such as B., have seen them as a valuable asset all their lives. The analysis of the language learning diaries below further illustrates how each student's personal experience has led him or her to form one of two goals in the foreign language classroom, namely to acquire as much as possible of the second language or to fulfill an other-imposed requirement as expeditiously as they can.

LANGUAGE LEARNING DIARIES

The language learning diaries give insight into students' actual language learning approaches, from specific strategies to general study habits. Each learner's degree of involvement with the L2 seems to reflect a basic orientation, formed as a result of the personal language learning histories descried above, namely either to genuinely acquire the L2, a goal consistently demonstrated by the effective language learners in the group, or to do only as much as necessary in order to fulfill the language requirement or to earn a certain grade. The three ineffective language learners participating in the study show themselves to consciously limit their efforts in learning the L2. Their language learning diaries all contain references to doing only what is required, such as, "Hopefully, it will be ENOUGH" (E.) and "I just want to do well ENOUGH to pass" (J.). M., the third ineffective language learner in the group, wants to do "well ENOUGH to get a good grade" on her final exam.

In each case, the ineffective language learners openly aim at doing just the amount of work they deem necessary to merit an acceptable grade, whereas the effective learners show through their actions, namely by consistently working harder than required, that their goal is to genuinely learn the L2. Consequently, effective and ineffective language learners differ markedly in their work habits. As opposed to the effective learners, who, by and large, made a greater effort than necessary and generally started to work on assignments early, an ineffective language learner, in this case J., confesses in his journal:

> It's 1:30 am. I just finished our homework that is due 9:05 Monday morning. Like usual, I put off all my homework all weekend until now. Actually I started research on my homework at 11:15 pm in the library after returning from bowling. Despite my late start I feel I did all right on the homework. I realize these study habits are wrong, but when it comes down to French or watching the NCAA Basketball Tournament, basketball wins outright. Now I'm forced to pull a possible all-nighter to catch up. C'est la vie!

While J.'s attempts at doing the minimum amount of work necessary to earn a passing grade are half-hearted, scattered, and therefore unproductive, B.'s effort, in comparison, is consistent and far exceeds course requirements. The most striking example of her elaborate and intensive language learning effort is her preparation for a required oral report. Whereas J., as will be shown below, spent a single evening on the same task by hastily translating an English encyclopedia article into French, B.'s research, only the first step in her systematic preparation, began eight full weeks before the actual talk. Almost two months before her oral presentation, B. reports:

> Yesterday I went to look for books in the library for my presentation in French class. Many descriptions for the books I looked at were in French, and I found myself actually understanding them. It felt very good. It felt good to be able to use other languages. At the end I borrowed five books, two of them in French. I think I'm going to at least try to use the French ones as much as I can.

B.'s satisfaction at using French whenever possible is equally prevalent among the other effective language learners. Instead of doing her research in English, which is what all three ineffective language learners did, B., over the course of two weeks, carefully prepared her talk following a process of outlining, elaborating, and simplifying, all in the L2. During this time period, B. reports that one day she

> rewrote the whole presentation, simplifying it to spoken form. When there were words that were too difficult to say, I tried to find other words to substitute them, so that it would be easier understood and also to say. (sic)

B.'s intention is to speak freely and clearly on the day of her talk, and through constant practice and the commitment of time and energy outlined in her journal, she achieves that goal:

> Every time I rehearsed my presentation, I found myself not following the script so much, but simplifying it more and more every time. Since I have memorized all the information in the script, when I present it, I'll simply say it as I think of it, in whatever form that comes to mind.

As one might predict, B.'s presentation was quite successful and provided her with further encouragement and satisfaction in language learning. J., in contrast, first thought about his oral project just a few days before it was due, and then only because of a scheduling change:

> I got a delay on my presentation. I guess they are running late so she has decided to move them back a week, so I have some extra time to put it together. Which means I'll probably still put it off until the last minute.

Indeed, the night before J.'s single most important class assignment is due, he makes the following entry:

> Tonight I have continued a long-standing tradition of waiting until the last minute to work on a project. I have researched, translated and tried to commit to memory my French oral project for tomorrow all tonight.

The differences in study habits illustrated above hold true for the other participants as well. The journals thus provide a clear link between student goals, formed in the course of their language learning history, and actual behavior. Moreover, the journals, as well as the class notes analyzed below, allow a glimpse at specific language learning strategies employed in the course of concrete L2 tasks, such as reaching a short story. The single most important language learning strategy, according to Rubin (personal communication), guessing or inferencing, comes naturally to an effective language learner such as B.:

> It took me a long time to read the story *La Parure*, but I found it less difficult than the previous ones. The length of the story scared me at first, but as I moved on, the story got me interested and I didn't feel the difficulty as much as before. There was a lot of vocabulary, too, so much that I didn't bother to check it all. I picked out the vocabulary that seemed important to me, and looked into the dictionary for only those words. For the rest of them, I only guessed since I didn't have the time, nor the patience, to check them all out.

While B. goes on to express her satisfaction about working her way through a challenging text, M., one of the ineffective language learners, experiences the same task quite differently:

> *La Parure* is a long story...Reading these stories is a long project. I have been told, "Just read it and you'll get the main idea." But I get about halfway through and then realize I didn't grasp anything but a couple of words. So I have to start over again looking up words that stump me.

This example illustrates the fact that even when ineffective language learners try to "do the right thing" and deploy a positive language learning strategy on a teacher's recommendation, their attempt is not necessarily successful. A possible explanation of this finding is that in the absence of the appropriate goal, namely to learn the L2, even what appear to be positive strategies may be unproductive. As discussed in the conclusion, such as claim has important implications with respect to the trainability of language learning strategies.

In addition to cognitive factors, such as strategy use on the part of effective and ineffective language learners, the diaries reveal striking affective differences. Even though all language learners are competitive and grade-conscious to some extent, a fact amply illustrated by Bailey (1983), the effective language learners in this study are able to use that tension to their advantage. When a learner feels that he or she "cannot compete" (J.), however, competitiveness can be debilitating and lead to withdrawal. On one such occasion, J. confesses:

My greatest fears have been realized. I totally screwed up my French exam. As it turns out, I am the only person who failed the stupid thing. It's my own fault for not studying, but I cannot help but feeling totally upset and dejected about the class and French. I don't feel like doing any French this week!

Just as success leads to increased effort on the part of effective learners, failure leads to avoidance in ineffective learners. J.'s next entry reads:

Tonight I tried to do the prestory so I can attempt to participate in class tomorrow. I got part of it done, but two things are preventing me from caring whether or not I finish it. One, I'm still dejected about my exam, and two, it's baseball season. The Phillies open their season tonight against the Pirates. My life has purpose again. Each spring I get excited about baseball season, and I tend to let my school work slip.

J.'s recent disappointment and long-standing work habits combine to keep him from seriously attempting to work his way out of a frustrating situation. Even when a greater effort is made by an ineffective language learner, as in the example below recorded by M., it may not lead to success;

Trying to read the story I keep looking up words I don't know. It's so annoying because after studying French for so long I feel I should know these words but I was absolutely clueless. Even if I didn't know the word, I remember all my previous teachers saying you don't have to know all the words to understand the sentence.

M.'s inability to remember lexical items may well stem from her reluctance to integrate them into some meaningful context. Her analytical approach to language study and lack of effective guessing strategies leave her frustrated and dissatisfied:

Today I fought with the dictionary. I hate that thing, it is so annoying looking up words and they give a list of five or six words.

Effective learners, as shown in the excerpts from B.'s diary, use more inferencing and with a higher degree of success partly because of a long-standing habit, and partly because they enjoy a text enough to become involved in just following the story. Reading as functional practice instead of deciphering is both more enjoyable and more productive as a strategy. The same is true for speaking extemporaneously in class as opposed to planning and translating every word ahead of time, another practice that distinguishes ineffective from effective learners.

The three effective language learners all profess a "learning by doing" philosophy and prefer functional tasks in the classroom. R., for instance, explains her active participation in class activities as follows:

> I believe that education is a participatory activity. While many college students seem to feel that by paying their tuition and being registered for a class they automatically will learn the information, I know that USING the information is the only way to actually accumulate and maintain the knowledge. I have always felt this way, and have always enjoyed learning because of this philosophy.

Both journals and class notes confirm that effective language learners do indeed focus on communicative activities in class, while ineffective learners reportedly feel intimidated by situations where functional language use is required. The ineffective learners all independently report that in the course of their language learning experience they felt more at ease in classes emphasizing grammar rules and rote memorization. Their journals and class notes further illustrate that preference for an analytical approach to language study including translation and memorization.

Reiss (1981) found effective language learners to be more conscious of, and willing to describe, actual strategies or learning techniques than ineffective ones. The journals analyzed here lend support to that distinction. While effective language learners give at least some concrete evidence of how they tackle individual learning tasks, ineffective learners often focus on the difficulty of motivating themselves to perform those tasks in the first place, especially in J.'s case. Fear of failure and frustration about a perceived lack of progress in the L2 are dominant themes as well.

The six journals analyzed for this study all offer insights into how each student's basic orientation towards language learning manifests itself as an actual approach to second language study. The degree of effort made, as well as the kinds of learning activities the students engaged in, together explain the degree of success they now enjoy. The diaries contain concrete evidence showing that one group of learners consciously chose to limit their acquisition of the L2 to what was required by the university, whereas their effective counterparts, motivated by their interest in foreign languages, chose to aim above and beyond course requirements. They worked to improve their L2 skills on their own, revising assignments even after they had been graded, and using the language whenever possible. This productive approach grows out of an apparent life-long orientation that views foreign languages as a useful, personal goal rather than being the result of superior language learning strategies alone.

CLASS NOTES

The students' class notes provide even more concrete evidence of each individual's study habits and specific learning strategies. Their analysis strengthens the claim made above that ineffective language learners rely heavily on translation and formal study, whereas effective learners focus on functional activities in and out of the classroom. Bialystok (1981) found that functional practice was far more effective than formal practice as a language learning strategy. Both reading and writing, productive functional tasks for the effective learners, were approached almost exclusively through translation and formal study by the ineffective language learners. Instead of writing and editing several drafts in the L2, as documented for the effective learners, the ineffective learners relied on a single English draft, as is the case for E. and M., or none at all (J.). E. and M. painstakingly translated their English compositions into French, almost as an afterthought, in order to produce a text in the L2. J.'s notes do not contain evidence of any external planning at all, but his improvised writing style, as shown below, is largely based on English as well.

In reading too, the ineffective learners relied almost exclusively on translation to decipher L2 texts. E. jots down between the lines complete verbatim translations of every reading worked on during the semester, a considerable effort which does not, however, increase his fluency in French. The analytical approach to language study exhibited by the ineffective learners stands in contrast to that of the effective learners, who read on and inference instead of constantly referring to glossaries and dictionaries. One of the effective language learners (R.) even goes as far as complaining about being forced to translate due to the difficulty of a task:

> Working on my essay on Haiti, I became discouraged...I depended on the dictionary too much for my liking. I felt kind of dumb, and a little uncomfortable about writing the essay in words that didn't come from me. I felt like I was not doing anything productive by copying words out of the dictionary. I would have gained more if we had learned a lot of vocabulary on the subject first, and then the French essay would have come more from me.

The alienation felt by this student is diametrically opposed to the relief expressed by the ineffective language learners when they find themselves in classes where a formal approach to L2 study, including translation, is accepted by the instructor.

Both journals and class notes illustrate how effective learners, unlike their ineffective counterparts, set specific study goals for themselves. While the ineffective language learners report that they "just study" indiscriminately, all three effective learners focus on likely exam topics while working on the L2. They actively regroup and organize lexical items, make lists and grammar charts, and underline important material. Two of the three effective learners use asterisks, and the third uses a color-coded underlining system to mark areas of knowledge judged to be especially important for upcoming exams. Nothing comparable was found in the notes taken by the three ineffective language learners.

Effective language learners are both highly organized and focused. They actively prepare for concrete tasks (such as writing an essay on a potential exam topic), whereas ineffective learners just scan their notes indiscriminately and make no observable attempt to manipulate the material in any functionally useful way. A journal entry by P., in contrast, illustrates the degree of specificity characteristic of an effective language learner's study of the L2:

> Today I prepared for the visit of our French boy by reviewing Cortina's *Conversational French*. I studied the vocabulary dealing with household words and meals. I reviewed in grammar the second person singular forms of verbs and the imperatives. Then I walked around the house briefly naming objects and having imaginary conversations with the boy—mainly my side. I also reviewed the students slang from my notes. I hope to follow a plan of study based on my conversations with Christophe.

As in this example, journals and class notes supplement each other in many instances and together offer a more complete picture of the language learning effort put forth by each learner. Effective and ineffective learners' approaches are shown to differ in kind as well as in degree of involvement with the L2. A comparison of notes taken in preparation for specific assignments and classroom activities demonstrates once again how ineffective language learners do only what is absolutely necessary, and sometimes not even that. J.'s preparation for an informal oral presentation in class looks as follows:

> ...*Maintenant je suis en entrêneur pour* Little League. *Les garcons ont dix et douse ans. Moi traville est enseigner les garcons les*

(rules), *et* sportsmanship. *Les* rules *de* Little League *est similer du* baseball *grande. Les* rules *differente est nous faisons* six innings. *Les garcons fallont joue deux* innings. *Autre* rules *est simplique. Les equipes du* (home) tube *dernier. Tres* strikes *le* batter *est finis. Tres* batters *finis et les equipe fini.*

The compensation strategies J. uses in this poorly researched passage might be beneficial in another context, such as an oral exam, where dictionaries and other resources are not available. In that case, the limited use of English and even Spanish lexical items might help the speaker to get his point across and keep the conversation flowing. The task above, however, was designed to involve students in collecting and acquiring vocabulary about a sports-related topic they were interested in. As a next step, the students were expected to communicate the information they had gathered to a small group. Instead of benefitting from the opportunity, J. makes up words, uses his L1 extensively, and improvises. R., on the other hand, takes full advantage of the task and prepares a concise, well thought-out statement. Even though it is not flawless, her presentation is carefully researched and contains a wealth of vocabulary not previously taught in class:

> *Je suis tres sportive, quand j'ai le temps. J'aime de regarder les sports aussi, quelquefois a la television, et quelquefois a le stade. Je joue au le football,*
> > *le ski nautique*
> > *le "volleyball,"*
> > *le baseball,*
> > *le "racquetball,"*
> > *le "bodybuilding" competitif,*
> > *le hockey sur glace, et*
> > *le hockey sur gazon.*
> *Quand j'ai eu huit ans, mes cousins m'ai enseignée de faire du patine, et de faire du hockey sur glace. quand j'etais en ecole secondaire j'ai apprendu de faire du hockey sur gazon. Le sport que j'aime le plus est le hockey. Maintenant, je n'ai pas le temps pour jouer a un equipe du hockey, mais j'ai le temps de joue beaucoup des autres sports de temps en temps.*

While J.'s notes are generally sketchy and often limited to items that had been written on the blackboard, all three effective language learners tend to elaborate on class material and add study notes or personal grammar outlines, such as the one below provided by R.:

L'Imparfait
<u>used</u> to describe recurring or habitual events. tells of states or conditions in the past. sets up background info.
<u>formation</u>
nous form (present tense) of verb
remove —ONS
add   —AIS   —IONS
          —AIS—IEZ
          —AIT—AIENT
Je parlais au téléphone quand Paul *est arrivé.*
   IMP.   P.C.

When taking lecture notes on the same topic, however, effective and ineffective language learners' notes are not necessarily distinguished by quantity. As a matter of fact, terseness, or a low ratio of words to propositions (Dunkel, 1988), is highest for B., an effective language learner. The notes taken by ineffective language learners sometimes contain more redundancy, as learners write down both pairs of cognates, such as "*alliés*—Allies" or even "*sabotage*—sabotage," and repeat new lexical items verbatim, only one day after they were first introduced.

The inability to retain such lexical items is a source of frustration for ineffective language learners such as M., who are quite conscious of their "forgetfulness." While effective language learners seem to integrate old and new material through active language use, ineffective learners do not link new information effectively to what they already know. In fact, such learners often behave as if they had no internal representation of the target language at all and were forced constantly to start over, with the L1 as their only point of reference. Thus, after almost three semesters of French at the university level, J. notes "*Je suis* = I am."

This lack of development observed in the interlanguage of ineffective language learners may well be due to the fact that in their effort just to fulfill a requirement they are not aiming at actually improving in the language. By focusing only on coping with the task at hand, learning becomes secondary to "getting by" or doing just enough for the moment. Little if anything is retained when completing a specific assignment is the only motive for contact with the L2 in the first place. Effective language learners, too, complete assignments and fulfill classroom obligations, but not as an end in itself. Since their goal is learning the language, they are more successful at transferring new knowledge to future tasks. Specifically, effective learners appear to benefit from correction in concrete instances, such as B.'s consistently accurate spelling of the adjective *culturel* after a single correction was made by her instructor. Another indication of the fact that effective language learners aim at getting better, not at getting by, is their detailed attention, documented in their class notes, to the error analysis provided by the instructor after each essay. Effective language learners do not view their effort as completed with the assignment of a grade, because their goal is to improve for the next opportunity. Ineffective learners, as might be expected, do not seem to pay attention to old work or build visibly on what they have accomplished on previous occasions. The goal of learning all, not just some, of the target language appears to be the driving force behind the ability of effective learners to draw on what they know and continue to build on it, which is the only way to acquire another language.

CONCLUSION

The case study of three effective and three ineffective language learners reported in this chapter explains differences in L2 achievement primarily as a function of student goals in the course of instruction. Such goals are shown to depend on a learner's social history and the use value ascribed to foreign languages in his or her environment. As a result of each learner's exposure to the world at large, documented in the language learning histories, language skills are seen either as a valuable asset or as an other-imposed requirement.

An analysis of the language learning diaries reveals that students who view language study only as a requirement openly limit their language learning effort to what they perceive as necessary to pass a given course or earn a certain grade. On the other hand, those students who have come to consider languages as valuable in and of themselves are shown to make a far greater effort to acquire the target language. This approach also differs in kind from the limited attempts at second language acquisition made by the ineffective language learners in this study.

Consistent differences in study habits and specific language learning strategies emerge when language learning histories, diaries, and class notes are analyzed and combined to elucidate and corroborate each other. The effective language learners, as a group, appear to engage in a personal and satisfying effort to acquire French that far exceeds course requirements. The ineffective language learners, on the other hand, report frustration and motivational difficulties while completing no more than the assigned course work. Although ineffective learners were less specific with respect to reporting particular language learning strategies than effective ones, a clear pattern is nevertheless revealed in the preceding analysis.

While ineffective language learners appear to cling to their L1 as a reference system and rely heavily on translation and rote learning, the effective language learners in the study favor language use and communicative activities in and out of class. They actively use the L2 when reading and writing, whereas the ineffective language learners seem to access and generate L2 texts exclusively via translation. In many instances, the efforts made by the ineffective language learners seem geared towards getting by rather than towards getting better, which makes them less receptive to error correction than their effective counterparts.

In light of these findings, this study questions the belief that positive learning strategies, in and of themselves, constitute the explanation of L2 achievement (see Oxford & Nyikos, 1989, among others). Attempts to train ineffective language learners to adopt specific strategies identified among effective learners have been less than successful (see Chamot & Küpper, 1989; O'Malley, Camot, Stewner-Manzanares, Russo, & Küpper, 1985; and Sutter, 1987), perhaps because they ignore students' motivation and personal histories. Researchers have to consider that, when originally observed in the "good language learner" studies of the 1970s (see Naiman, Fröhlich, Stern, & Todesco, 1978; Rubin, 1975, and Stern, 1975), those positive language learning strategies were used by successful students as a means to an end. If a learner's initial motive determines the quality of language study overall, it also influences the effectiveness of specific strategies. As shown above, J., for instance, uses excellent compensation strategies. The problem is that he does not improvise as successfully as he does in order to learn more of the language, but in order to avoid just that.

Apart from this reservation, the findings of this study confirm those of other language learning strategy researchers in many ways. Effective language learners do, in fact, inference where ineffective learners translate, and effective learners do engage in functional practice while ineffective ones prefer formal tasks. This study adds a caveat, however, namely that the positive language learning strategies observed among effective language learners are goal driven, systematic, and intuitively obvious. One has to question whether such originally voluntary behavior can readily be taught to ineffective language learners through language learning strategy training, independent of learners' goals and histories. The ineffective language learner M., for instance, did attempt to use a positive reading strategy recommended by her teachers, but to no avail. Cohen and Aphek (1981), too, report such isolated cases of positive strategies used by unsuccessful language learners.

Vygotskian psycholinguistic theory, with its claim that the initial motive for engaging in an activity is what determines its outcome, provides a useful framework for explaining why it may be so difficult to teach positive language learning strategies to ineffective language learners, and why the isolated use of positive language learning strategies on the part of ineffective language learners rarely leads to success. Just a Vygotskian psycholinguistic theory would predict, this study suggests that a student's goal in using a given language learning strategy helps determine its effectiveness. Consequently, this study cautions against the assumption that strategy training will automatically lead to better language learning and proposes that future language learning strategy research take students' goals and histories into account. Successful language learning depends on an individual's willingness to make every effort to acquire an L2 rather than on superior cognitive processing alone. Viewing foreign language skills as a valuable personal goal is a crucial trait of effective language learners. Each learner's social history is the key to goal formation, and, hence, to explaining success in second language acquisition.

REFERENCES

Bailey, K. (1983). Competitiveness and anxiety in adult second language learning: Looking at and through the diary studies. In H.W. Seliger & M.H. Long (Eds.), *Classroom oriented research in second language acquisition* (pp. 67–102). Rowley, MA: Newbury House.

Bialystok, E. (1981). The role of conscious strategies in second language proficiency. *Modern Language Journal, 65*, 24–35.

Burstall, C. (1975). Factors affecting foreign-language learning: A consideration of some recent research findings. *Language Teaching & Linguistics: Abstracts, 8*, 5–25.

Chamot, A.U., & Kupper, L. (1989). Learning strategies in foreign language instruction. *Foreign Language Annals, 22*, 13–24.

Chaudron, C. (1988). *Second language classrooms: Research on teaching and learning.* Cambridge: Cambridge University Press.

Cohen, A., & Aphek, E. (1981). Easifying second language learning. *Studies in Second Language Acquisition, 3*, 221–266.

Dunkel, P. (1988). The content of L1 and L2 students' lecture notes and its relation to test performance. *TESOL Quarterly, 22*, 259–281.

Festinger, L. (1957). *A theory of cognitive dissonance.* White Plains, NY: Row, Peterson, & Company.

Galperin, P.Y. (1980). The role of orientation in thought. *Soviet Psychology, 18,* 84–99.

Gardner, R.C., & Lambert, W.E. (1972). *Attitudes and motivation in second language learning.* Rowley, MA: Newbury House.

Henning, G. (1983). Oral proficiency testing: Comparative validities of interview, imitation and completion methods. *Language Learning, 33/3,* 315–332.

Naiman, N., Fröhlich, M., Stern, H.H., & Todesco, A. (1978). *The good language learner.* Toronto: The Ontario Institute for Studies in Education.

Oller, J.W., Jr. (1979). *Language tests at school.* London: Longman.

O'Malley, J.M., Chamot, A.U., Stewner-Manzanares, G., Russo, R.P., & Küpper, L. (1985). Learning strategy applications with students of English as a second language. *TESOL Quarterly, 19,* 557–584.

Oxford, R., & Nyikos, M. (1989). Variables affecting choice of language learning strategies by university students. *Modern Language Journal, 73,* 291–300.

Ramsey, R.M.G. (1980). Language-learning approach styles of adult multilinguals and successful language learners. *Annals of the New York Academy of Sciences, 345,* 73–96.

Reiss, M.-A. (1981). Helping the unsuccessful language learner. *Modern Language Journal, 65,* 121–28.

Rubin, J. (1975). What the 'Good Language Learner' can teach us. *TESOL Quarterly, 9,* 41–51.

Stern, H. (1975). What can we learn from the good language learner? *The Canadian Modern Language Review, 31,* 304–318.

Sutter, W. (1987). *Learning styles in adult refugees in North Jutland.* Denmark: County of North Jutland.

Vygotsky, L.S. (1978). *Mind in society: The development of higher psychological processes.* Cambridge, MA: Harvard University Press.

Vygotsky, L.S. (1986). *Thought and language.* Cambridge, MA: MIT Press.

Author Index

215

Subject Index

A

Accommodation, 58, 66–67
Act, 9
  moter, 9–10
  voluntary, 9–10
Activity Theory, 16–22, 29
  action, 7, 13, 17–22, 36–37, 174
    goal, 7, 9, 11, 13, 17–22, 29, 36, 43,
      44, 174, 197, 200, 202–203,
      206, 212
  activity, 4, 7, 17–19, 36–38, 42
    collective, 45
    communicative, 29
    concrete, 5
    joint, 58
    motive, 17–18, 21, 29, 36–37, 48,
      196
    roots of, 3–6
    sociocultural, 16, 21
    symbolic, 5
    versus task, 174–175
  operation, 17, 20–21, 36–37, 174
Appropriation, 10–11, 21, 39, *see also*
  Internationalization

B

Baby talk, 57
Backsliding, 79

C

Cloze test, 73, 76, 195
Communication
  asymmetric, 160
  conduit metaphor of, 34–35
  message model of, 34, 49, 147–148
  see also Dialogue

Consciousness, 3–5, 7, 21, 22
  co-knowledge, 38–39
Continuous access, 15–16, 188
Culture, 7, 9, 16, 28, *see also* Social
  context

D

Definition of situation, 13
Development
  child, 5–6, 10, 25, 117
    ontogenesis, 9–10, 118
  dialectic, 6, 50
  historical, 6
  interlanguage, 29, 35, 190
  law of cultural development, 11
  linguistic, 48–49, 52, 151
Dialogue, 12, 157, 160
  cognitive, 47
  versus monologue, 180

E

Egocentric speech, 14, 97, *See also*
  Inner speech, Private speech

F

Foreigner talk, 57
Fossilization, 28, 69–79
  definitions of, 69–70
  pedagogy, 70–71
  proficiency, 70
  research, 70

I

Inner speech, 13–16, 22, 28, 83, 104,
  118, 135–155
  first language, 82, 84, 90, 98, 100,
    153–155

219